Seven Myths of the Spanish Conquest

Seven Myths of the Spanish Conquest

MATTHEW RESTALL

OXFORD
UNIVERSITY PRESS

OXFORD
UNIVERSITY PRESS

Oxford   New York
Auckland   Bangkok   Buenos Aires   Cape Town   Chennai
Dar es Salaam   Delhi   Hong Kong   Istanbul   Karachi   Kolkata
Kuala Lumpur   Madrid   Melbourne   Mexico City   Mumbai   Nairobi
São Paulo   Shanghai   Taipei   Tokyo   Toronto

Copyright © 2003 by Oxford University Press, Inc.

First published by Oxford University Press, Inc., 2003
198 Madison Avenue, New York, New York 10016

www.oup.com

First issued as an Oxford University Press paperback, 2004
ISBN-13-978-0-19-517611-7

Oxford is a registered trademark of Oxford University Press

The Library of Congress has catalogued the cloth edition as follows:
Restall, Matthew, 1964–
Seven myths of the Spanish conquest / Matthew Restall.
p.   cm.
Includes bibliographical references and index.

1. Mexico—History—Conquest, 1519–1540—Historiography.
2. Spaniards—America—Historiography.
3. Latin America—History—Errors, inventions, etc.
4. Myth.
I. Title.
F1230 .R47 2003
980'.013'072—dc 21   2002192492

28   27   26   25   24   23   22   21
Printed in the United States of America
on acid-free paper

*To anyone
who has ever been my student;*

*to Jim and Felipe,
whose student I will always be;*

*and to Lucy,
tomorrow's student*

Contents

Acknowledgments

The names of these Seven Cities, which have not been discovered, remain unknown, and the search for them continues to this day.

—Pedro de Castañeda Nájera (ca. 1560)

The number seven has almost mystical qualities.

—*New York Times* (2002)

"There seem to be a lot of myths in this class," said the student, not without a hint of suspicion. Thus was the seed for this book planted, one spring afternoon in a Pennsylvania classroom.

What began as an attempt to respond to the student's comment and to adjust my undergraduate lectures accordingly soon developed into a book project—and the misconceptions and convenient fictions of Conquest history gradually settled into seven "myths" in seven chapters, constituting a seven-part argument against much of conventional wisdom on the Spanish Conquest in the Americas.

The book's seven-part structure seemed justified by the fact that the number seven has deep roots and symbolic significance in the history of the Americas, both Native American and Spanish. The origin myth of the Mexica included a tale of descent from seven lineages, who emerged from seven caves in a mythical location in the Mexican north.[1] The medieval law code that was the basis of Spanish law during the Conquest period was called *Las siete partidas* (The seven items). There were rumored to be seven cities of gold in Cíbola, a name given variously to northern South America before it was invaded and dubbed New Granada and to all or part of what is now the south and southwest United States—where Coronado searched in vain for the Seven Cities in 1540–42.[2]

My search for "seven myths" was not in vain, aided greatly the following spring (2001) by the experience of teaching a graduate seminar in the Pennsylvania State University History Department titled "Seven Myths of the Spanish Conquest." The idea was to write and teach on identical topics, allowing each process to stimulate and fertilize the other. It all worked out better than

I could possibly have hoped. Without the contributions of the seminar members in class and on paper (their essays are included in a special section of the bibliography), this book would have taken twice as long to write and been a vastly inferior product. I am most grateful to every one of them—Bobbie Arndt, Valentina Cesco, Iris Cowher, Jason Frederick, Gerardo Gutiérrez, María Inclán, Amy Kovak, Blanca Maldonado, Zachary Nelson, Christine Reese, Michael Smith, and Leah Vincent. I am also grateful to Gregg Roeber for encouraging and making possible my "Seven Myths" semester.

I was fortunate to spend the next spring (2002) as a National Endowment for the Humanities fellow at the John Carter Brown Library at Brown University, where finishing touches were put to the book manuscript. I am grateful to the library's director, Norman Fiering, to the staff, and to my fellow fellows for their generosity and many contributions. A number of friends and colleagues profoundly influenced my thinking on this topic or offered helpful comments on portions of the book. They include Patrick Carroll, Jack Crowley, Garrett Fagan, Michael Francis, Philip Jenkins, Grant Jones, Jane Landers, Juliette Levy, James Lockhart, James Muldoon, William Pencak, Carol Reardon, Helen Restall, Robin Restall, Tim Richardson, Guido Ruggiero, Susan Schroeder, Andrew Sluyter, and Dean Snow—and in particular Felipe Fernández-Armesto, Susan Kellogg, Kris Lane, and Neil Whitehead, all of whom gave me extensive written comments on the whole manuscript. Susan Ferber of Oxford University Press made line-by-line editorial suggestions that were as thorough as they were insightful. She is a true master of the red pen and I am most grateful for the resulting improvements made to every page.

Finally, I thank Helen, Sophie, and Isabel, for always understanding my need to finish "just one more sentence."

M.B.R.
State College, Pennsylvania
September, 2002

Those men . . . who have written not what they saw, but what they did not hear so well . . . wrote with great detriment to the truth, occupied only in dry sterility and with the fruitlessness of the surface, without penetrating into the reason of men.

—Fray Bartolomé de Las Casas (1559)

Mr. Writer, why don't you tell it like it really is?

—Stereophonics (2001)

To distinguish between the curved and the straight.

—Horace (ca. 30 B.C.)

I did not find out any more about this, and what I have written down is of little help.

—Fray Ramón Pané (1498)

Speaking with great majesty, seated on his throne, the Inca flung the book from his hands.

—Don Felipe Huaman Poma de Ayala (1615)

Introduction
The Lost Words of Bernal Díaz

It has been a shock for us to learn that we do not perceive the world
just as it is, and that our knowledge of the world is inescapably framed
by the concepts and language of our culture.

—Behan McCullagh (1998)

Historians today are priests of a cult of truth, called to the service of a
god whose existence they are doomed to doubt.

—Felipe Fernández-Armesto (1999)

Let the curious reader consider whether there is not much to ponder
in this that I am writing. What men have there been in the world who
have shown such daring?

—Bernal Díaz del Castillo (1570)

When Bernal Díaz first saw the Aztec capital he was lost for words. Years
later, the words would come, many of them, when he wrote a lengthy account of his experiences as a member of the Spanish expedition led by Hernán
Cortés against the Aztec empire. But on that November afternoon in 1519, as
Díaz and his fellow conquistadors came over the mountain pass and looked
down upon the Valley of Mexico for the first time, "gazing on such wonder-
ful sights, we did not know what to say, or whether what appeared before us
was real."[1]

Díaz's struggle to describe what he saw—the metropolis of Tenochtitlán,
studded with pyramids, crisscrossed with canals, seeming to hover on a lake
that was "crowded with canoes" and edged with other "great cities"—derived
from his shock at realizing that the world was not what he had perceived it to
be. Just as artists would for centuries draw pre-Conquest Tenochtitlán with
distinctly European features (see Figure 1), so did Díaz try to compare the
valley to European cityscapes of his experience, but could not. In the end, he
resorted to a reference to medieval fiction, so that the Aztec cities "seemed

Antient MEXICO

1 The Great Square. 2 The Temple. 3 Village of Tzapotepan. 4 Defence of the Royal Palace. 5. 6 The Menagerie House & Garden. 7 Aqueduct to supply y⁰ City. 8 Village of Tzapua or Tacuna, & The Great Lake.

like an enchanted vision from the tale of Amadis."[2] Cortés was likewise daunted by the challenge of finding a comparable city in the "old" world, likening Tenochtitlán to Córdoba, Seville, and Salamanca all in the same few pages.[3] But whether the Aztec capital was deemed to be more like Venice, Seville, or the fictional Amadis, the accounts by Díaz, Cortés, and the other Spaniards of what they saw and did in the Americas were inescapably framed by the concepts and language of their own culture.

As a result, a set of interrelated perspectives soon developed into a fairly coherent vision and interpretation of the Conquest—the sum of Spanish conquest activity in the Americas from 1492 to about 1700. While many aspects of the Conquest and its interpretation have long been debated—from the arguments of sixteenth-century Spanish ecclesiastics to those of professional historians today—most of the fundamental characteristics of that vision, and a surprising number of its details, have survived.

Cortés would be most gratified by the credit given to him for the fall of the Aztec Empire in many a website and textbook. The seven myths of the Conquest can all be found in the Cortés legend, in which his military genius, his use of superior Spanish technology, and his manipulation of credulous "Indians" and a superstitious Aztec emperor enable him to lead a few hundred Spanish soldiers to a daring conquest of an empire of millions —and thereby set an example that permits the rest of the Spanish conquests in the Americas. In the sixteenth century Cortés became the archetypal conquistador, and he remains so today.

At the same time, our understanding of the Conquest has become far more complex and sophisticated, owing not least to the increased availability of source documents written by Spaniards and Native Americans in the colonial period (that lasted from the sixteenth to early nineteenth centuries). It is true that in recent years historians have become increasingly concerned with the problem of subjectivity and our inability to escape it. Truth itself has been discredited as a concept relevant to historical investigation.[4] But the impossibility of being completely objective need not be so discouraging. In the realm of subjectivity things can get really interesting. The concepts of a particular culture, the way they are expressed, and the relationship between those words and reality, can lead to genuine insight into an historical phenomenon such as the Spanish Conquest—and a better understanding of how such a phenomenon has been understood over the centuries.

For example, Cortés becomes more interesting and more believable when his myth is explored and broken down. The realization that conquistadors

---

Facing page: *Fig. 1. Tenochtitlán, or "Antient Mexico," portrayed as more of a European city than a Mesoamerican one, complete with medieval towers and Old World oxen; from John Harris's* Voyages and Travels *(1744 [1705]).*

before and after Cortés behaved like him leads to other, equally fascinating stories. Awareness of the decisive role played by West Africans and native allies of the Spaniards enriches Conquest history and helps explain its outcome. The revelations that most conquistadors were not soldiers, and Native Americans did not believe Spanish invaders were gods, prompts investigation into the tangle of sources that both produced such misconceptions and permit alternative arguments.

This book is about the pictures painted by men like Díaz of the Spanish conquests in the Americas, and the pictures painted by historians and others who in the past five centuries have followed Díaz across the Atlantic and into Tenochtitlán and other places of wonder in the "new" world. The book's sources range from documents written by Spaniards, Native Americans, and West Africans who experienced the Conquest and its aftermath, to the tomes of academics produced in colonial and modern times, to Hollywood movies.

Each of the seven chapters articulates a myth about the Conquest, dissects it, and places it in the context of alternative sources of evidence. At its most basic level, the book juxtaposes false and accurate descriptions of the Conquest.[5] But the book is also more than that. In presenting historical interpretations of the Conquest as myths rooted in the cultural conceptions, misconceptions, and political agendas of their time, I am aware that I too am inescapably influenced by the concepts and language of my own culture. Beyond simply contrasting myth and reality, my analysis recognizes that myths can be real to their progenitors and that a supposed reality built by researching archival sources can also generate its own myths. This is therefore not just a book about what happened, but a book that compares two forms of what is said to have happened. One form is created at the time of the historical moment itself. The other form is germinated in archives and libraries, when historians write historical accounts that strive to achieve objectivity (even if it must always remain just out of reach).[6]

The term "myth" is used here not in the sense of folklore, of popular narratives and beliefs featuring religious systems and supernatural characters. Rather it is used to mean something fictitious that is commonly taken to be true, partially or absolutely.[7] Both of these meanings of "myth" have an ambiguous connection to "history." Ever since Plato set about exploding the myths of his day, Western thought has viewed history and myth as standing in opposition to each other; one is true, being the reconstruction of actual events and people who really lived, the other is fiction, being a construction of invented events and imagined people. However, this polarity is not always so clear. Plato sought to replace the "lies" of old myths with historical "truths" that were laced with new myths invented by him.[8] Historian Paul Veyne has argued that ancient Greek myths were "neither true nor fictitious because [they were] external to but nobler than the real world." Scholars of Mesoamerica, a civilizational area covering most of Mexico and Central America, assert that native people did not recognize such a distinction between myth and history. Instead Mesoamericans viewed the past in a way we would characterize as combining elements of myth and history. The great surviving text of the Quiché Mayas, the *Popol Vuh*, seamlessly blends mythic and historical components into one epic narrative, called "mythistory" by anthropologist Dennis Tedlock.[9]

Does this ambiguous relationship between myth and history, or their fusing into mythistory, undermine the quest to find truths about the past? In pursuing that quest, do we run the risk of following in Plato's footsteps and replacing old myths with invented truths or new myths? Are our truths really convenient fictions?[10] They may often be just that, but we can still examine the context and purpose of such fictions. We can compare the truths of the conquistadors to our truths about them, and as a result achieve a better understanding of the Conquest—even if that understanding does not pretend to be *the truth* in an absolute sense. Historical conclusions are not infallible, but when they are well evidenced and carefully argued they deserve to be taken as telling us something true about the world. We can question the truth claims of an historical narrative without going so far as to relegate it to merely one fiction among others.[11] There are always multiple narratives of any historical moment, but that does not mean that as interpretations they cannot tell us something true.

The Spanish writer Valle Inclán's famous aphorism "things are not how we see them but how we remember them" prompts us to be skeptical of eyewitness accounts like Díaz's.[12] But—more importantly—we are also reminded that within those memories history persists, myth is engendered, and truths of some kind await our discovery.

The moment in Bernal Díaz's narrative when he writes that he and his comrades were lost for words at the first sight of Tenochtitlán is a moment pregnant with interpretive possibilities. Perhaps the moment was created by Díaz in his old age, a product of his imagination. Perhaps it was a deliberate dramatization of an incredulity really experienced—but at a later date, when he was less exhausted, or his view of the valley was clearer. Perhaps the sensation of seeing something so new that it seemed unreal forced Díaz, in that moment of stunned silence, to open his mind to a larger vision of the world. Or perhaps he was simply terrified, as he hints later in his story, at the prospect of being one of a few strangers in a vast and potentially hostile city.

Although Díaz's silent awe does not last for long, he never completely fills in the moment, nor should we expect him to. The silences in Díaz's narrative include not only his own thoughts then and decades later, but also those of his Spanish comrades, the Africans they brought with them, and the central Mexican natives whom the Spaniards were forcing to take sides in a bloody civil war. And then there are the reactions of Díaz's readers, from his own time to today, reactions that fill silences throughout narratives such as his and thereby become part of the process of historical production.

The fact that there are so many phrases we can insert into Díaz's silent moment does not render the exercise of its exploration and reconstruction impossibly nebulous. Amidst the uncertainty and multiplicity of narratives, in such a moment and its interpretations, something true about the world can surely be discovered.

This book begins that endeavor with a critique of the idea that the Conquest was made possible only through the audacity and achievements of "great men"—the unique few to show such daring, to paraphrase Bernal Díaz. I argue in Chapter 1 that we can view the Conquest more clearly through the patterns created by the biographies of many Spaniards, rather than the lives of the supposedly exceptional few. The Spaniards who invaded the Americas followed procedures developed and standardized by generations of settlers. Their destinies were not determined by the bold genius of a handful of adventurers (to paraphrase the nineteenth-century historian William Prescott).[13] Chapter 2 tackles the myth that the conquistadors were soldiers sent to the Americas by the king of Spain. In fact, the conquistadors were far more varied in their identities, occupations, and motivations—and far more interesting—than that.

The myths of Chapters 3 and 4 are rooted in the accounts of the Conquest written by the conquistadors themselves. They were generated by specific political circumstances and cultural contexts, and yet, as with all Conquest myths, they have shown remarkable longevity. These are the notions that conquest was achieved and colonialism rapidly imposed, first, when native armies were defeated and Spanish cities founded, and second, by surprisingly small groups of Spaniards acting alone. Such narratives disguise the protracted and incomplete nature of the Conquest, as well as the crucial roles played by Native American "allies" and free and enslaved West Africans.

Chapter 5 navigates the reader through the rough waters of what I have termed the "myth of (mis)communication." This chapter argues that just as the Spaniards themselves fabricated the myth that they were able to communicate with native leaders, so have modern historians swung the pendulum too far in the opposite direction and generated a countermyth that emphasizes Spanish-native miscommunication. A middle ground between the two extremes allows a better understanding of how Spaniards and natives came to view each other's intentions. The topic of native roles leads us to that of native reactions. In Chapter 6 I take issue with the widespread misconception that the Conquest reduced the Native American world to a void.[14] In diverse and profound ways native cultures displayed resilience, adaptability, ongoing vitality, a heterogeneity of response to outside interference, and even a capacity to invert the impact of conquest and turn calamity into opportunity.

The final chapter discusses the ultimate myth, the foundational concept that has served for five centuries as the simplest—and most facile—explanation for the Conquest. This is the myth of Spanish superiority, a subset of the larger myth of European superiority and the nexus of racist ideologies that underpinned colonial expansion from the late fifteenth to early twentieth centuries.

The Epilogue is framed by the 1525 encounter of Cortés, Cuauhtémoc, the last Aztec emperor, and Paxbolonacha, the ruler of a small Maya kingdom. This episode, which has received little attention from historians, is presented here as illustrative of all the themes of the Conquest discussed in the book—viewed both through the seven myths and through their counterpoints. The myths surrounding Cuauhtémoc's death, which is the climax of the episode, function as metaphors for the larger myths of the Spanish Conquest.

Seven Myths of the Spanish Conquest

1

A Handful of Adventurers
The Myth of Exceptional Men

Mr. Christopher Columbus,
sailed the seas without a compass.
Well, when his men began a rumpus,
up spoke Christopher Columbus.
He said, 'There is land somewhere,
so until we get there,
we will not go wrong,
if we sing a swing song.
Since the world is round,
we'll be safe and sound.
Till our goal is found,
we'll just keep a-rhythm bound.'
Soon the crew was makin' merry.
Then came a yell,
'Let's drink to Isabel-la!
Bring on the rum!'
That music ended all the rumpus.
Wise old Christopher Columbus.

—Andy Razaf (1936)

The Conquest of Mexico and the conversion of the peoples of New Spain can
and should be included among the histories of the world, not only because it
was well done but because it was very great. . . . Long live, then, the name
and memory of him [Cortés] who conquered so vast a land, converted such
a multitude of men, cast down so many idols, and put an end to so much
sacrifice and the eating of human flesh!

—Francisco López de Gómara (1552)

When in ancient or modern times have such huge enterprises of so few
succeeded against so many? . . . And who has equaled those of Spain?
Certainly not the Jews nor the Greeks nor Romans, about whom most is
written.

—Francisco de Jerez (1534)

To such lengths of blind partiality will men be carried, who care less for the
truth of history than for the fame of its creatures.

—Aaron Goodrich (1874)

One of the great themes of historical literature over the past five centuries has been the assessment of the European discovery of the Americas as one of the two greatest events in human history. Perhaps the earliest such judgement made in print was the claim by the Paduan philosopher Lazzaro Buonamico in 1539 that nothing had brought more honor to mankind "than the invention of the printing press and the discovery of the new world; two things which I always thought could be compared, not only to Antiquity, but to immortality." A similar, better-known pronouncement was penned by Francisco López de Gómara, Hernán Cortés's private secretary and official biographer, in 1552. "The greatest event since the creation of the world (excluding the incarnation and death of Him who created it)," wrote Gómara, "is the discovery of the Indies [i.e., the Americas]."[1]

By the eighteenth century, the "discovery" had come to share its number one position with a related European achievement.[2] "No event," wrote the French philosopher Abbé Raynal in 1770, "has been so interesting to mankind in general ... as the discovery of the new world, and the passage to India by the Cape of Good Hope." Six years later the economist Adam Smith issued a bolder version of this assessment, stating that "the discovery of America, and that of a passage to the East Indies by the Cape of Good Hope, are the greatest and most important events recorded in the history of mankind."[3]

In the theme's most recent incarnation, the Discovery has acquired a distinctly modern companion. Writing near the dawn of the space age, in 1959, the intellectual historian Lewis Hanke focused not so much on the Discovery as the subsequent debate over Native Americans. "No matter how far rockets may reach into outer space," he asked, "will any more significant problems be discovered than those which agitated many Spaniards during the conquest of America?" In a similar vein, more than a decade after men walked on the moon, the semiotician Tzvetan Todorov declared that the voyages of the astronauts were of secondary significance because they led to "no encounter at all." In contrast, "the discovery of America, or of the Americans, is certainly the most astonishing encounter of our history."[4]

The connection between seafaring and spacefaring is made particularly explicit in the Smithsonian's National Air and Space Museum. In an exhibit titled *Where Next, Columbus?* the exploratory achievements of mankind are placed within a trajectory beginning with Columbus's transatlantic voyages, running through the European settlement of the North American West, and climaxing in space travel. One graphic from the exhibit even shows Columbus and the moon afloat in the same constellation.[5]

That image illustrates a second theme that has run parallel to the "greatest event" theme ever since the days of Columbus himself. This is the characterization of the European discovery and conquest of the Americas as the achievement of a few great men. This theme can also be summed up in a phrase that has appeared in print over and over—a handful of adventurers.

The roots of this interpretation run deep into the Conquest period itself, and versions of the phrase go back at least to the eighteenth century. Denis Diderot, for example, described the conquistadors as a mere "handful of men."[6] The version I have chosen as emblematic of the theme appears to have been coined in 1843 by the great nineteenth-century historian William Prescott. The Conquest of Mexico, wrote Prescott, was "the subversion of a great empire by a handful of adventurers."[7] Since then the phrase and variations upon it have become inescapable in the historical literature. The Conquest is the tale of "how a handful of Spaniards won two empires;" Cortés and Francisco Pizarro overthrew empires "leading only small bands of adventurers" with "no more than a handful of men"; the Conquest of Peru is achieved by "illiterate adventurers," or "by a mere handful of men," and that of Mexico by "a small contingent of Spanish adventurers" or "a motley bunch of Spanish adventurers."[8]

These two themes have inevitably given rise to a third. If history's greatest event—the European discovery and conquest of the Americas—was achieved by a mere "handful of adventurers," how did they do it? In the words of Francisco de Jerez, a conquistador of Peru who in 1534 published an account of the initial Spanish invasion of the Inca empire, "When in ancient or modern times have such huge enterprises of so few succeeded against so many?"[9] Historians writing today continue to repeat Jerez's question. "What . . . made so awesomely implausible a victory possible?" "How were small bands of conquistadores successful against powerful and populous polities?" "How could empires as powerful as those of the Aztecs or the Incas be destroyed so rapidly by a few hundred Spaniards?"[10]

The question represents "one of the most puzzling problems to have vexed historians."[11] Indeed, it is at the heart of this book, not only because the answers to it written before so often contain elements of all seven of the myths anatomized in these pages. It is also because the very posing of the question itself is profoundly misleading; it is the lid to the Pandora's Box of Conquest myths. Viewed within the circular confines of these three themes, the question of "how" answers itself. How could so few accomplish something so great? Because they themselves were exceptionally great men. This is the myth that is the focus of this first chapter.

⁀

In 1856 the Mexican artist José María Obregón completed a painting titled *The Inspiration of Christopher Columbus* (see Figure 2).[12] The painting captures the two principal elements of the Columbus myth—his brilliant use of the technology of the day, and, more importantly, the genius of his vision. The source of his inspiration is the ocean itself and what he somehow knows lies beyond it. Columbus gazes at the Atlantic horizon, seeing it not as a linear boundary but as a curved gateway to a new world.

This painting in fact tells us much more about the nineteenth century and views of Columbus in Obregón's day than it does about Columbus himself. In fact, the most exceptional thing about Columbus's geographical vision was that it was wrong. His achievements were the result of historical accident and his role in an historical process that was far larger than he was. Similarly, the Spaniards who subsequently crossed the Atlantic were part of a process peopled by many would-be conquerors. They and the people they encountered—not a mere handful of supposedly remarkable and great men—were responsible for the events that followed.

Among those Spaniards, Cortés and Pizarro are the best known. Indeed, the myth of exceptional men is centered on three monumental figures who still enjoy extraordinary name recognition almost half a millennium after their deaths. In a sense, the reputations of Columbus, Cortés, and Pizarro are justified. One discovered the Americas for early-modern Europeans, the other two led the initial expeditions that discovered and partially destroyed the two major empires that existed in the Americas in the early sixteenth century (the Mexica, or Aztec, and the Inca). As Columbus remarks in Sir Ridley Scott's feature film *1492: Conquest of Paradise*, summarizing his life's accomplishments: "I did it; you didn't."[13] Thus the Spanish empire in the Americas was made possible by the deeds of these three in the simplest sense; Spaniards needed to find the Americas and its major population centers in order to construct that empire.

Although using Columbus, Cortés, and Pizarro as larger than life characters that more or less explain the entire Conquest is clearly too facile, the simplicity of the model helps explain its incessant appeal. There seems to be a human impulse to personalize the past, to render complex processes intelligible and accessible by reducing them to emblematic characters and a narrative of their actions. The additional appeal of this reduction is that it gives the reducers a chance to shape the story and its protagonists. We shall see in a moment how this has occurred with respect to the examples of Columbus and Cortés.

My purpose is not to denigrate this technique of historical writing completely; after all, I use it myself in this book. Nor do I mean to create a narrative in which individual action is utterly subordinated to the larger structural forces and causes of social change. But in its absolute form the "great men" approach ignores the roles played by larger processes of social change. It fails to recognize the significance of context and the degree to which the great men are obliged to react to—rather than fashion—events, forces, and the many other human beings around them. The focus on a prominent few marginalizes the many other individuals whose lives were similar to those of the great save for the historical circumstances—that can often be described as historical accidents—that placed them in a different place and time. It likewise

Fig. 2. José María Obregón, The Inspiration of Christopher Columbus, *1856.*

renders virtually invisible the Native Americans and Africans who played crucial roles in these events and whose inclusion in the story of the Conquest makes it so much more interesting and, ultimately, more intelligible.

The complete explication of the myth of exceptional men will develop through all seven chapters, culminating in the myth to which it is most profoundly related, the myth of superiority. However, this chapter goes a long way toward explaining the myth through the related discussions of three sections. The first examines the role of Columbus in the myth's development. The second section traces the development of conquistador legends, focusing on Cortés as the most lauded of them all, from the myth's sixteenth-century roots to the present. The third and final section of the chapter details the seven principal elements of conquistador patterns of action—the procedures that were not exclusive to the visionary or brilliant few, but were the standard practices of all the Conquest's Spanish protagonists.

The Obregón painting of Columbus would probably be seen by most viewers today not as a true historical portrait, but as an allegory. One could argue that while Columbus may not have spent much time staring at the Atlantic (except perhaps when he was crossing it), he was surely inspired by its possibilities. Likewise, the Berry/Razaf song is on one level a witty ditty of the swing era and not to be taken too seriously. On the other hand, its humor only makes sense if the listener can be depended upon already to have a perception of Columbus as sagacious and visionary. The lyrics are a parody of that sagacity, for his hitting upon the idea that a mutiny can be averted by throwing a party (hardly an original or visionary notion) is only funny if one knows that he is "wise old Christopher Columbus" for more historically significant reasons.[14]

One of these reasons is what historian Felipe Fernández-Armesto has called "the infamous canard," namely Columbus's allegedly exceptional knowledge of the world's sphericity. As he sings in the song, "Since the world is round, we'll be safe and sound."[15] This legend is similarly the reference point to the opening scene of Scott's *1492: Conquest of Paradise,* in which Columbus, in a pose reminiscent of the Obregón painting, is sitting on the rocks looking out to sea. One of his sons is with him, a young boy whom Columbus instructs to watch a ship disappear over the horizon. His father, meanwhile, is peeling an orange. Again, whether the viewer takes the scene as accurate historical depiction or dramatic allegory, it only works because of the filmmakers' reasonable assumption that the viewer anticipates the significance of the orange. Sure enough, when the fruit is peeled and the ship disappears, Columbus spells out his brilliant connection between the shape of the orange and that of the world—"What did I tell you? It's round. Like this. Round!"[16]

One historian, Jeffrey Burton Russell, has written an entire book about this aspect of the Columbus myth, tracing it back to Washington Irving's 1828 account of the *Life and Voyages of Christopher Columbus*. Irving vividly described a 1486 debate in Salamanca between Columbus and a gathering of the wise men of Spain, professors, friars, and other senior churchmen who cited ancient authorities in support of their contention that the earth was flat. Columbus, bold visionary, risked condemnation as a heretic to defend his position on the earth's roundness. This scene was repeated in various forms by historians for the next hundred years.

The problem was, it was largely fiction. The Salamanca meeting, which occurred either in 1486 or 1487—and only two of whose wise men can be identified for certain—actually concerned the size of the ocean to the west, with Columbus erroneously arguing that the distance from Spain to Asia was shorter than the authorities claimed. "All agreed that what the Admiral was saying could not possibly be true," one of the professors present later testified. They were right in this, and in their belief that the earth was round, a belief shared by all educated Europeans of the day. Although Samuel Eliot Morison pointed out in his widely read 1942 biography of Columbus that the flat-earth Salamanca debate was "pure moonshine," the myth had caught hold and still resists being uprooted today.[17]

As Umberto Eco recently observed, most people, when asked "what Christopher Columbus wanted to prove," will answer that "Columbus believed the earth was round, whereas the Salamanca sages believed it was flat and hence thought that, after sailing a short distance, the three caravels would plunge into the cosmic abyss."[18] But although the men of Salamanca were right (about the earth's size), they were also wrong (about what lay to the west). And although Columbus was wrong (about the earth's size), he was also right (that sailing west led to land). In the end, it was not the vision and genius granted to Columbus by later myth makers that allowed him to stick doggedly to his error and still turn out to be right, it was rather (in Eco's phrase) "thanks to serendipity."[19]

It may have been serendipity, yes, but also historical process. In order to understand how Columbus fits into the myth of exceptional men, he must be placed in the dual context of two distinct historical processes. The first of these is the fifteenth-century process of Portuguese expansion into the Atlantic. The second is the nineteenth-century process whereby the modern myth of Columbus was constructed in the English-speaking world.

Columbus had profound Portuguese connections. Although he was Genoese and the sponsor of his voyages across the Atlantic was Queen Isabella of Castile, Columbus spent much of his life from the 1470s on in Portugal. In the late 1470s he married the daughter of a Portuguese Atlantic colonist, and he repeatedly sought royal Portuguese patronage before and after first approaching the Castilian monarch.

These Portuguese connections have tended to be ignored in popular representations of Columbus for various reasons. One is the obvious fact that Columbus's eventual contract with Isabella led to conquests in the sixteenth-century Americas that were far more Spanish than Portuguese. Another is the cliché-ridden history taught in schools, one rooted in the nineteenth-century development of the Columbus myth.[20] But Columbus himself is also to blame. His years spent as a foreigner peddling erroneous ideas about the size of the world fostered a sense of individual distinction tinged with paranoia, one he did not hesitate to promote on paper. "The image of the lonely man of destiny," as Fernández-Armesto has written, "struggling against prevailing orthodoxy to realize a dream that was ahead of its time, derives from his own self-image as a friendless outsider, derided by a scientific and social establishment that was reluctant to accept him." [21] As a result, Columbus's own writings have provided fodder for the formation of legends and myths about him— including the omission of the Portuguese context.

This context is so important because it is by looking at Portugal before and during Columbus's years there that one can see the degree to which the transplanted Genoese navigator had neither a unique plan nor a unique vision nor a unique pattern of previous experience.[22] Many others created and contributed to the expansion process of which Columbus became a part. Beginning 200 years before Columbus crossed the Atlantic, southern European shipping broke out of the Mediterranean into the Atlantic. The Vivaldi brothers, most notably, set off from Genoa in 1291 on what turned out to be a one-way voyage west across the Atlantic. Then, in the fourteenth and early fifteenth centuries a new zone of navigation was created that was bordered by the Azores in the north, the Canary Islands in the south, and the Iberian-African coasts in the east.[23]

Finally, from the 1420s on, a further stretch of exploration and navigation into the mid- and west Atlantic was created and charted. In the 1450s and 1460s, Flores, Corvo, the Cape Verde Islands, and the islands of the Gulf of Guinea were explored. The Madeiras and Canaries were settled and turned into sugar-plantation colonies and by 1478 the former was the largest sugar producer in the Western world. Maps of the time show how important and extensive was the discovery of Atlantic space; speculation about the lands and features of the ocean was the most noteworthy feature of fifteenth-century cartography.[24]

Although men from Italian city-states were involved from the start, and Castilians increasingly participated in the process (especially, from the late-fourteenth century on, in hostile competition for control of the Canaries), it was Portugal that dominated this expansion. Italian navigators were systematically and most effectively co-opted by the Portuguese monarchy (later joined by the Flemish), permitting the new Portuguese empire to control Atlantic settlement (except for the Canaries) and the agenda of expansion.[25]

This agenda featured a steady mapping of the African coastline with a view to rounding the foot of the continent and charting a route to the East Indies. By 1486 the Portuguese were so confident of imminent success that their ambassador to the Vatican, Vasco Fernandes de Lucena, pitched their endeavors to Pope Innocent VII during his coronation as something worthy of immediate blessing. Portuguese exploration to date allowed the ambassador "to perceive how many and how large accumulations of fortunes and honors and glory will befall not only all of Christendom but also . . . this most sacred See of Peter." The pitch worked, and the following year the pope issued one of his so-called expansion bulls condoning Portuguese imperial ambitions.[26]

Columbus tried to become part of this process with growing desperation in the 1480s and 1490s. He failed for so long because he lacked the connections and persuasive ideas of other navigators. Even after he succeeded in crossing the Atlantic and returning, the extent of his success was questioned and questionable within the context of the time. The islands he had found (in the Caribbean) fell within the zone assigned to the Portuguese by the 1486 papal bull. And although in 1494 the papacy brokered a Portuguese-Castilian treaty that redefined these zones, it became increasingly apparent during the 1490s that Columbus had not found the much-sought sea route to the East Indies—but had been lying about it to Queen Isabella. Then, in 1499, Vasco da Gama returned from his successful voyage around the Cape and it became clear that the Portuguese had won the competition after all.

Columbus's career was irreversibly damaged. His claim to have found islands off the coast of Asia, and thus the coveted sea route to that continent, rang hollow in the face of mounting evidence that these were new lands entirely. Columbus seemed to be lying for the sake of his contractual rewards. Perceiving the extent of his failure and his duplicity, the Castilian crown dispatched an agent to the Caribbean to arrest Columbus and bring him back to Spain in chains. Although he was later permitted to cross the Atlantic, he was forbidden to revisit the Caribbean and was stripped of the titles of Admiral and Viceroy of the Indies—titles he had fought to be included in his original contract and arguably the chief goal of his career. Meanwhile, those titles were conferred by the Portuguese crown upon da Gama.[27]

The fact that it was Columbus's voyages, not da Gama's, that would lead to the changing of world history was not to the Genoese's credit. His discoveries were an accidental geographical byproduct of Portuguese expansion two centuries old, of Portuguese-Castilian competition for Atlantic control a century old, and of Portuguese-Castilian competition for a sea route to India older than Columbus himself. Furthermore, had Columbus not reached the Americas, any one of numerous other navigators would have done so within a decade.[28] Most obviously, the Portuguese Pedro Álvares Cabral explored the Brazilian coast in 1500, likewise arriving there in an attempt to reach Asia (by rounding the Cape). In 1499 Alonso de Ojeda had sailed to the Venezuelan coast, accompanied by the Florentine Amerigo Vespucci, who also crossed the Atlantic under Portuguese license two or three times in 1501–1503 (and in 1508 became the chief pilot of Castile). Because Vespucci's letters made for much better reading than Columbus's and were published and sold well in the years immediately following his voyages, it was his name that a German cartographer assigned to Brazil in a map of 1507—a name that caught on and was applied to all the "Americas."[29]

The "unfairness" of this naming, and the irony of the phrase "Columbus discovered America," has not been lost on historians.[30] But it is an important reflection of the fact that in his lifetime—and for decades, to some extent centuries, afterward—Columbus was correctly perceived as a briefly fortunate but unexceptional participant in a process involving many southern Europeans.

Indeed the image of Vespucci taking the credit for Columbus's achievements should be tempered by the fact that the Florentine's fame came after the Genoese's death. Columbus did not live to see "America" named. The two explorers were friends, in fact, colleagues in the large Iberian community of navigators who were collectively responsible for the two seafaring feats that would one day be hailed by the likes of Abbé Raynal and Adam Smith as history's greatest events. Amidst the self-pity of his final years, Columbus lamented the lack of approbation heaped upon himself and his friend Vespucci, for whom he wrote that "Fortune has been adverse . . . as for so many others. His labors have not brought him the benefits they deserve."[31]

The decline of Columbus's fortunes after 1499 was not only the result of his losing the race to the East Indies, but also a product of his marginal status as a Genoese and a man of the sea in an ethnocentric Castilian world where Italians and sailors tended to be derided. He was also hampered as a "Spanish" settler and administrator by notions of colonial procedure that were derived more from Portuguese models than Castilian ones; the Portuguese emphasized trading posts, the Castilians permanent settlements. As a result, he was fated to be pushed aside by colonial-era historians just as he was by royal officials during his lifetime. When Gómara eulogized the conquest of the Americas as mankind's greatest moment since the coming of Christ, he not only had in mind Cortés, rather than Columbus, as the personification of that achievement, but he even denied the Genoese his role as first discoverer.[32] Toward the end of the sixteenth century Columbus began to appear in Italian epic poetry, and in the following century there emerged two complementary images of him, both rooted in his own writings but now given the romantic veneer characteristic of legend formation. One such image saw Columbus as an instrument of providence, the other portrayed him as an unappreciated visionary, an unjustly mocked heroic dreamer—as in Lope de Vega's 1614 play, *El Nuevo Mundo descubierto por Cristóbal Colón*

(The New World discovered by Christopher Columbus). Nevertheless, the Genoese remained a distant second, if that, to Cortés as the principal symbolic hero of the Discovery and Conquest.[33]

All of that began to change with the tricentennial of Columbus's first landfall in the Americas. Significantly, it was not in Spain or Latin America, but in the young United States, that this rehabilitation and reconstruction of the navigator took place. Certainly the new republics of Latin America did not ignore Columbus as a symbol ready for appropriation—one of these nations was named after him, and two Caribbean colonies fought over his remains.[34] But it was in Boston, Baltimore, and New York that celebrations were held on 12 October 1792. It was North American historians, such as Washington Irving, who generated interest in Columbus among English-speaking readers of the nineteenth century. And it was Italian and Irish immigrants and their descendants in the United States who in the late nineteenth century created solidarity organizations centered on an image of Columbus as an emblematic Catholic immigrant.[35]

Academic and popular interest in Columbus gathered pace in both North America and Europe as the four hundredth anniversary of his first voyage approached. These culminated in two colossal celebrations of the quadricentennial in Madrid in 1892 and Chicago in 1893. Years of preparation, millions of pesetas and dollars spent, hundreds of related events, millions of visitors and participants, all had the effect of so thoroughly creating a Columbus in the popular mind on both sides of the Atlantic that he survives to this day. In 1912 Columbus Day became an official holiday, and by 1992 it generated a public controversy almost as great as the celebrations of a century earlier. Yet whether the Genoese explorer is vilified or celebrated as hero, our Columbus—the one of present-day myth, history, and debate—is not a fifteenth-century man, but a nineteenth-century one, with a twentieth-century veneer.[36]

☞

If Columbus is the principal icon of the Discovery, Cortés is the principal icon of the Conquest. How did Cortés—and to a lesser extent Francisco Pizarro and other conquistadors—become elevated to icons by history?

The Mexican historian Enrique Florescano has observed that the Conquest gave rise to "a new protagonist of historical action and narration: the conquistador" and with him "a new historical discourse" that featured "a new manner of seeing and representing the past."[37] The historical discourse of the conquistadors may have been new in the sense of its application to the Americas, but it was actually based on a genre of document developed by Iberians before they reached the New World. This genre was the report that conquerors sent to the crown upon completion of their activities of exploration, conquest, and settlement. Such reports had a dual purpose. One purpose was to inform the monarch of events and newly acquired lands, especially if those lands contained the two elements most sought as the basis for colonization—settled native populations, and precious metals. The other purpose was to petition for rewards in the form of offices, titles, and pensions. Hence the Spanish name for the genre, *probanza de mérito* (proof of merit).[38]

The very nature and purpose of *probanzas* obliged those who wrote them to promote their own deeds and downplay or ignore those of others—to eliminate process and pattern in favor or individual action and achievement. Most of Conquest mythology can be found in these reports—the Spaniards as superior beings blessed by divine providence, the invisibility of Africans and native allies, the Conquest's rapid rush to completion, and above all the Conquest as the accomplishment of bold and self-sacrificing individuals.

Probanzas are also important because so many were written. Literally thousands sit in the great imperial archives in Seville, and still more are in Madrid, Mexico City, Lima, and elsewhere. In addition to documents declaring themselves to be *probanzas* and conforming strictly to its conventions, there were also other types of reports that featured most of the characteristics of *probanzas*, including *relaciones* (reports or accounts), *cartas* (letters), and *cartas de relación*. Typically *probanzas* and *relaciones* were addressed to the king, although sometimes other royal officials were approached directly as intermediaries.

Only the best-connected petitioners had a hope of the king himself reading their letters. Most such reports were brief—a page or two—wooden, formulaic in style, given scant attention by royal officials, then shelved until their rediscovery by twentieth-century historians. Many, no doubt, have never been read. But an influential minority were widely read either through publication as conquest accounts, or by being worked into colonial-period histories. For example, the famous letters by Cortés to the king, which were in effect a series of *probanzas*, were published shortly after reaching Spain. They so efficiently promoted the Conquest as Cortés's achievement, and sold so well in at least five languages, that the crown banned the *cartas* lest the conqueror's cult status become a political threat. The letters continued to circulate, however, and later admirers traveled like pilgrims to Cortés's residence in Spain. The Cortés cult was further stimulated by Gómara's hagiography of 1552—that the crown attempted to suppress too.[39]

There was plenty of precedent to the publication of *probanza*-like letters and to crown intervention in their distribution or suppression. Within months of Columbus's return to Spain from his first Atlantic crossing, a "letter" putatively written by him but actually crafted by royal officials based on a document by Columbus was published in Spanish, Italian (prose and verse versions), and Latin. It promoted the "discovery" as a Spanish achievement that cast favorable light on the Spanish monarchs and on Columbus as their agent.[40] Significantly, it also made the letter originally written by Columbus, who as a Genoese would have been less familiar with the Iberian genres, look more like a Spanish *probanza*.

Probably the best known of Conquest accounts, Bernal Díaz's narrative of the Conquest of Mexico, is seldom recognized for what it was—a monumental *probanza* whose absurd length (over 600 pages when later printed) counterproductively assured it would not be read by the king, as indeed it almost certainly was not. Perhaps Díaz had lost hope in the efficacy of the more conventional *probanza,* having penned a number of them earlier in his life. Requesting a pension in 1552, for example, he declared that he wrote to "your majesty as a loyal servant, the best I can, because for thirty-eight years I have served you." And six years later, he asked "to give account of who I am so that your majesty might deign to do me fuller favors." But despite coming from a family of good social standing, Díaz's connections proved to be a barrier rather than a conduit to those "fuller favors." As a relation of Diego Velázquez (early patron and then great enemy of Cortés), he was denied due reward in Mexico in the 1520s by Cortés, and suffered almost as much as a marginalized settler in Guatemala in the decades that followed.[41]

Perhaps Díaz's age at the time of his book's completion was such that he cared less about official royal reaction and more for the satisfaction of the creative process and the opportunity to pen countless jabs at Gómara, whose account Díaz judged with damning simplicity to be "very contrary to what happened."[42] In this sense, his account is more akin to a modern history book. Yet the structure, tone, and thrust of Díaz's text remain profoundly rooted in the conventions of the *probanza*. As one Díaz scholar, Ramón Iglesia, has commented, "his book is an unrestrained list of merits and services."[43]

Why did Díaz feel the need to list such "merits and services?" His dissatisfaction with his lot, his paltry share of the spoils of the conquests of Tenochtitlán and highland Guatemala, and his desire to set the record straight for posterity are only part of the answer. The larger context to his expectations and his choice of format for expressing himself is the culture of patronage in sixteenth-century Spain—a system of social, political, and economic networks that underlay almost all Spanish activities in the Americas and that nurtured the written culture of the *probanza*.

Royal patronage not only helps explain the first stage in the development of the great men myth—the *probanza*—but also the second, which is the body of literature comprising the chronicles or histories written in the colonial period. The dividing line between the two is blurred, but this is central to my point: the *probanza* evolved into the chronicle, *probanzas* were used as the basis of histories, and historical works adopted the conventions of the *probanza*. The most notable of those conventions was the way in which individuals were treated, especially the heroes to whom the Conquest could be attributed.

This treatment of individuals was in effect promoted by the crown. But, paradoxically, the crown also sought to suppress it. Official chronicler positions, created in 1532 and 1571, were intended to control the dissemination of information about the Conquest.[44] Such efforts were in vain. Part of the problem was that the Spanish crown lacked the centralized control and bureaucratic reach of the modern state—precisely the reason that attempts were repeatedly made to control the production of historical literature. More significantly, perhaps, was the fact that the culture of the *probanza*—its way of portraying the Conquest and its protagonists—became in the sixteenth century the dominant historical discourse, the conventional way in which Spaniards viewed and represented the Conquest.

The ultimate purpose of that representation was justification. The eyewitness accounts, such as Cortés's letters or Jerez's narrative of the massacre at Cajamarca, framed the justification of personal actions and roles within a larger context of imperial justification. The later writings of the chroniclers further developed the theme of justification into an ideology of imperialism that represented the Conquest as a dual mission, bringing both civilization and Christianity to the Americas. In the great sixteenth-century histories by Gómara, Antonio de Herrera, and Gonzalo Fernández de Oviedo the succession of discoveries and conquests are part of a providential plan to bring the true faith to the whole world. The Spaniards are obviously the agents of that divine plan, and the most prominent conquistadors are thus presented as God's principal agents.[45]

Cortés emerged in the sixteenth century as the most recognizable of God's agents for several reasons. One was the impressive nature of the Mexica empire and the subsequent importance of central Mexico to the Spanish empire. Another was the rapid publication and wide circulation (despite royal attempts at censorship) of Cortés's letters to the king, which argued unambiguously that God had directed the Conquest of Mexico as a favor to the Spanish monarchy. The blessed status of Cortés himself was heavily implied; in one letter he uses the Spanish term *medio* (medium or agent), to describe his providential role.[46] A third was the supportive spin placed on Cortés and the Conquest by the Franciscans.

Friars of the Order of St. Francis were the first Spanish priests into the Mesoamerican regions that would become the colonies of New Spain. In competition with the Dominicans, to a lesser extent other orders, and later the secular clergy (priests who were not members of an order), the Franciscans remained central to the activities of the church throughout colonial Spanish America. In central Mexico, Yucatan, and other parts of New Spain, sixteenth-century Franciscans were the driving force behind efforts to convert native peoples and build a colonial church. The roles that natives themselves played in that process, and the writings generated as a result by both friars and

natives, gave rise to an extraordinary body of literature that was foundational to the academic discipline of ethnography.[47]

The Franciscans saw Cortés's support of their entry into Mexico and their
activities in the earliest colonial years as being crucial to their mission, and as
a result contributed much to the formation of his legend. One such friar, Toribio
Motolinía, who was one of the famous first Franciscan Twelve into Mexico,
asked the emperor in a letter of 1555, "Who has loved and defended the Indians
of this new world like Cortés?" Motolinía (who took his name from the Nahuatl
for "poverty") was partly reacting to the writings of Bartolomé de Las Casas,
who had attacked Cortés and who, significantly, was a Dominican. The likes of
Las Casas, the Franciscan told the emperor, sought through exaggerations, errors, lies, and simple ignorance to obscure "the services [Cortés] did God and
your majesty." Above all, "through this captain, God opened the door for us to
preach his holy gospel, and it was he who caused the Indians to revere the holy
sacraments and respect the ministers of the church."[48]

Even Bernardino de Sahagún, the Franciscan who had preserved an important Mexica account of the Conquest as the final book of his epic twelve-
volume *General History of the Things of New Spain,* later rewrote the account
into "a paean of praise to Hernán Cortés and a justification of the Spanish
victory."[49] The original 1579 version reflected the perspectives of the Mexica
of Tlatelolco (a subordinate municipality within the capital that was
Tenochtitlán and then Mexico City). Sahagún claimed that his 1585 revised
version was still a native perspective that simply corrected "certain mistakes."
But the historian Sarah Cline has convincingly shown how the revisions promoted the attitudes of Sahagún and the other early Franciscans toward the
providential role of Cortés in leading the Spaniards into Mexico in 1519 and
inviting the Franciscans in 1524. The 1585 version thus had a political purpose,
at a time when the early Franciscan agenda was under attack from other Spaniards, and it reveals to us how the Cortés legend continued to be perpetuated
long after his death.[50]

The Franciscans saw the Conquest as a great leap toward the conversion of
all mankind and the subsequent second coming of Christ. This millennial vision influenced Cortés himself, inspiring him to make further expeditions in
the 1520s north to Baja California and south into Honduras. It also contributed to his legendary status among humanists and other intellectuals who frequently gathered at his house in Spain in his final years. These included Juan
Ginés de Sepúlveda, whose extreme negative views on "the Indians" pitted
him against Las Casas and would bring him infamy in twentieth-century academic circles. In 1543 Sepúlveda depicted the Conquest as epitomized by "a
noble, valiant Cortés" and "a timorous, cowardly Montezuma." Also included
in the Madrid group was Cervantes de Salazar, whose 1546 ode to Cortés (the
dedication to a dialogue on the dignity of man) compared him to Alexander,
Julius Caesar, and St. Paul.[51]

Here and facing page: *Figs. 3 and 4. Frontispieces to Gabriel Lasso de la Vega's* Cortés
valeroso, y Mexicana *(1588). The two images contrast the "invincible" man of arms at age
63, eyes heavenward, with the young ruff-collared man of letters, eyes on the reader; the
Cortés coat of arms is complete with the icons of status, Lasso de la Vega's is a plain shield.*

Another member of the circle was Gómara, whose account of the Conquest took the form of a hagiography of Cortés, who emerges as an idealized
figure to whom the entire Discovery and Conquest is subject; his narrative
begins and ends with the birth and death of Cortés.[52] Although Bernal Díaz
claimed that his own account was inspired in part by the errors he perceived
in Gómara's book, he nevertheless portrayed Cortés as a flawed but larger than
life figure—the flaws serving only to add a ruggedness to his heroism.[53] Although there were many accounts of the Conquest published during the colonial centuries, most giving the likes of "the great Cortés" the kind of adulatory
treatment he received in Gabriel Lasso de la Vega's *Cortés valeroso, y Mexicana*
(Valiant Cortés) of 1588 (see Figures 3 and 4), the three by Cortés, Gómara,
and Díaz remained the most influential.[54] Their effect was to magnify Cortés
as the emblematic conquistador, and to make the Conquest of Mexico a sym-

bol and model of the entire Conquest, with Columbus and Pizarro placed partially in Cortés's shadow and other conquests and conquistadors almost entirely eclipsed.

For centuries, the standard sources on the Conquest and related topics were the reports of Columbus and Cortés, similar accounts by other conquistadors, and the colonial histories based on them.[55] These tended to conform to the conventions of Spanish imperial ideology, with many of the more controversial texts not being published until after the colonial period. The longer works of Las Casas, for example, the *Historia general de las Indias* (General History of the Indies) and *La Apologética historia sumaria* (The Apologetic History) saw print in 1875 and 1909 for the first time, and Motolinía's *Historia de las Indias* (History of the Indies) and his *Memoriales* (Memorials) were not published until 1848 and 1903, respectively.[56]

Yet the nineteenth century hardly unraveled the colonial-era development of the myth of Cortés and the other "great men" responsible for the Conquest. This was in large part due to the third chronological stage in the development of this chapter's myth—the success of the histories of the Conquests of Mexico and Peru by William Prescott. Like Gómara's account, Prescott's narrative of the Mexican story ends not with the fall of Tenochtitlán, but later with the death of Cortés. As Prescott admitted, "The two pillars upon which the story of the conquest mainly rests are the Chronicles of Gómara and of Bernal Díaz." For Prescott, these two balanced each other, so that while Díaz "freely exposes [Cortés's] cunning or cupidity, and sometimes his cruelty, he does ample justice to his great and heroic qualities." [57]

Prescott's books repackaged the Conquest myths that were rooted in the *probanzas, relaciones,* and *cartas* of the conquistadors, and reworked them into an ideology of imperial justification by the colonial chroniclers. He presented them to an audience eager to read that a "handful" of Europeans, because of their inherently superior qualities, could triumph over numerous barbarous natives despite the odds and hardships. [58] This audience was well fed on a diet of the nineteenth-century European and North American versions of imperial and expansionist ideology. Prescott's Spanish Conquests were credible and comforting, while the Catholicism of the conquistadors allowed the Protestant author and readership alike a facile explanation for the occasional, unfortunate excess or act of cruelty.

Although Prescott wrote his histories of the Conquest a century and a half ago, they remain in print and are still read. [59] Furthermore, his influence is widely visible, combined as it is with the larger cultural impetus (one that influenced Prescott himself) toward depicting European conquests as achievements personalized by great leaders. [60] A fine example of the longevity of Prescottian perspectives on the Conquest is Hugh Thomas's *Conquest,* which has sold well in many languages since it was first published in 1995. Although Thomas uses some native sources and did some original archival research, his book is overwhelmingly based on Spanish sources and projects a traditional Spanish perspective on events. As suggested by the subtitle—*Montezuma, Cortés, and the Fall of Old Mexico*—the book reproduces Bernal Díaz's gripping narrative by similarly emphasizing the intrigues and decisive impact of the Spanish and native Mexican leaders, in particular the former. [61]

Thomas's book contains the chief elements of that Conquest perspective running back through Prescott and Gómara to Cortés himself and the *probanzas* of the conquerors. Those elements are the structuring of the Conquest into a clear narrative that leads inexorably to victory, an explanation of the Conquest that ultimately testifies to the civilizational superiority of the Spaniards, a glorification of Cortés, and an endorsement of the myth that a few great and exceptional men made the Conquest possible. [62]

Shortly after landing on the coast of the Gulf of Mexico in 1519, in a move routinely hailed as bold and brilliant, Cortés burned his ships. Actually, he did not. The ships were scuttled and at least one was merely grounded. But in 1546 Cervantes de Salazar referred in print to Cortés's ship-burning and the image took hold.[63]

The myth of the burning ships not only reflects the existence of numerous little legends within the larger myths, but also illustrates how every move of Cortés's has been taken as indicative of his exceptionality.[64] With respect to the destruction of ships, Francisco de Montejo did the same thing in 1527 on the coast of Yucatan.[65] Arguably this was in imitation of Cortés, and no doubt Cortés did influence other conquistadors through their common experience of the invasion of the Mexica empire or through reading the published editions of his letters to the king. However, too often, without any direct evidence, the actions of conquistadors after the 1519–21 invasion of Mexico are taken as deliberately imitating Cortés, while pre-1519 patterns are ignored.

The classic position is summed up well in this sentence written in 1966 by Charles Gibson, one of the most eminent colonial Latin American historians of his generation: "Although no other conquistador rivaled Cortés in military skill or in the capacity to control the conquest aftermath, all subsequent campaigns were in some measure modeled upon the conquest of the Aztec empire."[66] This image of Cortés as both exception and archetype has been articulated in various forms by numerous scholars, who see Cortés as "incomparable" in his particular combination of skills, as "a remarkably gifted man" who is "the first to have a political and even a historical consciousness of his actions." Without Cortés, "there might very well have been no Conquest," as he "was the one who created the dream of gold and new power which intoxicated all those who followed him."[67]

In fact, Cortés followed Conquest procedures that had Iberian roots predating the Conquest and were consolidated during the Caribbean phase of Conquest (1492–1521). These routines were further developed in the sixteenth and seventeenth centuries not because all conquistadors mimicked Cortés— although some may have imagined they were emulating him—but because Spaniards were concerned to justify their actions and give them a legalistic veneer by citing and following approved precedents. The Conquest pattern was a procedure followed by many, not the exceptional actions of a handful.[68]

The first aspect of Conquest procedure was the use of legalistic measures to lend a veneer of validity to an expedition. Such measures typically included the reading out of a legal document, such as a conquest license or the so-called Requirement—the request for submission that was rather absurdly to be read to native communities or armies before hostilities took place. Also included was the declaration of a formal territorial claim. Finally, typical legalistic measures included the founding of a town. Spaniards placed great emphasis on city-dwelling, equating it with civilization, social status, and security, and so the gesture was imbued with reassuring symbolism for the conquistadors. It also permitted a given group of conquistadors to turn themselves into a *cabildo* (town council) and thereby acquire standing sufficient to make certain kinds of resolutions, laws, and other legally valid decisions.

The most famous instance of this is the founding of Vera Cruz on the Gulf of Mexico coast by Cortés and his fellow captains. The cabildo thereby created wrote immediately to the crown, stating that "to all of us it seemed better that a town with a court of justice should be founded and inhabited there in the name of your Royal Highnesses, so that in this land your Majesties might possess lordship as in your other kingdoms and domains."[69]

In fact, the purpose of the imaginary Vera Cruz was not to set about building a town but to create a new basis of authority to replace that given to Cortés by his patron, the governor of Cuba. This case is famous but not unique; conquistadors routinely "founded" towns and cities during the course of explorations and invasions, settlements that were not built at that moment, if ever, but that figuratively marked the countryside as legally claimed and possessed by the expedition leaders. Early Caribbean cities such as Santo Domingo and Havana were founded two or three times before becoming permanent settlements. Francisco de Montejo founded at least four settlements on the coast of Yucatan named after his home town of Salamanca; only one was ever actually built and none retained that name, but the putative foundings gave a legalistic veneer to Montejo's claims that his expeditions were going better than they actually were.[70]

The purpose of Vera Cruz as a town that existed in 1519 in name only leads us to the second aspect of Conquest procedure—the appeal to a higher authority, typically and ideally the king himself. In the passage quoted above, the Vera Cruz *cabildo*, obviously representing the interests of Cortés and his faction within the expedition, state that founding a town is "better" than carrying out the orders of Diego Velázquez, the governor of Cuba and patron to Cortés and his expedition. These orders were, in the rather snide words of the letter to the crown, "to acquire as much gold as possible and, having acquired it, return with it to the island of Fernandina [Cuba] in order that it might be enjoyed only by Diego Velázquez and the captain [Cortés]."[71] By supporting a different course of action, Cortés is thus portrayed as selflessly giving up this collaborative enjoyment with Velázquez, to the crown's benefit. In fact, Cortés needed the direct approval of the crown in order to claim governorship of whatever lands he was able to conquer. His strategies did not so much reflect his allegedly exceptional political skills, but rather the nature of his legal position. Simply put, Velázquez held the crown's license to explore (and was about to receive a license to conquer) and to become governor, Cortés needed that license. To that end, he betrayed Velázquez, wrote directly to the king, sent agents to argue his case at court, and scuttled the remaining ships to prevent Velázquez loyalists from

slipping back to Cuba to warn him—all logical, predictable, standard conquistador responses to the situation.[72]

One of the agents sent to Spain was Francisco de Montejo. He likewise sought
to circumvent the patronage of Cortés and acquire directly a license to conquer from the king. Thus while campaigning at court in the early 1520s on
behalf of Cortés, Montejo also lobbied to have Yucatan defined as a territory
separate from Mexico with himself the recipient of a license to conquer it—
that he received in 1526.[73] Similarly, the roots of the Conquest of Peru can be
found in expeditions of exploration under Francisco Pizarro and Diego de
Almagro sent out along the Pacific coast by Pedrarias de Avila, governor of
Panama and Nicaragua. Voyages of 1524–28 along the northern Pacific coast of
South America convinced Pizarro that the region contained enough wealth
and native population to be worth making the arduous return voyage to Spain
to acquire his own license to conquer. Pedrarias had died, but it was important
to Pizarro that he shut out potential rival claims from the governor's successor, Pedro de los Ríos, and from Pizarro's own partner, Almagro.[74]

Returning from Spain in 1530 with a long list of titles and honors for himself, and none for Almagro, it was clear that Francisco Pizarro had stabbed
his partner in the back. Although the two men remained partners with a
fatally bitter competitiveness (Pizarro had Almagro executed in 1537 and four
years later Almagro's son had Pizarro assassinated), Pizarro's apparent treachery should not been seen as an individual character trait. Nor should Almagro's attempts to take southern Peru from Pizarro be seen solely in terms
of personal rancor. Both men were simply following standard procedures in
order to attain the ultimate goal of every conquistador—royal confirmation
of the governorship of an imperial province. As Francisco Pizarro wrote in a
letter a few days before he was murdered, the governorship of Peru "is the
most important thing to me and for which I have always clamored, since without it all my hardships and services will have been in vain."[75]

Another example of an appeal to the king as typical Conquest procedure
took place when Gonzalo Pizarro (Francisco's brother) led a vast expedition
east from Quito across the Andes and into Amazonia in 1540. The terrain got
the better of the Spaniards and their African and native auxiliaries, and as the
death toll mounted the expedition ground to a halt. One of the company's
captains, Francisco de Orellana, was sent ahead by river to find food. He and
his small party never returned, instead successfully navigating the Amazon all
the way out to the Atlantic and eventually making it to the Caribbean and then
Spain. Pizarro, meanwhile, waited for weeks before struggling back to Quito.

According to Orellana, the river's current made it impossible for him to
return to Gonzalo Pizarro and the main body of expedition survivors. According to Pizarro, Orellana deliberately and treacherously abandoned him.
Colonial chroniclers took Pizarro's side, and subsequent historians followed

their cue. Prescott, for example, accused Orellana of abandoning his "unfortunate comrades . . . in the wilderness;" the "glory of the discovery" of the Amazon was "barren [and] surely not balanced by the iniquitous circumstances which attended it." In the 1950s the English writer George Millar wrote an *apologia* for Orellana, whose reputation for centuries, complained Millar, had been that of "a cad if not a coward." Historians over the past half century have done little to build upon Millar's obscure efforts to undo Gonzalo Pizarro's labeling of Orellana as "the worst traitor that ever lived." Most have simply ignored him, and Michael Wood's sympathetic attention to him in his recent *Conquistadors* television series and book is unusual.[76]

Yet Orellana's actions were neither heroic nor treacherous. Regardless of whether he was or was not able to return upriver to Pizarro, his willingness to go ahead alone, his subsequent defense of his actions, and his acquisition in Spain of a conqueror's permit to return as *adelantado* (licensed conqueror) to the Amazon (where he soon died) all conformed to the well-established patterns of conquistador behavior.[77]

#3

The purpose of Gonzalo Pizarro's expedition over the Andes was to locate the source of gold usually embodied in the legend of El Dorado (a mythical ruler or city of gold)—bringing us to the third routine aspect of Conquest procedure. This was the search for precious metals, preferably gold, with silver a close second. This aspect of Conquest procedure has probably least often been depicted as the exceptional or original strategy of Cortés or one of the other well-known conquistadors. On the contrary, it has been accurately seen as a concern of all members of Spanish expeditions. But it has certainly been misunderstood, to the extent that Spanish "thirst for gold" represents one of the many little legends or mini-myths of the Conquest. The conquistadors have been depicted as "driven by the lust for gold" or by a "greed" for it that "is strongly reminiscent of the collective psychosis that seized upon California gold diggers in the mid-nineteenth century." In the words of another scholar, "It never occurred [to Spanish colonists] to do anything but look for gold, and this frantic search for precious metals, jewels, and pearls prevented them from engaging in any productive economic activity."[78]

Such a perspective fails utterly to understand the nature of the early colonial economy and the role played in it by precious metals. The "most important thing" to Pizarro was not gold, but the governorship. However, he needed to find gold in order for there to be a governorship worth having. Put in the larger context, Spaniards had no interest at all in the metal per se, any more than we treasure credit cards as objects. The finely worked gold artifacts collected at Cajamarca and other places were melted down in the *fundición*, a routine that immediately followed all such acquisitions and that allowed shares to be paid out, debts settled, and further supplies and credit procured. It was the value and buying power of gold and silver that Spaniards cared for. They conceived of the precious metals as money—often referring to shipments of them as *dineros*—and as the basis of the credit system that supported so much conquistador activity.[79]

If Spaniards seem at times single-minded in their quest for these metals, this was because gold and silver were not just the preferred source of wealth, but the only items whose value in relation to their transportability made the entire Conquest and colonial endeavor possible. No other New World product even came close to being as valuably nonperishable, divisible, and compact. Rather than being a barrier to "productive economic activity," gold and silver from the Americas and its pursuit by Spaniards underwrote the Conquest and virtually all subsequent economic activity in the New World (let alone altering the economic and political history of Europe).

Almost as determinedly as they sought gold, Spaniards looked for native populations. One aspect of this complex process was the need to acquire native allies—the fourth standard Conquest procedure. This strategy was necessitated by the fact that Spanish expeditions were always outnumbered by the native peoples of the regions being invaded, and that Spaniards were often ignorant of both region and people. Allies were potential sources of invaluable information. They also provided crucial support in the way of provisions and porters to transport them. Above all, native allies provided military assistance, offsetting the potential imbalance of numbers during battle and allowing the Spaniards to pursue a classic divide-and-conquer strategy. This was by no means an original or exceptional strategy as pursued by Cortés or by Pizarro; every conquistador sought native allies, as many and as soon as possible.

The fifth routine aspect of the Conquest was the acquisition of a particular category of native ally—the interpreter. Much has been made of Cortés's use of a Nahua noblewoman as his interpreter—the famous Malinche—often giving the impression that she was an example of Cortés's superior strategic skills. Yet Cortés was only following procedure and had quite predictably been keeping his eyes out for a potential interpreter ever since first sighting the mainland. To that end, he had gone to some trouble to rescue Gerónimo de Aguilar, shipwrecked seven years earlier on the Yucatec coast, on the reasonable assumption that Aguilar had learned the mainland native language.[80] But Aguilar could only speak Yucatec Maya, not Nahuatl, the language of the Mexica empire, so Cortés continued to search. That Malinche could speak Maya and Nahuatl was pure luck, but she was soon taught Spanish anyway.

As with many of these patterns, the routine search for an interpreter can be traced back to the earliest days of the Conquest. Columbus seized and acquired native guides beginning with his first voyage, guides who were obliged to learn Spanish immediately and therefore could soon be called upon to act as interpreters. Seven Caribbean natives were brought back to Spain in 1493 to be instructed as interpreters. Five soon died, but the others returned with Columbus on his second voyage. After these two apparently died, the quest for interpreters continued. In 1502, for example, a Central

American native was captured, christened Juan Pérez, and trained specifically for this purpose.[81]

Examples abound from then on. Hernández de Córdoba, acting "in an entirely expected manner" (as historian Hugh Thomas observes), took two prisoners off the Yucatec coast in 1517, either nicknaming or baptizing them Melchor and Julián, and tried to make interpreters of them. Julián reluctantly cooperated and returned to the coasts of Yucatan with the Grijalva expedition of following year, but died soon after. Melchor resisted (that Gómara would later read as lack of couth). Although he too accompanied Grijalva, Melchor escaped at the first opportunity when brought along on Cortés's expedition. Other interpreters, some Spanish but the vast majority native, pop up periodically in the accounts of these expeditions. For example, there is the native Jamaican woman found on the Yucatec coast; a Nahuatl speaker captured by Grijalva, baptized Francisco, and used by Cortés; the Shakori native of South Carolina, interpreter for Vásquez de Ayllón, who called him Francisco de Chicora and took him to Spain; the Spanish page Orteguilla, assigned by Cortés to Moctezuma during the emperor's captivity, who soon became bilingual; and Gerónimo de Aguilar, the shipwrecked Spaniard rescued by Cortés after eight years among the Mayas.[82]

Many others followed in later decades. For example, the Conquest role of Martinillo, an Andean interpreter, allowed him to become don Martín Pizarro. Gaspar Antonio Chi enjoyed a long career in sixteenth-century Yucatan as both a Maya nobleman and the colony's Interpreter General.[83] The fates of native interpreters like Malinche, Martinillo, and Chi owed much to their own abilities, but they also reflected the fact that the quest for interpreters and their relative acceptance into colonial society was a fundamental and ubiquitous Conquest pattern.

The sixth aspect of Conquest procedure was the use of display violence, or the theatrical use of violence. Despite the assistance of native allies (and interpreters), and the use of African auxiliaries, Spanish-led forces often remained outnumbered and seriously threatened by the native peoples whose lands they were invading. Despite evidence of numerous massacres by Spaniards and the routine enslavement of the seminomadic peoples of the Caribbean and Central America, for the most part Spaniards did not seek to decimate or enslave native peoples but rather to subdue and exploit them as a more or less compliant labor force. A standard means of pursuing such subjugation was to employ dramatic displays of concentrated violence in order to terrorize a native group and convince them of the efficacy of cooperation with Spanish demands. Theatrical and terrorizing techniques appear again and again in the records of Conquest expeditions.[84]

These include the severing of the right hands (or sometimes the arms) of native prisoners, often by the hundreds;[85] the killing of women and, if necessary, sending the corpses home; and the mutilation or killing of select individuals, most typically by fire or by setting mastiffs on them, in front of native witnesses.[86] Another technique was the massacre of unarmed natives, whose effect was magnified if women, children, and the elderly were killed (as in the Cortés-led massacre in Cholula), or if the victims were celebrants in an important native festival or ritual (as in the Alvarado-led massacre in Tenochtitlán), or if the victims were confined by space or crowded tightly together (as in both of the above cases as well as the Pizarro-led massacre of Atahuallpa's entourage). As John Ogilby put it in 1670, Spanish expeditions advanced with "fear conquering more than slaughter."[87] If these examples use terror more than theater, more theatrical tactics and techniques were intended to confuse or impress. These included the attaching of bells to horses; the sounding of trumpets in conjunction with the firing of guns; and the use of cannons to blow apart trees or buildings.[88]

One particularly theatrical form of display violence was the public seizure of a native ruler (the seventh aspect of conquistador procedure). The move by Cortés that has been commonly judged his most bold, his "most startling decision," in Todorov's words, is the seizure of Moctezuma following the Mexica emperor's welcoming of the Spaniards into Tenochtitlán.[89] While the Spaniards were themselves prisoners of the Mexica within one of the palaces in the city center, they kept Moctezuma their prisoner in order to guarantee their safety. The ploy worked for a while, and then when Moctezuma was no longer useful to the Spaniards, they murdered him— later claiming that a stone thrown by one of the emperor's own people had dealt him a fatal blow on the head. Much has been made of the genius and even the supposed originality of this strategy, with Cortés being given all credit and Moctezuma denounced for allowing it to happen.

Such analysis, however, fails to recognize that Spaniards routinely took native rulers hostage. Pizarro's famous capture of Atahuallpa at Cajamarca in 1532 is either taken to be as exceptional and ingenious as Cortés's seizure of Moctezuma or assumed to be an imitation of the Mexican case.[90] In fact, the leaders at Cajamarca—Pizarro, Benalcázar, and Soto—were all 20-year veterans of the Conquest of Panama and Nicaragua, where they had been capturing native rulers long before any Spaniard even knew Mexico existed.[91] And shortly before the march to Cajamarca, Pizarro had captured and held hostage the native ruler of Puná Island, Tumbalá.[92]

What made Atahuallpa's capture unique was simply a matter of scale— the extent of Atahuallpa's empire, the size of his entourage, the quantity of gold and silver with which he was "ransomed" (the Spaniards executed him anyway). But his capture as a strategy was by no means original. Indeed, the practice was instinctive to Spaniards from the start of the Conquest. When, in 1493, the Haitian native lord Guacanagarí appeared to slip from Columbus's control, the Spaniards on the expedition demanded that they be allowed (in the words of Las Casas) "to take Guacanagarí prisoner, but the Admiral would not do it."[93] However, Columbus's uncertainty as to how to control and treat the natives soon allowed standard Spanish practices to become dominant. A year later another Haitian lord, Caonabó, was publicly executed, and thereafter Spaniards routinely captured, ransomed, tortured, and executed native rulers throughout the Caribbean islands and later the adjacent mainland.[94]

Four decades after Columbus's first voyage, and shortly after Atahuallpa's capture at Cajamarca, one of the men present, Gaspar de Marquina, sent his father a letter attached to a gold bar acquired from the Inca ruler's ransom. Gaspar casually mentioned that the Spaniards had captured one of the local "great lords," and "with him prisoner, a man can go by himself 500 leagues without getting killed."[95] Thus, in a nutshell, Marquina unwittingly conveyed both the routine nature and causal efficacy of the capture of native leaders.

Just as prominent conquistadors such as Cortés and Pizarro were not original in their decisions and actions, nor were the Spaniards in their general conformity to the routine aspects of the Conquest employing unique tactics. Many of these aspects were part of the patterns both of Native American and western European imperial expansion and warfare. In the decades before the major Spanish invasions of the American mainland, Castilians and their neighbors had developed conquest practices and routines through the acquisition of a string of possessions in the southern Mediterranean, northern Africa, and the Caribbean.[96] During this same time, the Mexica and Inca had likewise developed standard procedures through the rapid creation of extensive empires, the former stretching from northern Mexico to the edge of the Maya area, the latter ranging from Ecuador to Chile.

Yet the larger contexts of conquistador activities have been overwhelmed by a view of the Conquest that has dominated our historical discourse on its events and protagonists, a view that gives primacy of cause and explanation to a handful of exceptional men. Collective achievement, of course, is less appealing both to the participants and to those later reading about it as the human impulse is to look for the heroes and villains. Explaining the Discovery and Conquest in terms of the vision of Columbus or the genius of Cortés would no doubt have delighted both men, but it has been a barrier to a fuller understanding of this "greatest event since the creation of the world." Fortune may have been "adverse" to Columbus, as he claimed was true of his friend Vespucci, but history has not—nor has it been to Cortés and Pizarro.

2

Neither Paid Nor Forced
The Myth of the King's Army

If the Romans subjugated so many provinces, it was with greater or equal numbers of people, in known territories, provided with the usual sustenance, and with paid captains and armies. But our Spaniards . . . were never more than two or three hundred and even less. . . . And the many times they traveled, they were neither paid nor forced but went of their own will and at their own cost.

—Francisco de Jerez (1534)

Then a few days after [Governor Pedrarias] died, we got news of how Governor Francisco Pizarro was coming to be governor of this kingdom of New Castile. And so, hearing this news and having few prospects in Nicaragua, we came to this district, where there's more gold and silver than iron in Biscay.

—Gaspar de Marquina (1533)

I gave to the *adelantado* [my husband, Francisco de Montejo] a great quantity of money for the costs of the people and fleet that came to these provinces for their conquest and pacification, which assistance the *adelantado* took and thus carried out that conquest, as is common knowledge.

—Doña Beatriz de Herrera (1554)

When Columbus returned on his second voyage to the Caribbean island that he had named Hispaniola, he was accompanied by a Spanish army. At least, this is the impression given by a dramatic scene in the 1992 movie *1492: Conquest of Paradise*, in which Spanish soldiers line up on the beach in disciplined ranks, in uniforms and with standard-issue weapons, banners waving, awaiting a drum roll before marching forward.[1]

This same impression is repeated in movies, illustrations, textbooks, and scholarly publications. According to this common portrait, the first Spanish invaders and settlers pursued careers "through the military" and constitute "forces" that "march" under the "command" of their captains, who plan and execute "military operations." All are part of "Spain's war machine." Most persistently, they are "soldiers." Cortés sets off with "three hundred foot soldiers."

He talks to "his soldiers," and he gives away his interpreter and lover, Malinche, "to one of his soldiers." In addition to the predominance of military terminology to describe Spanish expeditions and the ubiquitous use of the term "soldier" to describe the conquerors, the Spanish royal state is typically granted a monolithic, directive role in Spanish expansion.[2] The sum of all this is what I have called the "myth of the king's army."

⟋⟍

In the eyewitness account by Francisco de Jerez of the 1532 events at Cajamarca— the Pizarro-Atahuallpa encounter and subsequent massacre of Andeans—the conquistador reminds his readers that the Spaniards did *not* constitute an army. Jerez's point of reference was not the Spanish army, for such a thing was still ill defined even in Europe in the 1530s, but the Roman army of ancient times. The triumph of the Pizarro-led Spaniards, in what Jerez most prematurely calls "the conquest of Peru," is thus presented as even more extraordinary and impressive precisely because it was not the achievement of "paid captains and armies."[3]

Other accounts by Spaniards who participated in Conquest campaigns confirm Jerez's assertion. For example, some modern historians who refer to the "soldiers" who invaded the Mexica empire quote the letters written by Cortés himself, thereby lending apparent authenticity to the use of the term. But the word always turns out to have been inserted by historians or by Cortés's English translators; where the Pagden edition has "three hundred foot soldiers," Cortés himself writes *trescientos peones*, "300 men on foot."[4] Cortés not only avoids the word "soldier" but reveals in his letters to the king, despite his efforts to portray himself as firmly in charge, that the men following him are as much a motley bunch of individuals as Jerez's compatriots at Cajamarca would be.

If the conquistadors themselves made it clear in the 1520s and 1530s that no armies were sent by the king of Spain to the Americas during these decades, what is the origin of the myth? Are we simply influenced by our own senses of what modern armies are like? No doubt this has much to do with the perpetuation of the myth. We are accustomed to legal, armed activity being the monopoly of highly institutionalized national forces. Understanding sixteenth-century Spanish expeditions requires a leap of imagination.

But the myth also has roots in military developments in Spain in the mid-to-late sixteenth century and the changes in terminology that accompanied those developments. The 1615 illustration of Atahuallpa's seizure at the top of Figure 5 seems to contradict Jerez's eyewitness description and show the men of Cajamarca as soldiers. In fact, tracking the use of *soldado*, the Spanish term for "soldier," is revealing. Cortés does not use it in the 1520s, nor does

Fig. 5. Title page to the sixth volume of Antonio de Herrera's
Historia General de los Hechos de los Castellanos (1615).

Pedro de Alvarado writing of his invasion of Guatemala in the same decade, nor does it appear anywhere in the official 64-page report of the division of gold and silver among the men at Cajamarca in 1533 (or in a 1557 copy of that report).[5] In the account of the Conquest of Yucatan by the Franciscan friar Diego de Landa, the phrase *soldados españoles* appears just once. As the surviving version of the account is a compilation of excerpts and summaries made in the late seventeenth century, this could be a later addition. However, as Landa's original, long-lost manuscript was written around 1566, the single use of "soldiers" could also reflect the gradual shift in terminology and Spanish perceptions of who conquistadors were.[6] In one collection of letters written by conquistadors and other Spanish settlers in the Americas between 1520 and 1595, only one of the 36 documents uses the word "soldier." Significantly it was written relatively late and by a new arrival—in 1556 by a Spanish woman, doña Isabel de Guevara, in the recently founded town of Asunción, Paraguay.[7]

Bernal Díaz uses *soldado* often in his narrative of the Conquest of Mexico, but his book was drafted around 1570, finished in 1576, and edited for its first publication in 1632.[8] By this time, a century after Jerez had written of the events at Cajamarca, the conquistadors were well on the way to becoming soldiers. They certainly looked the part in Herrera's title-page illustrations (see Figure 5), and in the Conquest paintings that were fashionable in seventeenth-century Mexico. In Figure 6, for example, Cortés appears at the head of a fully armored and well-organized military force that includes galleons, cavalry, and artillery. Conquistadors were soldiers and nothing else when Ilarione da Bergamo heard of the Conquest from Spaniards in Mexico in the 1760s,[9] by which time engravings and paintings of Columbus and Spanish conquistadors routinely showed them in full armor, backed by uniformed soldiers.[10] In the nineteenth century the terminology of "soldier" and "army" was unquestioned (even though a close read of Prescott's histories, based as they were in large part on early colonial accounts, reveals a wealth of evidence as to the true nature of the conquerors). In the early twentieth century, books on the Conquest tended to include illustrations that further perpetuated the myth. For example, the 1923 frontispiece to Francisco de Icaza's "biographical dictionary" of the conquistadors depicts the first settlers coming ashore as a unit of professional soldiers with standard-issue dress and equipment.[11]

The gradual adoption of *soldado* in the late sixteenth century, and the assumption that soon followed that the early conquistadors were soldiers, related to broader shifts in the way Europeans waged war. Significantly it was the Spaniards—and close behind them their archenemies of the day, the French— who led the way in creating what historians have come to call the "military revolution." This revolution took many forms. For one, the size of military forces grew dramatically; whereas Ferdinand and Isabella had taken Granada in 1492 with 60,000 men, their grandson Charles V besieged the German city

Fig. 6. "Veracruz N2": The arrival of Cortés in Veracruz and the reception by Moctezuma's ambassadors. The second painting in the Strickland/Kislak Conquista de México *series, Mexican School, seventeenth century. Cortés, Bernal Díaz, and Marina (or Malinche) are identified by number.*

of Metz in 1552 with 150,000. By the end of the century, Spanish (and French) armies had again more than doubled in size.

Furthermore, developments in artillery meant that numbers of guns, tonnage of gunpowder used, and gunner numbers doubled three times over during the century. Artillery was just one aspect of the revolution in firearm technology and the tactics and strategy with which weapons were used. Finally, campaigns grew longer as well as larger and more complex, so that war became a permanent state of affairs; there were just nine years of peace in sixteenth-century Europe. Created by Castilian expansionism, Spain had only just become a loosely defined nation at the end of the fifteenth century. Yet within decades, Spain's Hapsburg rulers had acquired a European empire stretching from Italy to the Netherlands to the Canary Islands. Thus because Spain was not the only concern of its Hapsburg kings, they were obliged to maintain multiple, large forces—that were dedicated well into the seventeenth century to crushing French, Dutch, English, and German Protestant opposition to Hapsburg hegemony over Europe.

All of this might be taken to show that the conquistadors really were soldiers in a Spanish war machine. But this was not so. During the foundational decades of Spanish expansion, from the first Caribbean settlements of the 1490s to the spread of conquest expeditions throughout much of the American mainland in the 1530s, the military revolution was still in its genesis. Most of the important technological changes—the invention of the musket, the use of volley-fire techniques; the building of faster, larger, and better-armed ships—would not occur until the second half of the century. And while the numbers of men at arms grew dramatically in the sixteenth century, that growth was even greater in the seventeenth. By 1710 there were 1.3 million Europeans at arms.

Perhaps most significantly, only in the seventeenth century were permanent, professional armies created of the kind that we associate with the term "army" today. Such armies were loyal to a state, rather than an individual leader. They evolved as nation-states came into being and concepts of citizenship took shape. It was thus not until long after the heyday of the conquistadors that the European states, Spain included, achieved the level of centralization and institutionalization to be able to field forces in which the majority of men were trained, salaried, permanent, veteran soldiers with uniforms and standard-issue weapons. Even then, this was an ideal by no means always realized.[12]

In addition, these changes were driven by wars in Europe and it was there that professional armies developed and changes were implemented. In the sixteenth century, Spain lacked the resources to dispatch large forces and significant quantities of weapons across the Atlantic. The formal fleet system linking Seville to the American colonies was not well established until the 1550s. It also lacked the motive to do so, as serious European competition in the Americas did not develop until the next century. Furthermore, Spain's involvement in European conflicts was increasingly complex and challenging during the sixteenth century. Spain's response to the tactical, logistical, and technological demands of these conflicts has been hailed by military historians as remarkable and revolutionary. But Spanish conquest endeavors in the Americas were peripheral to this process and cannot be attributed to Spain's admittedly foundational contributions to the military revolution in Europe.[13]

Finally, Spaniards soon learned that the New World required different military methods. In his 1599 book, *The Armed Forces and Description of the Indies*, the Spanish captain Bernardo de Vargas Machuca argued that in the Americas the patterns and practices of European warfare were irrelevant. Called by one prominent military historian "the first manual of guerrilla warfare ever published," the treatise proposed that linear formations, hierarchical units, and permanent garrisons be abandoned in favor of small, covert fighting units dedicated to search-and-destroy missions carried out over several years.[14]

Vargas Machuca seemed unaware that much of what he was advocating had already been common practice among Spaniards in the Americas for a century. Cortés's 500 men and the 168 at Cajamarca were relatively large companies of conquistadors. Beyond the central regions of Mesoamerica and Peru, most expeditions comprised less than 100 Spaniards (almost always outnumbered by African slaves and servants and by Native American "allies"). Their tactics included display violence and the treacherous treatment of native rulers. Search-and-destroy threats were usually made and often carried out. Furthermore, when Spanish imperial authorities did begin to establish a network of permanent garrisons and other features of a professional standing army in the seventeenth century, their purpose was not to enforce colonial rule over Native Americans but to defend the empire from English, French, and Dutch pirates. Nor did the descendents of conquistadors man such units, which were overwhelmingly black or *pardo* militias—that is, small companies of enslaved and free Africans and free "coloreds" (men of mixed Spanish-African descent).[15]

In short, the Spanish Conquest was not carried out by soldiers sent by the king, as the conquistadors themselves were well aware. But the military revolution that developed in Europe in the sixteenth and seventeenth centuries altered subsequent Spanish perceptions of the early conquerors. Modern historians followed suit, likewise influenced by assumptions regarding the nature of men at arms. Thus the conquistadors, long after their deaths, all became soldiers.

If the conquistadors were armed and in some sense organized and experienced in military matters, is it not accurate enough to call them soldiers? One military historian has said as much, arguing that although "few of the men who fought . . . in the conquest of Peru were soldiers . . . militarily useful skills, values, and patterns of socialization were so deeply embedded and so widespread in early sixteenth-century Spanish society that the distinction is, from our standpoint, functionally unimportant."[16] To an extent, this was true. But arguably such skills and values were equally widespread among other Europeans, and, for that matter, among native groups such as the Mexica.

Furthermore, the conquistador acquired his martial skills not from formal training, but from conflict situations in the Americas. Expedition members tended to be recruited in recently founded colonies, creating a relay system of conquest that meant most participants already had some experience in the New World. For example, of the 101 Spaniards at Cajamarca whose pre-1532 experience is recorded, 64 had prior Conquest experience and 52 had spent at least five years in the Americas.[17] But none of this amounted to formal training.

The conquistadors' lack of formal training was paralleled by a lack of formal ranking. Spanish forces in Europe at this time were led by commanders from the high nobility and organized into various ranks (the names of some being the root of English terms of rank—*cabo de colonela* for "colonel," for example, and *sargento mayor* for "sergeant major").[18] In contrast, conquistador groups were headed by captains, the sole named rank and one that varied in number, with the other men divided only into those on horseback and those on foot—the latter rising to the former simply through the purchase of a horse. The record of the division of spoils at Cajamarca listed the men in two categories only, *gente de a cavallo* (people on horseback) and *gente de a pie* (people on foot).[19]

If conquistadors identified themselves not as soldiers, but as men on foot or on horseback, how else did they see themselves? How did they become conquistadors? And why did they end up fighting in the Americas?

The beginning of an answer to these questions is implied by Jerez's remark that the invaders of the Inca empire were "neither paid nor forced." A fuller answer is suggested by the words of one of Jerez's compatriots at Cajamarca, a young Basque Spaniard named Gaspar de Marquina, who sent the following letter to his father in Spain from Cajamarca in July 1533:

> Sir, I want to tell you the story of my life since I came to these parts. You already know how I went to Nicaragua with Governor Pedrarias as his page, and I was with him until God was pleased to take him from this world. He died very poor, and so all of us dependents [*criados*] of his were left poor too, as the carrier of this letter can very well tell you when he sees you. Then a few days after he died, we got news of how Governor Francisco Pizarro was coming to be governor of this kingdom of New Castile. And so, hearing this news and having few prospects in Nicaragua, we came to this district, where there's more gold and silver than iron in Biscay, and more sheep than in Soria, and great supplies of all kinds of food, and much fine clothing, and the best people that have been seen in the whole Indies, and many great lords among them. One of them, who rules over 500 leagues, we have prisoner in our power, and with him prisoner, a man can go by himself 500 leagues without getting killed; instead they give you whatever you need and carry you on their shoulders in a litter.[20]

The prisoner to whom Marquina rather casually refers is none other than the Inca, Atahuallpa, but Marquina is more concerned with conveying to his father the enormity of his own reversal of fortune. He skips over months of travel, hardship, uncertainty, and a great battle, in order to create the contrast within one paragraph between his low point after Pedrarias's death and his present high point. From his letter it is clear that Gaspar de Marquina is not a professional soldier, but a page, a fully literate, high-ranking servant, first of the governor of the colony of Nicaragua and then of the governor of Peru (that despite the events at Cajamarca, was not really conquered and certainly not colonized by 1533). He is in the "Indies" of his own free will, pursuing opportunity—in order, the rest of the letter reveals, to return to his father in

Spain a wealthy man and, most likely, take up a career as a notary or merchant. He pursues that opportunity through his connection to important patrons, successfully attaching himself to another when one dies without apparent benefit to Marquina. (Incidentally, by the time his father received the letter, and the gold bar accompanying it, Gaspar had been killed in a skirmish with native Andeans.)[21]

Spaniards, then, joined conquest expeditions not in return for specified payments, but in the hope of acquiring wealth and status. They were, in the words of historian James Lockhart, "free agents, emigrants, settlers, unsalaried and ununiformed earners of *encomiendas* and shares of treasure."[22] An *encomienda* was a grant of native American labor. The holder, or *encomendero*, had the right to tax the natives of a given community or cluster of towns in goods and labor. Such grants allowed the recipient to enjoy high status and often a superior lifestyle among his fellow colonists. The first *encomenderos* were men who had fought to win their grants, but they were not soldiers. As there were never enough *encomiendas* to go round, the most lucrative grants went to those who had invested the most in the expedition. Lesser investors received lesser grants or simply a share of the spoils of war.[23] Had Gaspar de Marquina lived longer, he might have won for himself a modest *encomienda*. At the very least his future share of the spoils of conquest would have doubled due to the horse he purchased with his newly won wealth in Cajamarca (and upon which he was killed). To some extent, all participants were investors in commercial ventures that carried high risks but potentially the highest of returns. Spaniards called these ventures "companies." While powerful patrons played important investment roles, it was the captains who primarily funded companies and expected to reap the greatest rewards. As the governor of Panama, Pedrarias de Avila, told King Charles of early Conquest expeditions into Nicaragua and Colombia, "it was done without touching your majesty's royal treasury."[24] The spirit of commercialism thus infused conquest expeditions from start to finish, with participants selling services and trading goods with each other throughout the endeavor. The conquerors were, in other words, armed entrepreneurs.

Marquina refers to himself as a page (*paje*), and a dependent (*criado*). An Englishman of the day would have called him either a "servant" or a "creature," although no English word fully conveys the way in which a *criado* was both subordinate and a real member of the household. The identity of Marquina's patrons and other details of his life also give us a sense of his social status within the broad category of *criado*. Fully identifying a conquistador can thus take multiple sources of information. Conquistadors had various reasons to identify themselves in writing, but their self-identities did not necessarily match those given to them by others, and they shift according to circumstances. The circumstances under which the identities of each conquistador company were recorded were seldom the same. Still, these records help us to know the conquistadors better.

For example, following the founding of the city of Panama in 1519, the 98 Spanish conquistador-settlers were asked to contribute to such a record, to which 75 responded (see Table 1). Only two of them claimed to be professional soldiers whereas 60 percent claimed to be professional men and artisans, occupations from the middle ranks of society. A similar analysis of the conquerors of the New Kingdom of Granada (today's Colombia) is less precise as to occupations and probably exaggerates the numbers of middle-ranking men. Nevertheless, the data clearly show that men of some means or property, professionals, and entrepreneurs of some kind predominated.[25]

Comparable information on Peru's conquistadors is likewise patchy, but sufficiently revealing. Of the 47 of the 168 men at Cajamarca who gave their occupations, it is clear that these men were not professional soldiers, but professionals and artisans who had acquired various battle experience and martial skills. The 17 artisans included tailors, horseshoers, carpenters, trumpeters, a cooper, a swordsmith, a stonemason, a barber, and a piper/crier.[26] The same kinds of artisans had also accompanied Francisco de Montejo on

Table 1: The Occupations of the Conquistadors of Panama, Peru, and the New Kingdom of Granada (Colombia)

	Panama (1519–22)	Peru (1532–34)	Colombia (1536–43)
Low nobility	2 (3%)		10 (7%)
Merchants			4
Artisans	20	17	13
Aides, secretaries, and similar employees	15	2	10
Professionals	4	6	12
Ecclesiastics		1	
Notaries	2	4	9
Rentiers	2		2
Shipowners	1		5
Royal officials	1		7
Other leaders			31
Horse owners			44
Slave owners			2
(Middle ranking totals)	(45 [60%])	(43 [92%])	(139 [90%])
Farmers	16		1
Sailors	10	2	
Soldiers	2		3
Artillerymen		2	
(Plebeian totals)	(28 [37%])	(4 [8%])	(4 [3%])
TOTALS	75 (100%)	47 (100%)	153 (100%)

Source: Lockhart, *Cajamarca*, 1972: 38; Avellaneda, *Conquerors*, 1995: 91, 93.
Note: These numbers do not represent all members of these expeditions, only those for whom there is such information. The methods and circumstances in which the original information was gathered were not standardized, and the table should thus be viewed as giving an approximate impression.

his first expedition into Yucatan in 1527, along with the usual professional men—merchants, physicians, a couple of priests, and a pair of Flemish artillery engineers. An unspecified number of the artisans and professionals invested in the company were confident enough of its outcome to bring their wives (although, following customary practice, these Spanish women probably remained with the merchants at the last Caribbean port before Yucatan was reached).[27]

In addition, Conquest records often contain information on the age and birthplace of conquistadors. It is available, for example, for 1,210 members of the original expeditions to Panama (84 men), Mexico (743), Peru (131), and Colombia (252). The makeup of each expedition was similar, with an average of 30 percent from the southern Spanish kingdom of Andalusia, 19 percent from neighboring Extremadura, 24 percent from the core kingdoms of Old and New Castile, and the remainder from other regions of the Iberian peninsula. Other Europeans were rare, restricted to the odd Portuguese, Genoese, Flemish, or Greek man. In age, the conquerors ranged from teenagers to the occasional 60-year-old. The average age of the men who went to both Peru and Colombia was 27, with the vast majority in their twenties or early thirties.[28]

In terms of education, again the range was broad, from men who were completely illiterate and uneducated to the occasional man of considerable learning. Although the availability of and attention given to conquistador narratives certainly gives the impression that the conquerors were handy with a pen if not well read,[29] the fully literate were among the minority in Spain as among conquest expeditions. Literacy rates among the conquerors and early settlers were slightly higher than average rates in Spain, if only because few farmers and other plebeians were among the migrants. The classic eyewitness narratives—Bernal Díaz and Cortés on Mexico; Gonzalo Jiménez on Colombia; Francisco de Jerez and Pedro Pizarro on Peru—are classics in part because they are rare. Most conquistadors wrote or dictated "merit" reports in the standardized style of the *probanza*, and about a quarter of the conquerors of Peru and Colombia were unable to sign their names. Despite the myth that literacy gave Spaniards an advantage over Native Americans, members of conquistador companies could probably read and write no better than the most literate native societies, such as the Mayas. Most Europeans and Mayas were semiliterate, with minorities being fully literate and fully illiterate. The correlation between social status and literacy among conquistadors was not as close as might be expected. The colonial chronicler Juan Rodríguez Freyle, a Bogotá native, claimed that some city council members of the New Granada settlements used branding irons to sign documents.[30] Most famously, the chief early conquistador of Peru, Francisco Pizarro, remained illiterate all of his life.[31]

The excerpt from Marquina's letter pointed to networks of patronage that bound individuals and groups of families together, often from the same Spanish town or region, through social ties, political alliances, and economic activities. Central to such networks was the tension between inequality and codependency among its members. Patrons and dependents, senior and junior members, relied upon each other to represent their interests in ways appropriate to their means and standing in society. In the context of conquest companies, patrons organized and made major financial investments in expeditions, calling upon their dependents to man the companies and in turn to recruit additional participants, investment, and supplies. Simple recruitment—the persuasion of relative strangers that the risks of a conquest venture were worth the potential gains in wealth and social status—was thus subordinate to patronage-based recruitment.

An important dimension to the pattern of patronage-based recruitment was the way it perpetuated the chain of conquest. As Marquina's story illustrates, most conquests and newly founded colonies served as stepping stones to other conquest enterprises. Certainly, some expeditions were assembled in Spain, but most originated in one Spanish colony in order to conquer an adjacent territory. Even if a company was assembled in Spain, it was likely to be launched from a colonial site. Gonzalo Jiménez's 1536–38 expedition into Colombia, for example, comprised hundreds of young recruits brought from Spain, but it was in Santa Marta, on Colombia's Caribbean coast, that specific plans were made and veteran conquistadors added to the company—largely through the patronage networks of Jiménez himself and his patron, Santa Marta's governor, don Pedro Fernández de Lugo.[32]

The most vivid way to illustrate this pattern is to follow the links of patronage that made up the chains of the Spanish Conquest. One section of one of these chains began in the year 1518 on the island of Cuba, where Governor Diego Velázquez was deciding who should lead a third expedition of exploration to the mainland. This was not intended as a great enterprise of conquest. That was supposed to come later, led by Velázquez himself, when a license for such had come through from Spain—a license that (like Columbus's contract of 1492) would ensure Velázquez the governorship of the conquered mainland. This expedition would pave the way and required someone close to Velázquez, a man willing to finance most of the company and be bolder than the leaders of the first two voyages along the Yucatec and Mexican coasts. Velázquez's first choice, a nephew of his, turned him down. The expedition would be too expensive, he said. His second and third choices, both his cousins, likewise declined, unwilling to risk the comfort of their *encomiendas* on Cuba for a trip into the unknown.[33]

Governor Velázquez's fourth choice was his one-time secretary, a native of Medellín, Extremadura, who had fought alongside Velázquez during the Conquest of Cuba and received an *encomienda* from him, and who had asked Velázquez to be godfather to his illegitimate *mestiza* (mixed-race) daughter. In a letter of 1519, Velázquez described this man as *criado mío de mucho tiempo* (a long-time dependent of mine). His name was Hernán Cortés.[34]

The two conquistadors of Cuba had had their differences, but even these stemmed from their patronage-based relationship. Cortés had seduced one of the maids-in-waiting to Velázquez's wife, and the governor had forced Cortés against his will to marry her. Now, in the autumn of 1518, Cortés made such efficient use of his own and Velázquez's networks of patronage, as well as his persuasive powers of simple recruitment, that the governor tried to stop the expedition—fearing that Cortés would break his connection to his patron and appeal directly to the king.[35]

Velázquez's fears were well founded, not just because that was precisely what Cortés did, but because this was standard conquistador practice. Indeed, even before the climax of his two-year war of conquest against the Mexica empire (1519–21), Cortés was obliged to tolerate efforts by other leaders of the company under his patronage to make their own marks on the mainland. The nature of patronage relations and the relay system of conquest meant that it was inevitable that the *criados* of Cortés would before long seek to become their own men—or rather, more direct *criados* of the king. But there were different ways to do this. Cristóbal de Olid, one of Cortés's valued captains in the war against the Mexica, showed how not to do it; he so infuriated his patron that in 1525 Cortés traveled by land all the way from Mexico to Honduras in order to see Olid beheaded. Other captains from the original Cortés expedition succeeded in carving out their own colonies, namely Francisco de Montejo and Pedro de Alvarado.

Francisco de Montejo was one of the early settlers of Havana and a *criado* of Velázquez. He was recruited by Cortés to be a major investor and captain on the expedition, having played a similar role and provided a well-stocked ship on the ill-fated Grijalva expedition to the mainland coast earlier in 1518. It was Montejo's good fortune, however, to avoid almost all the fighting of 1519–21 and yet still receive a share of the spoils appropriate to his investment and status—an *encomienda* in the Valley of Mexico. This was because Montejo was chosen by Cortés to fight the political battle in Spain while Cortés himself set out against the Mexica empire. In July 1519 Montejo sailed from the Mexican coast across the Atlantic with a cargo that included letters and gold for Cortés's family and, most importantly, numerous "gifts" for the Spanish emperor and a letter predictably requesting Cortés's appointment as governor of everything he could conquer. Velázquez heard of Cortés's treachery and sent a ship on an unsuccessful transatlantic chase after Montejo.

Some sources suggest that Montejo, playing a double game, himself leaked the news to the Cuban governor.[36]

In fact, Montejo was playing a triple game. While he remained for a time prepared to switch sides back to Velázquez, should occasion require it, he also persisted in arguing Cortés's case in Spain for over three years. At last, in October 1522, the emperor ruled in Cortés's favor, granting him the governorship of New Spain, although Cortés did not receive word of this until the following September.[37] By this time, the Mexica empire was no more, Cortés had been the effective ruler of Mexico for over two years, and Montejo had been assigned in absentia the lucrative *encomienda* of Azcapotzalco. Meanwhile, Montejo was busy laying the groundwork for his own, independent conquest career. In 1526 these efforts paid off, and Montejo was given a conqueror's license for Yucatan, whose coast he had sailed twice, with Grijalva and Cortés, and that he hoped would turn out to contain another Tenochtitlán or something like it.

Comments by Diego de Landa, the bishop of Yucatan, on Montejo's activities in Spain are revealing, both for their defensive tone and for their insights into how conquistadors relied on personal enterprise, rather than royal backing, to finance expeditions. Wrote the Franciscan:

> During the time that Montejo was at court he negotiated for himself the conquest of Yucatan [i.e., the license that would grant him the governorship should he conquer the region], although he might have negotiated for other things, and received the title of *adelantado* [licensed conqueror]. . . . He then exchanged marriage vows with a lady of Seville, a rich widow, and was thus able to gather 500 men whom he embarked in three ships.[38]

Later, this rich widow, doña Beatriz de Herrera, came looking for Montejo in Mexico. According to Landa: "The *adelantado* had married doña Beatriz de Herrera secretly in Seville, and some say that he denied her, but don Antonio Mendoza, the viceroy of New Spain, intervened and as a result he [Montejo] received her."[39] Doña Beatriz de Herrera would write to the king in 1554, in one of a series of petitions for a royal pension, that she had been the principal investor in Montejo's company. She claimed to have been left "in extreme poverty" after giving him "a great quantity of money" to cover the costs of the company.[40]

Thus armed with a conqueror's license and his new wife's fortune, Montejo's hopes were high. But there was no Maya empire, and his first invasion of Yucatan proved to be a disaster. Only 18 months after reaching Cozumel in the autumn of 1527, he was forced to withdraw to Mexico with the bedraggled survivors of his company. He returned later in 1529 with more Spanish recruits, African slaves, and hundreds of armed Nahuas, native warriors from his Azcapotzalco *encomienda*. But by 1534 the Spaniards were still battling Mayas and controlled barely any territory. In putting together both his expeditions, Montejo had made use of his own network of patronage, as well as the related Cortés network. One such associate was Alonso de Ávila, who had been with Montejo back in the days of the 1518 Grijalva company and had then fought with Cortés against the Mexica. However, the principle of reciprocity and mutual interest was at the heart of the Spanish patronage system. During two invasions, stretching over seven years, Montejo had failed to deliver to his associates and dependents any investment returns. Therefore, when in 1534 word reached Yucatan of the events at Cajamarca of 1532 and the gold and silver acquired in Peru, Montejo's company fell apart. As he himself wrote to the king, "with the great news that came of Peru, all the [Spanish] men went away and depopulated all the [colonial] towns of the land."[41]

Some of these men, like Ávila, judging that they had missed the Peru boat, returned to Mexico.[42] Those who followed the third Montejo invasion of Yucatan, this one led by his son and nephew, would end up in the 1540s with *encomiendas* of Mayas. But many of the Yucatan veterans went to Peru, seeking new patrons and better opportunities. And some of them ended up in the company assembled for a 1534 invasion of Ecuador by Pedro de Alvarado—whose career took him to southern Mesoamerica and into South America.

Pedro de Alvarado had captained a vessel owned by Velázquez on the 1518 Grijalva expedition and that year apparently joined his fellow Extremaduran Cortés with much enthusiasm. Although he was not one of Cortés's original 11 captains, he rose to prominence during the many military encounters of the long trek from the coast to the Valley of Mexico. Alvarado was a loyal Cortés *criado* but had a reputation for impetuosity and belligerence. His assertion of independence in Tenochtitlán in 1520 proved fatal to many of his compatriots. During Cortés's temporary absence from the city, Alvarado had ended the Spanish-Mexica standoff and initiated a bloody massacre that led to weeks of hostilities climaxing with the desperate Spanish flight that the conquistadors dubbed *La Noche Triste* (The Tragic Night). Yet Alvarado served his patron and his compatriots well in the final months of siege and assault on Tenochtitlán, and in 1522 Cortés granted him the first major *encomienda* in the immediate environs of Tenochtitlán–Mexico City, the native Nahuas of Xochimilco.[43]

In accordance with Conquest patterns, the following year Alvarado led a major expedition down into Guatemala—either sent by Cortés or with his blessing, depending on one's perspective. In addition to Spanish recruits, many from the Mexican wars, African slaves, and Nahuas from his *encomienda*, Alvarado also took his three brothers, two of his cousins, and other members of a patronage circle he had cultivated as an *encomendero*.[44] Through a classic divide-and-conquer strategy, Alvarado played the two major native groups of the highlands off against each other, the Quiché Mayas and the Cakchiquel Mayas. Although Alvarado and his relatives achieved the rapid submission of these two groups, as well as the neighboring Tzutujil, in just two months of fighting in 1524, the wars of conquest in highland Guatemala would drag on for a decade.[45] As was often the case, the quick Spanish victory was a myth that masked years of conflict among Spaniards and among natives as well as between them.

The prolonged hostilities had multiple causes: the fragmented and diverse nature of native polities in the highlands; excessive Spanish demands and actions that were frequently counterproductive to the imposition of colonial rule; and Alvarado's apparent view of Guatemala as little more than another stage in his Conquest career. Both loyal to Cortés and yet keen to replace him—typical of patronage patterns in the Conquest—Alvarado communicated by letter with his patron regularly. He set off to Chiapas in 1525 in a vain attempt to meet up with Cortés on the latter's Honduras trip, and the following year traveled to Honduras himself at Cortés's request. However, earlier in 1526 Alvarado had gone half way to Mexico on the strength of reports that Cortés had died and a faction of fellow veterans from the Mexican wars was ready to make Alvarado governor of Mexico.[46]

His uneven commitment to Guatemala, and the problems inherent to divided Spanish colonists attempting to "pacify" divided highland Mayas, helps to explain why Alvarado's response to early news of the lands and potential wealth of South America was to use his resources and status to form another large Conquest company. Despite his *encomiendas* in Mexico and Guatemala and his confirmation in 1530 as governor of the latter, Alvarado set his sights on Peru as early as 1531. But his ambitions should also be seen in the larger context. As free agents seeking opportunity both through patronage networks with compatriots and in competition with other Spaniards, the conquistadors were seldom committed to any one region. Just as they were not sent by the king to conquer as his soldiers, nor were they sent to settle as his colonists. Both king and conquerors talked much about settlement, but more as a means to the extraction of wealth than an end unto itself. Alvarado's apparent restlessness was entirely consistent with the logic of Conquest patterns.[47]

Alvarado's well-financed expedition brought veterans from the Conquest wars in Mexico, Yucatan, Guatemala, other parts of Mesoamerica, and even the Caribbean, to Peru. It did not represent the first links in the chain of conquest into South America, but through its personnel it further connected Andean events to conquests in the north. In view of Pizarro's success in 1532–33, the Guatemalan governor's purpose in 1534 seems to have been either to bypass Pizarro and sieze Cuzco or to carve out a separate colony in the northern territories of the Inca empire, the region of Quito (today's Ecuador). This never happened, for the simple reason that Diego de Almagro, one of Pizarro's captains, rushed north to meet Alvarado. Rather than fight, the two conquistadors made a deal. Although Alvarado was paid to disband his expedition and return to Guatemala, even richer than before, Almagro was permitted to recruit men from Alvarado's company. As Almagro was in the throes of breaking patronage ties to Pizarro and acquiring his own as-yet-unconquered governorship in the southern Andes, many of these men ended up fighting in Chile's conquest wars.[48]

Thus did two relay systems or chains of conquest—forged by the ties of patronage and the impetus of individual opportunity—begin as one in the Caribbean, run to Mexico, diverge into Yucatan and Guatemala, and then converge again in northern Peru, where they met another one, the Pizarro-Almagro chain that came from Panama and ran down the Andes into Chile.

The variety of identities, experiences, and life stories in the "Indies" renders the concept of the typical conquistador somewhat nonsensical. But if we were to create such a figure, constructed from the averages and patterns of conquistador biographies, he would be a young man in his late twenties, semiliterate, from southwestern Spain, trained in a particular trade or profession, seeking opportunity through patronage networks based on family and home-town ties. Armed as well as he could afford, and with some experience already of exploration and conquest in the Americas, he would be ready to invest what he had and risk his life if absolutely necessary in order to be a member of the first company to conquer somewhere wealthy and well populated. He would not in any sense be a soldier in the armies of the king of Spain.

The armed Spanish entrepreneurs that our imagined typical conquistador represents were not, of course, the only members of conquistador expeditions, although their own accounts and those of so many historians since have given that impression that they were. It is thus to the other conquerors, largely invisible in such accounts, that we turn in the next chapter.

3

Invisible Warriors
The Myth of the White Conquistador

The Indian empire was in a manner conquered by Indians.

—William H. Prescott (1843)

The conquistadors say that the Tlaxcaltecs deserve that His Majesty grant them much favor, and that if it had not been for them, they [the Spaniards] would all have been dead, when the Mexica repulsed the Christians from Mexico, and that the Tlaxcaltecs offered them a haven.

—Fray Toribio de Benavente Motolinía (1540)

Napot Canche was governor of the *cah* [Maya town] here in Calkini; it was on his palace patio that the tribute was delivered to the captain, Montejo, when he and his soldiers arrived here. . . . Their swine and their Culhuas [Mexica] arrived first; the captain of the Culhuas was [a Mexica named] Gonzalo.

—The Title of Calkini (1579)

I . . . black resident [*de color negro vecino*] of this city . . . was present at all the invasions and conquests and pacifications which were carried out.

—Juan Garrido (1538)

About eight years ago . . . having in my possession as my slave one Juan Valiente, a Black, and wishing to treat him kindly and being confident that he would conduct himself properly, I granted him permission . . . to go to Guatemala and Peru and wherever else he might wish to go and earn . . . whatever might be his share, providing that he keep an accounting of it and bring it all back to me within four years.

—Alonso Valiente (1541)

The image is a familiar one. Thousands of native warriors swarm like bees upon the vastly outnumbered conquistadors, who against all odds fend them off and survive to fight another day. This familiarity is rooted in part in the larger context of the Western colonial experience, whose mythology is punctuated by tales of barbarian hordes miraculously repulsed (even if temporarily) or crushed—the Capture of Atahuallpa, the Siege of Vienna, the Alamo, Custer's Last Stand, Rorke's Drift.

But the image is also familiar specifically with respect to the Spanish Conquest. This is because it is so ubiquitous in the most widely read accounts of the invasion, particularly those of the Conquest of Mexico, from Bernal Díaz and Cortés to Prescott—the last a best-seller in the days when history still taught "that Europeans will triumph over natives, however formidable the apparent odds."[1] It is, of course, a corollary to the handful-of-adventurers image, and is thus equally central to the conquistadors' own portrait of the Conquest.[2]

This image tells us much about the Spaniards, but it leaves out critical aspects of the story. There is no doubt that the Spaniards were consistently outnumbered by native enemies on the battlefield. But what has so often been ignored or forgotten is the fact that Spaniards tended also to be outnumbered by their own native allies. Furthermore, the "invisible warriors" of this myth took an additional form, that of the Africans, free and enslaved, who accompanied Spanish invaders and in later campaigns equaled or exceeded them in number.[3]

In the 1760s an Italian friar of the Capuchin order named Ilarione da Bergamo traveled through Mexico, later writing up an account of his journey. Ilarione's brief references to the Conquest, based on his conversations with Spaniards in Mexico and his reading of the popular histories of the time, give us some sense of the state of Conquest myths in the late eighteenth century. Ilarione's understanding is that the greatly outnumbered conquistadors could only pull off their remarkable feat owing to their superior weaponry, the handicapping superstitions of the "wretched Indians," and the interventions of providence. The Capuchin friar's perspective reflects that of colonial Spaniards, a view encapsulated by Bernal Díaz's pithy explanation of one typical encounter—"The Indians were charging us in such numbers that only by a miracle of swordplay were we able to drive them back and re-form our ranks." Notably still absent in Ilarione's day, as in Díaz's, are natives or Africans fighting alongside the Spaniards.[4]

Yet a careful search through the many sources on the Spanish invasion of Mexico reveals numerous casual references to the participation of native allies. For example, during his 1524 invasion of highland Guatemala, Alvarado wrote two letters to Cortés, the first making no reference to native allies, the second mentioning just once, in parentheses, that his force comprised 250 Spaniards "and about five or six thousand friendly Indians."[5] Even Prescott, influenced in so many ways by the sixteenth-century Spaniards upon whose accounts he relied, realized that "it would be unjust to the Aztecs [Mexica] themselves, at least to their military prowess, to regard the Conquest as directly achieved by the Spaniards alone."[6]

"You have arrived here in Tenochtitlan! Be strong, Tlaxcalans and Huejotzin-cans!" Thus begins one of the sixteenth-century songs written in the central Mexican language of Nahuatl and known as the *Cantares Mexicanos* or *Songs of the Aztecs*. It is an ambiguous celebration of the role played by warriors from Tlaxcala and Huejotzingo in the siege and capture of the Mexica capital of Tenochtitlán. In the first two cantos, these natives are aided by the Spaniards and their weapons in "destroying the city, destroying the Mexica." In the third canto the Mexica temporarily turn the tide of battle. But in the fourth, although they seize a captive for sacrifice, the Mexica "are surrounded," and in the fifth and final canto the Mexica ruler Cuauhtémoc is captured and cuck-olded by Cortés.[7]

The disposition of the song is thus unclear. The historical fact of Tlaxcalan victory is certainly not avoided, but the Mexica seem to claim some kind of covert victory through the perpetuation of high status, as symbolized by Cuahtémoc's former child bride, doña Isabel, "who sits beside you, Captain General [Cortés]," and her half-Spanish child. As the Mexica, Tlaxcalans, and Huejotzincans were all Nahuas, the song's lyrics present the war as a kind of civil or local conflict, between rival city-states within the same ethnic and lin-guistic area. The Spaniards play important roles, but secondary ones as agents of native ambition whose eventual triumph really isn't a triumph—a "victory" whose flawed and partial nature is ripe for parody because the Spaniards seem unaware of its incompleteness. Symbolically, at the point of apparent Mexica defeat in canto four of the song, the Mexica capture and sacrifice a Spaniard named Guzmán "as much-valued tribute to Tenochtitlán."[8]

This spin on the Conquest as a native civil war resulting in an incomplete Spanish domination offers an alternative to the predictably hispanocentric perspective of the Spaniards, and is one that is readily found in native sources. It also reveals a dimension of the Spanish invasions so central to their out-come that without it the Conquest cannot be sensibly understood. The *Song of the Aztecs* evokes both aspects of this native dimension—the insertion of Spaniards into a native civil war, and the use by Spaniards of native allies in further expeditions outside the homeland of those natives.

The first of these is most obviously illustrated by the role of the Tlaxcalans. As the Mexica (or Aztec) empire expanded across central Mexico in the late fifteenth and early sixteenth centuries, the small city-state of Tlaxcala man-aged to maintain a precarious independence, even after it became surrounded by towns subjugated to the Mexica. Located roughly halfway between the Gulf coast and Tenochtitlán, Tlaxcala represented both a major hurdle and a crucial opportunity for the Cortés-led expedition of 1519. At first the Tlaxcalan political faction hostile to the Spaniards dominated the response to the ar-rival of the foreigners, who suffered a series of violent confrontations. Had such hostilities persisted, Cortés would have been forced to retreat east and seek an alternative route or strategy.[9]

But Spanish survival and the impression made by their weapons allowed the Tlaxcalan faction in favor of making an anti-Mexica alliance with Cortés to come to the fore. As these Tlaxcalans rightly judged, with Spanish assistance they would be able to destroy the Mexica empire and its capital city (see Figure 7). As Prescott deftly puts it: "The first terrible encounter of the Spaniards with the Tlascalans, which had nearly proved their ruin, did in fact insure their success. It secured them a strong native support on which to retreat in the hour of trouble, and round which they could rally the kindred races of the land for one great and overwhelming assault." We cannot be sure how many native allies Cortés had, but by any estimate they outnumbered Spaniards many times over. Gómara stated that Cortés first arrived in Tenochtitlán with 6,000 such allies. According to prominent Conquest historian Ross Hassig, the final siege and assault on the Mexica capital was carried out with 200,000 native allies, "even though they went virtually unacknowledged and certainly unrewarded."[10]

Fig. 7. Spaniards with Tlaxcalan allies battle Mexicas, who are throwing stones; from fray Bernardino de Sahagún's General History of the Things of New Spain *or* Florentine Codex *(1579).*

Cortés, not surprisingly, claimed that the Tlaxcalan role resulted from a strategy of his own devising. Seeing the animosity between the Tlaxcalans and the Mexica, Cortés saw "the opportunity to subdue them more quickly, for, as the saying goes, 'divided they fall.'"[11] Historians of various kinds have followed Cortés's cue, up to the present. The semiotician Tzvetan Todorov, for example, characterizes the divide-and-conquer strategy as an "endeavor" in which the Spaniard "succeeds very well."[12] The point, of course, is not that Cortés did not attempt to exploit native rivalries and divisions—clearly he did—but that his endeavor must be properly contextualized.

Two contexts are particularly important. One is that of native politics. The Tlaxcalans and other Nahuas and native Mesoamericans endeavored as much as Cortés and often with equal success to exploit the situation in the pursuit of immediate political goals. Tlaxcala's neighbor, Huejotzingo, had long resisted incorporation into the Mexica empire and likewise assisted the Spaniards in the Conquest. Indeed the Huejotzincans later wrote to the king of Spain that they had never opposed the Spaniards and had been better allies than the Tlaxcalans, who "in many places ran away, and often fought badly." In contrast, they asserted "we helped not only in warfare, but also we gave them [the Spaniards] everything they needed."[13] The Huejotzincans, in other words, were not passive tools of Cortés's strategy; rather they sought to use the Spanish presence to promote their interests and pursue rivalries first against the Mexica and later against the Tlaxcalans.

The other context is that of Spanish actions elsewhere. The search for native allies was one of the standard procedures or routines of Spanish conquest activity throughout the Americas. Pedro de Alvarado entered highland Guatemala in 1524 not only with thousands of Nahua allies but also expecting to be able to take advantage of a Mexica-Tlaxcala type rivalry; the two major Maya groups of the region, the Cakchiquel and the Quiché, had both sent ambassadors to Mexico City a year or two earlier. As a result, for the rest of the decade, a brutal civil war ravaged the highlands as the Spaniards used these groups against each other and against smaller Maya groups, while periodically turning with violence upon these native "allies."[14] Conversely, Spaniards under the Montejos sought desperately to make sense of regional politics in Yucatan in order to exploit or establish a similar division, being forced in the end to make a series of often unreliable alliances with local dynasties such as the Pech and Xiu. These Maya noble families controlled relatively small portions of Yucatan, and the Spaniards never achieved control over the whole peninsula.[15]

The most obvious example of how Spaniards sought native allies, looked for native divisions, and benefited enormously from them is the Inca civil war. Smallpox spread into South America faster than Europeans did, so the disease had preceded Pizarro into the Andes, killing the Inca ruler Huayna Capac and his heir before Spaniards entered their empire. Two brothers,

Atahuallpa and Huascar, then took control of the northern and southern halves of the empire, respectively, in an uneasy peace that collapsed into civil war after two years. Had Pizarro arrived in northern Peru just a few months later, he most likely would have found a united Inca empire under Atahuallpa's rule. But Pizarro's timing was accidentally perfect, and he was able to insinuate himself into the conflict. Although seized by Pizarro, Atahuallpa sought to turn his captivity to his advantage by using the Spaniards against his brother Huascar. Alliances and betrayals proliferated and soon both Inca rulers were dead.[16]

Their successor, Manco Inca, was supposed to be a Spanish puppet, but he soon rebelled. However, four years of Inca disunity during the Pizarro-Almagro invasion had given the Spaniards a steady enough supply of native allies to permit Spanish survival in the region. Manco's great siege of Cuzco in 1536 would probably have resulted in the elimination of Pizarro's forces were it not for his Andean allies. These were initially less than 1,000 but grew to over 4,000 later in the siege as two of Manco's brothers and other nobles of the same Inca faction came over to Pizarro's side. These allies saved the Spaniards from starvation, rescued individual Spaniards, acted as spies, and fought along with Spanish horsemen in sorties against the besiegers.[17] Their assistance enabled Pizarro and his company to survive until Almagro's relief force arrived. Native support not only saved Pizarro in 1536, it also allowed the Spaniards to survive long enough to establish a permanent foothold in the Andes and to begin to build colonies.

As the Andean conquests fanned out from centers of the former Inca empire to the southern and northern regions of South America, native warriors and servants proved equally invaluable. The taking of native allies from one zone of conquest to the next was a practice established at the very onset of Spanish activity in the Americas. Caribbean islanders were routinely carried between islands as support personnel on conquest expeditions, and then brought to the mainland in the campaigns into Panama and Mexico. For example, Cortés brought 200 native Cubans with him to Mexico in 1519.[18]

When the Spaniards under Cortés left the Gulf coast and headed toward central Mexico, native Cempoalan warriors and porters accompanied them, and Tlaxcalans, Huejotzincans, and others later became part of a vast support force that greatly outnumbered the Spaniards. The Huejotzincans continued to fight alongside Spaniards and provide other services as the Conquest stretched out over the 1520s and 1530s. As Huejotzingo's rulers would inform the king in 1560, "we never abandoned or left them. And as they went to conquer Michoacan, Jalisco, and Colhuacan, and at Pánuco and Oaxaca and Tehuantepec and Guatemala, we were the only ones who went along while they conquered and made war here in New Spain until they had finished the conquest; we never abandoned them, in no way did we hold back their warmaking, though some of us were destroyed in it."[19]

In fact, the Huejotzincans were not the only Nahuas to fight in other regions of what became New Spain. Montejo brought hundreds of warriors from Azcapotzalco, in the Valley of Mexico, to Yucatan. One Maya account of the Spanish invasion offers a revealing commentary on their use as a vanguard force. Following a series of military encounters in the region, the Spaniards entered the important town of Calkini in 1541 to accept the nominal submission of the local Maya rulers. The description of that ritual by the rulers of Calkini remarks pointedly that the Nahuas—called Culhuas by the Maya after Culhuacan, the town that had once dominated the Valley of Mexico—arrived first. The Maya account also noted that the leader of the Culhuas had been baptized Gonzalo, that their force brought along a herd of pigs (an animal introduced by the Spaniards), and that they were the ones who gathered up the tribute goods offered to the Spaniards.[20]

There is no hint of racial solidarity between Nahuas and Mayas in this account, nor should any be expected. Spaniards lumped different native groups together as "Indians," but to the Mayas of Calkini, the Culhuas were as foreign as the Spaniards. They were invaders to be repulsed or accommodated, as circumstances allowed, just as if they had come alone as part of the Mexica imperial expansion into Yucatan that never happened but may have eventually occurred had the Spaniards not appeared.

Nor was there a sense of Maya ethnic solidarity in the sixteenth century. In time, Mayas from the Calkini region and other parts of Yucatan would accompany Spaniards into unconquered regions of the peninsula as porters, warriors, and auxiliaries of various kinds. Companies of archers were under permanent commission in the Maya towns of Tekax and Oxkutzcab, regularly called upon to man or assist in raids into the unconquered regions south of the colony of Yucatan. As late as the 1690s Mayas from over a dozen Yucatec towns—organized into companies under their own officers and armed with muskets, axes, machetes, and bows and arrows—fought other Mayas in support of Spanish Conquest endeavors in the Petén region that is now northern Guatemala.[21]

Ideally, these auxiliaries came more or less voluntarily (that is, they were not enslaved) and in large numbers, as was the case with Montejo's "Culhuas" in Yucatan. However, native groups who were not accustomed to providing tribute or organized labor services to lords, such as the semisedentary peoples of the Caribbean and southern Central America, resisted these arrangements. The Spanish response was to enslave such peoples. The enslaving of Native Americans was soon banned by the Spanish crown, who viewed native slavery as contributing to the extinction of most Caribbean native groups, as being made redundant by African slavery, and as being unnecessary among mainland sedentary societies (where organized labor systems already existed). But in the early decades of the Conquest, natives routinely accompanied Spaniards as slaves on expeditions to other regions, mostly, but not solely, in the Caribbean. Native slaves from Nicaragua participated in the Conquest of Peru, for example. They fought and provided other services alongside other natives and Africans, both slaves and free servants. Natives tended to outnumber Africans, as most of the latter were costly slaves purchased from transatlantic traders. While the men fought and transported supplies, there were also native women who cooked and acted as female company and lovers for the Spaniards, had children by the Europeans, and settled with them as servants in their new colonial residences.

That Spaniards expected to have several native or black auxiliaries, and that they considered it a great hardship to go without them, is evidence enough of their important role in the Conquest. "Two years is long enough to go about begging without servants," wrote one conquistador, a member of the Pizarro company who almost starved on Gallo Island, off Ecuador, while awaiting reinforcements and supplies. "I will need [someone] for the practice of my trade, and also someone to serve me," he told his brother, "that is, a Black or a good Indian man and woman, because if I should buy them here it would cost a great deal."[22]

Whether as squads of Huejotzincan warriors helping to topple the Mexica empire, a Nahua from Azcapotzalco leading his men into a Maya village, or an enslaved native Nicaraguan woman serving a conquistador in Peru, native peoples are everywhere in the Conquest alongside the Spaniards. One symbolic illustration of their omnipresence is found in the first couple of conquest festivals performed in Mexico. The first took place in Coatzacoalcos, on the Gulf coast, late in 1524. The occasion was the entry into the town of the Cortés-led expedition en route to Honduras, and the festival was a welcome in the form of (in Bernal Díaz's words) "triumphal arches, and certain [mock] ambushes of Christians and Moors, and other grand entertainments and dramatized games." As an anticipatory celebration of Cortés's Honduran triumph, the festival was full of irony, as not only were almost all the celebrants natives, but in reality Cortés was leading an overwhelmingly native army against rebellious Spaniards under one of his old captains, Cristóbal de Olid.

The return of Cortés to Mexico City in 1526 occasioned the second such festival on record. Again the dances, games, and mock battles all featured native celebrants, supposedly commemorating Spanish triumphs but very clearly also representing their own complex roles in the incomplete Conquest. As Díaz dryly observed, during the festival the lake that then still surrounded Mexico City was "full of canoes and Indian warriors in them, according to the manner in which they were accustomed to fight against us in the time of Guatemuz [Cuauhtémoc]."[23]

Festivals of conquest and reconquest not only offer insights into the roles placed by native warriors on both sides of the Conquest wars, but also depict other oft-ignored participants—such as Africans. For example, the performance of the "Conquest of Rhodes" was staged in Mexico City in 1539, in response to news of an anti-Ottoman truce signed the year before by the Spanish and French monarchs. The play was an elaborate affair whose vast sets were constructed by "more than fifty thousand workmen" (Africans and local natives), according to Bernal Díaz. It anticipated imminent Mediterranean victories (that remained wishful thinking), but portrayed local historical events too— thousands of native Nahuas and possibly other Mesoamericans played both the attackers and defenders during the siege of Rhodes, with "Cortés" the leader of the Christian forces.

For the Spanish audience, this was the main event, but the native and black participants and audience must have seen the play that preceded the siege as equally significant. This opening spectacle featured three artificial forests stocked with real animals, who were "hunted" by bands of native warriors. The native actors reflected both the medieval European "wild men" tradition and the Mesoamerican tradition that juxtaposed "civilized" central Mexican Nahuas with "barbarous" Mesoamericans (the Chichimecs and others of the frontiers of the Mexica empire and then New Spain). The hunt soon became a battle between these two groups, a conflict that was made more complex but then resolved by the arrival of a cavalry of "more than fifty black men and women" (Díaz again), led by a black king and queen.

The presence and role of Africans was surely open to interpretation by the diverse population of early Mexico City. For Spaniards, African and native roles underscored the Conquest's reduction of non-Spaniards to armed agents of colonialism or to mere playactors in military conflict. For natives, the black role was bittersweet, being both a reminder of African military roles in the Spanish invasion and a parody of that invasion through its representation as entirely African—monarchy included. For Africans, their entrance into the play on horseback must have been a proud celebration of their military prowess, of a conquistador status so seldom permitted public recognition. All those present must also have been reminded that barely 18 months earlier, in the autumn of 1537, an unknown number of the 10,000 Africans already resident in Mexico City had allegedly plotted a slave revolt and crowned a rebel black king. This slave monarch, along with other black leaders, had then been publicly executed—and was surely resurrected, in the minds of the city's blacks, in the form of the festival's African king.[24]

Whatever their identity or perspective, none of the inhabitants of Mexico City in 1539 would have viewed a black presence in that year's festival of conquest as incongruous. All took for granted the fact that Africans too had participated in the real Conquest. Indeed, Africans were ubiquitous not only to the Conquest of Mexico but also to the entire endeavor of Spanish invasion and colonization in the Americas. Because the majority of such Africans arrived as slaves, and because of their subordinate status in the increasingly ethnocentric Castilian worldview, the widespread and central role of blacks was consistently ignored by Spaniards writing about the Conquest. As with so much else in the evolution of the Conquest into a collage of myths, subsequent historians and others consolidated this marginalization. Evidence of black roles is thus scattered and often opaque, but when the pieces are put together, it is incontrovertible.

Among the evidence that can be pieced together is the life story of one seemingly extraordinary black conquistador, Juan Valiente.[25] Although we have no direct information on Valiente's youth, he was almost certainly born in West Africa around 1505 and purchased as a very young man by Portuguese traders from African slavers on the coast. He then became part of the great wave of people and supplies that entered Mexico in the wake of the Spanish invasion and the fall of the Mexica empire. After being purchased by a Spaniard named Alonso Valiente, the young African was baptized and brought to his new master's house in the newly founded city of Puebla around 1530. Not surprisingly, Juan Valiente grew restless in his position as an enslaved domestic servant. Whether he pursued various strategies to stretch the bounds of his servitude we do not know, but in 1533 he was able to convince his owner to let him go and seek opportunity as a conquistador for a period of four years, "providing that he keep an account of [his earnings] and bring it all back me [his owner]." The African would have kept a notarized record of this agreement on his person at all times to avoid being arrested as a slave in flight.

Valiente arrived in Guatemala in time to join Pedro de Alvarado's expedition to Peru. Alvarado's extensive company of Spaniards, natives, and Africans was stopped in northern Peru by Diego de Almagro, then still Pizarro's partner, in 1534. Almagro bought out Alvarado, but those who had followed the latter had the option of joining the former. Valiente chose to switch companies, and by 1535 he was fighting down in Chile with Almagro. Mortality rates were high in the Conquest, but those who survived often saw their fortunes improve dramatically. This was true for Valiente, despite his technical status as a slave. By 1540 he was again (or still) in Chile, but now as a captain, a horseman, and a vested partner in Juan de Valdivia's company. Ongoing campaigns against Chile's native Araucanians during the 1540s brought further rewards—an estate outside Santiago, which city he helped Valdivia found, in 1546, and four years later an *encomienda*, a grant of tribute-paying natives. Meanwhile, Valiente had married a Juana de Valdivia, possibly a native servant but more likely a former African slave of the governor's.[26]

During these decades the black conquistador's owner, Alonso Valiente, still 4,000 miles away in the Mexican city of Puebla, had not given up on his

investment. Although Juan Valiente's permit of travel required him to return and turn over the spoils of conquest to his master after four years, an
updated version was dispatched upon the expiration of the original agreement. It probably never reached the slave, as four more years later, in 1541,
Alonso had yet to hear from or of Valiente. In that year he sent his nephew
on a wild goose chase to find the slave and bring him back or negotiate a
good price on his manumission.[27] Interestingly, Valiente had not forgotten
the agreement with Alonso either. Despite his success as a conquistador and
his ability to live as a free man in Chile, his technical status as a slave troubled
him enough that he commissioned a royal official in 1550 to purchase for
Valiente his legal freedom either in Lima or in Puebla. But the official ab-
sconded to Spain with the funds. Finally, five years later, Alonso Valiente
received news of his slave's career, and made yet another attempt to recover
a return on his investment. But by then the black conquistador and
encomendero had been killed by Araucanians at the 1553 battle of Tucapel.

The life of Juan Valiente certainly seems extraordinary—the stuff, even, of
fiction. But every aspect of it can be related to the larger patterns either of
Spanish conquistador activity or of the African experience in early Spanish
America. As a black West African brought against his will to the Americas in
the sixteenth century, Valiente was hardly unique. The transportation of West
Africans as slaves out of their homeland, which had been a part of trans-
Saharan trade for centuries, became an increasingly important part of the
new Atlantic economy in the late fifteenth century. The Discovery would
take the slave trade in a new direction and serve to magnify it considerably,
so that over the four centuries ending in 1850 some 12 million men and women
from West and Central Africa would be loaded onto transatlantic slave ships.
Although the Portuguese, and later the British, dominated this trade,
Castilians were involved as early as the fifteenth century. The first black Africans brought to the Americas probably arrived by 1502, and in 1510 the king
of Spain authorized the first large shipment of Africans slaves—250 destined for Hispaniola. By century's end, roughly 100,000 Africans had been
shipped to the Spanish-American colonies.[28]

The obvious purpose of the Atlantic slave trade was to meet labor demands, and the most infamous of slave occupations in the New World was
that of plantation worker. But while Spaniards did set up sugar and other
plantations worked by African slaves, their colonies were primarily built in
areas of heavy native settlement and relied upon native labor. Thus the black
slaves of Spaniards in the colonies tended to function more as personal auxiliaries—as domestic servants, as assistants in commercial enterprises, as

symbols of social status—just as in the Conquest they were personal auxiliaries of individual Spanish conquistadors. They were servants who were, by
necessity, armed; by fighting and surviving they usually earned their freedom and became conquistadors in their own right.

Juan Valiente arrived in the New World too late to be a part of this pattern
in the Caribbean and Mexico, but other Africans were there alongside the
first Spaniards. Juan Garrido, for example, born in West Africa about 1480,
was in Lisbon and Seville in the late 1490s and arrived in the Caribbean in
1502 or 1503 (see Table 2). He later claimed to have crossed the Atlantic as a

Table 2: The Life of Juan Garrido, a Black Conquistador

ca. 1480?	Born in West Africa and probably sold as a slave to Portuguese traders
ca. 1495?	Becomes a Christian in Lisbon; later moves to Seville (may have gained freedom in Lisbon or Seville)
ca. 1503	Crosses Atlantic to Santo Domingo, probably as a servant or slave of a Spaniard named Pedro Garrido
1508–19	Participates in the Conquests of Puerto Rico and Cuba, in the supposed Conquests of Guadalupe and Dominica, and in the Discovery of Florida; is otherwise resident in Puerto Rico
1519–21	Member of the Conquest expedition into central Mexico, probably as a servant of Pedro Garrido and later Hernán Cortés (or, less likely, in the retinues of Juan Núñez Sedeño [1519] or Pánfilo de Narváez [1520])
1521	Builds a commemorative chapel on the Tacuba causeway near the site of the heavy Spanish and allied losses of 1520
1521–23	Resident, adjacent to his chapel, on the outskirts of Mexico City; plants the first three seeds of wheat to be grown in New Spain
1523–24	Member of the Antonio de Caravajal expedition to Michoacán and Zacatula
1524–28	Resident in Mexico City; on 10 February 1525, he is granted a house-plot within the rebuilt city; 1524–26 holds post of doorkeeper (*portero*) and for a time is also crier (*pregonero*) and guardian of the Chapultepec aqueduct
1528	Heads a gold mining expedition, complete with black slave gang, to Zacatula
1528–33	Resident in Mexico City
ca. 1533–36	Member of the Cortés expedition to Baja California, in charge of and co-owner of a squad of black and native slaves intended for mining
1536–ca. 47	Resident in Mexico City, where he dies; leaves a wife and three children (one of whom may have been the Juan Garrido resident in Cuernavaca in 1552)

Sources: AGI, *México* 204, fs. 1–9; Icaza, *Diccionario*, 1923, I: 98; Gerhard, "A Black Conquistador,"
1978; Alegría, *Juan Garrido*, 1990; Altman, "Spanish Society," 1991: 439. Note: A version of this table
first appeared in Restall, "Black Conquistadors," 2000: 177.

free man, although he more likely acquired his freedom in the Caribbean. Between 1508 and 1519 he fought in the Conquests of Puerto Rico and Cuba, in raids on other islands, and in the Discovery of Florida. Back in 1502 the governor of Hispaniola, Nicolás de Ovando, had brought Africans to act as auxiliary conquerors, but when they did the opposite and joined the native resistance on the island, he banned further importation of black slaves. The ban had little effect; Spaniards took as many Africans on expeditions as they could afford.[29] Garrido was by no means the only black conquistador to accompany Ponce de León into Puerto Rico, nor was he the only one to invade Cuba with Diego Velázquez—who in 1515 wrote to the king that "many black slaves" had participated in the Conquest there.[30]

Valiente and Garrido were typical of black conquistadors in a number of ways. They both appear to have been African born. Only a minority of blacks in the Conquest were born in Spain or Portugal (examples are Juan García and Miguel Ruíz—see Tables 3 and 4), and only much later in the Conquest were there American-born black soldiers. Both acquired freedom as a result of their military experiences, Garrido legally granted the status, Valiente effectively taking it and only denied its legal confirmation by the exigencies of long-distance communication in sixteenth-century Spanish America. Both were about 28 years old when their conquistador careers began, perhaps closer to 30 when they first actually fought in the New World. While Spanish conquistadors were on average in their late twenties, their black counterparts tended to be a few years older, probably because less Hispanized younger Africans were less likely to be trusted with armed roles by Spaniards and more likely to be placed in danger as "arrow fodder." Finally, both men were baptized Juan, the Christian name of more than half the black conquistadors on record, highlighting the Spaniards' lack of imagination in baptizing slaves.[31]

Where Valiente and Garrido differed was primarily in the timing of their arrival in the New World. Garrido's early arrival meant he participated in the major Caribbean and Mexican conquests. A generation later, Valiente reached Mexico and Peru right after the initial phases of conquest, and thus ended up fighting in a more peripheral region.

In 1519 Juan Garrido joined the Cortés expedition to the mainland, and in the 1520s was one of the founding residents of Mexico City. Garrido later wrote to the king that he "was the first to have the inspiration to sow wheat here in New Spain and to see if it took; I did this and experimented at my own expense."[32] Another first attributed to an African in Mexico was the bringing of smallpox to the mainland. Francisco de Eguía, one of the black slaves on the Narváez expedition of 1520, allegedly died of the disease soon after landing on the Mexican coast.[33]

Unlike later expeditions, Africans did not participate in the Conquest of Mexico in the hundreds, for as Bernal Díaz observed, "at that time Blacks and horses were worth their weight in gold."[34] But Garrido and Eguía were

probably among dozens of blacks among the Spaniards who invaded the
Mexica empire. One was Juan Cortés, a slave named after his owner. Juan
Sedeño also had his own African servant. The Ramírez brothers, who later
followed Alvarado to Guatemala, each brought a horse and a black slave to
Mexico.[35] Both Spanish and native sources make references to the black presence, albeit typically without providing specifics. The Dominican chronicler, Diego Durán, for example, mentions various "servants and blacks," while
the native account compiled by Sahagún (known to us as the *Florentine Codex*) simply notes that with the Spaniards "came some blacks, who had crisply
curled dark hair."[36] Two of the illustrations in Durán's account depict a black
African beside Cortés (see Figure 8).[37] Such drawings are probably intended
not to represent specific individuals but rather the presence of a number of
black servants and slaves on the expedition, all of whom would have fought
and, if they survived, emerged as veteran conquistadors like Garrido.

As the first major conquest on the mainland, the Conquest of Mexico
helped to inspire and finance a flurry of Spanish expeditions through the
Americas. All included African slaves and servants, many of whom, like Juan
Garrido and Juan Valiente, became or continued to fight as conquistadors
(see Table 3). These expeditions can be placed in two groups, one part of the
chain or relay system of conquest that radiated out from central Mexico, the
other part of the chain of conquest that ran into South America.

Illustrative of the first chain—that ran up into the Mexican far north and
down into southern Mesoamerica as far as Honduras—is Garrido's continued

*Fig. 8. Cortés, accompanied by a black servant or slave and various Spaniards, being
received by Moctezuma, accompanied by two Mexica lords; Plate 58 in fray Diego de Durán's*
The History of the Indies of New Spain *(1581).*

experience of exploration and conquest in New Spain after the fall of Tenochtitlán. He participated in expeditions to the Mexican regions of Michoacán and Zacatula in the 1520s, and to Baja California with Cortés in the 1530s. By this time blacks on such expeditions had begun to number in the hundreds, sometimes outnumbering Spanish company members; Cortés took over 300 to Baja California.[38]

While Garrido periodically left central Mexico for the north, Valiente chose to go south, to Guatemala. Alvarado had taken Africans into the Maya highlands in 1524, and they continued to arrive steadily in the years that followed, most as slaves, many to join the sizeable black underclass in the Guatemalan capital, some to seek Conquest opportunity as did Valiente.[39] In 1533 the buzz in the colonies was all about Peru and the much-heralded Montejo expedition into Yucatan was in ruins. Had the timing of Spanish discoveries and fortunes been different, or had Valiente arrived in Guatemala before Peru's discovery or as late as 1540, he may have chosen to go to Yucatan instead. There he would have found dozens of Africans on the early Montejo campaigns, and perhaps over a hundred on the final invasion of the 1540s. These included an African baptized as Sebastián Toral, who won freedom for his efforts and raised a family as one of the first settlers of the colonial Yucatec capital of Mérida—whose black and Spanish populations were almost equal in number around 1550.[40]

When Juan Valiente joined Alvarado's vast but short-lived expedition to Peru in 1534, he traveled with 200 other African slaves, servants, and a small number of voluntary members like himself. In opting to stay in South America, he effectively jumped from one chain of conquest to another. The latter chain had begun in the Caribbean and the southern regions of Central America in the 1510s (see Table 3),[41] extended down into greater Peru in the 1530s, and then out into the margins of South America—as illustrated by Valiente's career in Chile from the late 1530s into the 1550s.

Juan Valiente's movements and motives thus made him an unexceptional member of the African diaspora that was part of Spanish expansion in the sixteenth century. This was as true of the South American portion of his life as it was of his earlier years in the Americas. Just as Garrido was not the only black conquistador of Mexico, nor was Valiente the only African in Peru and Chile in the 1530s. There were two blacks with Pizarro's company at Cajamarca, Juan García and Miguel Ruíz, both of whose biographies can be reconstructed in modest detail (see Tables 3 and 4). These two, however, were free mulattos who had voluntarily joined the expedition. There were unknown numbers of other blacks, mostly African-born slaves, who accompanied this and subsequent expeditions into the Andes. Indeed, the only casualty on the Spanish side during the capture of Atahuallpa was a black slave of Jerónimo de Aliaga's.[42]

Table 3: Life Patterns of Some Black Conquistadors

Name	Birth Place and Status	Places of Conquest Activity	Recompense for Fighting
Juan Garrido	Africa or Portugal, black slave	Mexico, Zacatula, and Baja California	Manumission; various minor posts; house site in Mexico City
Sebastián Toral	Africa(?), black slave	Yucatan	Manumission; tax exemption
Pedro Fulupo	Africa(?), black slave	Costa Rica	Unknown
Juan Bardales	Africa, black slave	Honduras and Panama	Manumission; 50-peso pension
Antonio Pérez	North Africa, free black	Venezuela	Horseman; made captain
Juan Portugués	Africa or Portugal, black	Venezuela	Unknown
Juan García	Spain, free mulatto	Peru	Footman's share of gold and silver at Cajamarca; a share at Cuzco
Miguel Ruíz	Spain, free mulatto	Peru	Horseman's share of gold and silver at Cajamarca, a posthumous share at Cuzco
Juan Valiente	Africa(?), black slave	Peru, Chile	Treated as free; horseman; made captain; an estate and *encomienda*
Juan Beltrán	Spanish America, free mulatto (black-native)	Chile	Confirmed as fort captain at Villarica; an *encomienda*

Sources: AGI, *México* 204, fs. 1–9; Icaza, *Diccionario*, 1923, I: 98; Gerhard, "A Black Conquistador," 1978; Alegría, *Juan Garrido*, 1990; AGI, *México* 2999, 2, f. 180; Meléndez and Duncan, *El Negro*, 1972: 25; Herrera, "People of Santiago," 1997: 254; Oviedo y Baños, *Historia*, 1967 [1723]: 347, 390, 394, 438–39; Cieza de León, *Peru*, 1998 [1550]: 243; Lockhart, *Cajamarca*, 1972: 6–15, 380–84, 421–22; Boyd-Bowman, "Negro Slaves," 1969: 150–51; Sater, "Black Experience," 1974: 16–17; Vásquez de Espinosa, *Compendium*, 1942 [1620]: 743–44.
Note: A version of this table originally appeared in Restall, "Black Conquistadors," 2000: 174.

The Conquest account by Pedro de Cieza de León, a young Spaniard who spent 15 years (1535–50) as a conquistador-chronicler in South America, is typical of how Spanish sources both ignore and reveal black roles. Cieza de León never provides the total number of blacks in any one company, nor does he name any of the Africans who fought or traveled with him, but on 19 occasions he mentions their presence. Thirteen of these references are to blacks in Peruvian expeditions; six in Chilean ones; seven are to Africans starving or freezing to death in the northern Andes or Chile. Valiente would certainly have been on at least one of these journeys and must have been lucky to survive.[43] The remainder of Cieza de León's references are to notable incidents that reveal the black presence, despite the chronicler's failure to otherwise record it. An African discovered fresh water for a company led by Alvarado's cousin, Diego, in the Ecuadorian interior; an African saved Almagro's life; native Andeans attempted to wash the color off a black slave; a mulatto messenger had a finger cut off by Manco Inca, the Inca ruler who succeeded Atahuallpa.

Other sources produce a similar litany of incidents that add up to overwhelming evidence of the black presence in the Peruvian Conquest. The first four non-natives to see the Inca capital of Cuzco in 1533 included a black man (he returned to Cajamarca leading a train of Andean porters carrying precious metals). During Manco Inca's 1536 siege of Cuzco, blacks labored to extinguish the fires on the roof of the royal palace as fast as attacking Andeans set them. A force sent from Hispaniola to relieve the defenders included 200 Africans with military experience—a veritable squadron of black conquistadors.[44]

Cieza de León also recorded the presence of blacks on a disastrous expedition into Colombia in the 1530s that the chronicler barely survived. Conquistadors eventually did manage to establish a colony there, which they named New Granada; one of their number was Pedro de Lerma, a mulatto who achieved full-fledged conquistador status. Scores of other blacks, most of them slaves, played various roles in all the Conquest expeditions into New Granada. When a group of them rebelled during one expedition, the governor, Luis de Lugo, ordered their genitals to be cut off. One died. Likewise there were Africans with the infamous Lope de Aguirre, with Diego de Ordaz on the Orinoco, and with Diego de Losada on the Conquest of Caracas (one of whom, Antonio Pérez, was a veteran captain).[45]

Just as Juan Garrido has been called Mexico's only black conquistador, so has Juan Valiente been called "the lone Negro conqueror of Chile."[46] Yet the evidence for Mexico, Chile, Peru, Colombia, Venezuela, and elsewhere shows that these men were by no means alone. And if the number of Africans on earlier expeditions was in the dozens or hundreds, there were soon thousands of black men and women in core colonies such as Peru—even while the Conquest continued. Between 1529 and 1537 the Pizarro brothers were granted 258 licenses to import African slaves to Peru, and in 1534 Alvarado brought 200 more Africans (many of whom, like Valiente, remained). But many more blacks arrived illegally, including 400 slaves shipped from Panama to Peru in just one six-month period in 1535. As the Conquest wars of the 1530s slid into the Spanish Peruvian civil war of the 1540s, the total number of blacks in Peru grew to some 2,000, and by the early 1550s to 3,000.[47]

In addition to there being so many other Africans in Peru and Chile, Valiente's experience in the military was shared by other blacks. The names of some of the many other blacks who fought in Chile have survived—an African named Felipe fought at Marihueni, a Juan Fernández fought at Cañete, and Juan Beltrán played so vital a role in the Conquest of Villarica that he was appointed its garrison commander.[48] Elsewhere in the Americas the written record offers brief insights into the hard years of frequent combat that must have characterized the lives of black conquistadors. Juan Bardales, for example, claimed that he took 106 arrow wounds in Honduras and saved the life of his Spanish captain (see Table 3).[49]

The king eventually granted Bardales a pension, as he did Toral, black conqueror in Yucatan, remarking that "he helped place that province under our command."[50] This seems like grudging recognition of services rendered, and Spaniards seldom acknowledged the importance of African combat roles; yet it is also clear that Spaniards tended to view Africans as "very good at fighting," as one official put it.[51] There are several reasons why this perception rose. Black slaves had served for centuries in the Middle East, North Africa, and the Iberian peninsula. Most black Africans were enslaved through warfare, and thus many already had combat experience. Finally, Africans in the Americas were motivated to develop martial skills not only to survive but also as a means to acquire freedom, which was a black conquistador's standard reward.[52]

Spaniards thought that two categories of Africans were especially pugnacious, Muslims in general and Wolofs in particular, who were consequently feared and distrusted on the one hand, and respected and valued on the other. For example, in royal legislation of 1532 Wolofs (who came from the Sénégal river region of West Africa) were called "arrogant, disobedient, rebellious, and incorrigible." Juan de Castellanos, a sixteenth-century Spanish poet who lived for a while in Puerto Rico, wrote that "The Wolofs are skillful and very warlike / With vain presumptions to be knights."[53] Black conquistadors who were deemed by Spaniards to be both militarily skillful and loyal were lauded as paragons. One such conqueror was Juan Beltrán, a mulatto of African and Native American descent, whose career in sixteenth-century Chile had become legendary by the time Vásquez de Espinosa wrote of him in 1620. This "valiant captain," wrote the Spanish traveler, "is worthy of eternal memory for his great deeds among those savages. He was very deferential toward the Spaniards, and very obedient and loyal to them. With the Indians he was fearless; they stood in awe of him and respected him, to such a degree that the mere mention of his name was often enough to intimidate the Indians and put their forces to flight."[54]

Beltrán fought for many years in Chile until his Araucanian enemies managed to kill him, and Valiente likewise died in battle against the same Native Americans when in his late forties. Beltrán and Valiente were not typical of black conquistadors, in that they continued to play active roles in combat, whereas most black conquerors fought and then settled into positions in the new Mesoamerican and Andean colonies.

Spaniards associated a limited number of occupations with Africans and mulattos, stereotypical roles reinforced by repeated Spanish placing of blacks in these positions. The most common was that of street or town crier (*pregonero*), a post held by both Juan García (Table 4) and Juan Garrido; Lima's crier in the 1540s, Pedro de la Peña, was black too. Other functions typically assigned to blacks were those of constable, auctioneer (Pedro de la Peña was one too), executioner, piper (Juan García again), and master of weights and measures (García yet again). Perhaps the most typical position of all was that of doorkeeper or guard (*portero*), a position held by Garrido in Mexico City and Sebastián Toral, one of Yucatan's black conquistadors, in Mérida. The *portero* summoned the Spanish city councilors, set out tables and chairs, and stood guard at the door during meetings.[55]

It is not clear if Valiente ever held these positions, although it is likely that he would have, had he stayed in Peru or arrived early enough in Mexico or Guatemala to fight there. Because such posts were usually assigned in the wake of initial Conquest wars, and Chile's Conquest was an interminable affair, Valiente probably remained a conquistador, rather than a post-Conquest *pregonero* or *portero*. Furthermore, Valiente's survival on the frontier allowed him to rise to a social level denied men of African descent in core colonies such as Mexico, Guatemala, and Peru. Buying a horse and becoming a captain was not common for an African, but not unheard of. Being granted an estate and then an *encomienda* was rare on the frontier and simply never happened in core areas. Indeed, the only solid evidence of blacks being given *encomiendas* that I have found is from Chile, where in addition to Valiente, Juan Beltrán and two mulattos named Gómez de León and Leonor Galiano received them.[56]

More often, blacks were expected to live on the margins of the new Spanish towns and to fill marginal posts. Less common was the decision of Juan García, who took his share of the early spoils of the Conquest of Peru and returned to Spain, where he lived to be an old man. As a free Spanish-born mulatto and a member of the exceptionally profitable company that acquired gold and silver at Cajamarca in 1532–33 and at Cuzco in 1534, he had the luxury of that option. Yet as a black man, he was also escaping the murmurs of resentment that had begun to circulate in Lima over his parvenu status.[57] Certainly, Africans were valued in the Spanish Conquest, but only if they settled after the Conquest for

Table 4: The Life of Juan García, Black Conquistador

ca. 1495?	Born free, near Jaraicejo (near Trujillo, Extremadura, Spain), probably of mixed black-Spanish parentage though later referred to by other Spaniards as "black"
1530	Recruited in Trujillo to join the Pizarro expedition to Peru; leaves behind his wife and two daughters
1531–34	Footman member of the Pizarro Conquest expedition that leaves Panama in January 1531; holds the posts of crier (*pregonero*) and piper (*gaitero*) and is made responsible for weighing gold and silver at Cajamarca; present at the division of gold and silver at Coaque in 1531, at Cajamarca in 1533 (where he buys an enslaved native Nicaraguan woman from a fellow conquistador), and at Cuzco in 1534
1534–35	One of the founding citizens of Spanish Cuzco, where he then resides
1535–36	Travels to Lima, where he spends time preparing his return to Spain, then to Nombre de Dios (Panama) and back to Extremadura; takes with him his share of gold and silver and probably his illegitimate daughter and her native Andean mother, one of his servants
1536–45	Lives in the Jaraicejo-Trujillo area to at least 1545, calling himself Juan García Pizarro; date of death unknown

Sources: Lockhart, *Cajamarca*, 1972: 6–15, 380–84; Cieza de León, *Peru*, 1998 [1550]: 243.
Note: A version of this table first appeared in Restall, "Black Conquistadors," 2000: 186.

free but subordinate lives as gatekeepers, like Garrido and Toral, or fought willingly until their deaths, like Beltrán and Valiente.

The final chapter of Juan Beltrán's life serves to illustrate most evocatively the role played by black and native combatants in the Spanish Conquest. For "his sterling character and his bravery" in the conquest and founding of a Spanish town at Villarica, according to the colonial chronicler Vásquez de Espinosa, the new governor assigned Beltrán to oversee the construction of a fort outside the town and then named him its captain. He also "presented him with five hundred Indians," for whom "he was a valiant governor and captain . . . and they were very obedient to him. He made himself respected and feared in all the neighboring provinces, into which he made long *malocas* or raids, bringing back great prizes."[58] Vásquez de Espinosa's purpose was to eulogize Beltrán, but in doing so he revealed a "Spanish" Conquest in which a black captain led native warriors against other Native Americans. Whether in the heart of the Mexica empire or down on the Chilean frontier, the Spaniards were by no means the sole conquistadors.

4

Under the Lordship of the King
The Myth of Completion

By divine will I have placed under the lordship of the King and Queen, Our
Lords, an other world, thanks to which Spain, once called poor, is now the
richest [of nations].

—Christopher Columbus (1500)

It is in fact the conquest of America that heralds and establishes our present
identity; even if every date that permits us to separate any two periods is
arbitrary, none is more suitable, in order to mark the beginning of the
modern era, than the year 1492, the year Columbus crosses the Atlantic
ocean. We are all direct descendents of Columbus, it is with him that our
genealogy begins, insofar as the word *beginning* has a meaning.

—Tzvetan Todorov (1984)

But many kingdoms and provinces were not totally or entirely conquered, and
there were left among other provinces and kingdoms great portions of them
unconquered, unreduced, unpacified, some of them not even yet discovered.

—Juan de Villagutierre Soto-Mayor (1701)

Some wars have two names. What Russians call the Great Patriotic War is known
in the West as the Second World War. The Mexican-American War is, to those
south of the border, the War of the North American Invasion. But the Conquest of Mexico has no other name. Nobody has ever called it, at least in print,
the War of the Spanish Invasion, or the Spanish-Mexica War. The same is true
for the Conquest of Peru, the Conquest of Yucatan, and so on.

   These conventional titles to the components of the Conquest are taken
for granted as simple, neutral descriptions. But they are hardly that. For in
assigning "conquest" to the entire process of Spanish exploration, expansion, discovery, and invasion, that process is placed within a framework in
which events move inexorably toward the inevitable climax of Spanish victory. Conquest history turns on symbolic Spanish accomplishments—such as
a particular victory (or massacre) or the founding of a city. The years of those

events have consequently become the milestones that mark the transition from barbarism to civilization (in Spanish minds), the shift from pre-Columbian or pre-Conquest to colonial (in the academic terminology of today).

This vision of the Conquest originated with the conquistadors themselves and has survived more or less intact up to the present. Sixteenth-century Spaniards consistently presented their deeds and those of their compatriots in terms that prematurely anticipated the completion of Conquest campaigns and imbued Conquest chronicles with an air of inevitability. The phrase "Spanish Conquest" and all it implies has come down through history because the Spaniards were so concerned to depict their endeavors as conquests and pacifications, as contracts fulfilled, as providential intention, as faits accomplis. Such depictions are the roots of what I have called the "myth of completion." This chapter will examine two related reasons the Spaniards did this. The first of these was the Spanish system of patronage, contract, and reward—beginning with Columbus and his insistence until his death that he had fulfilled his contract by discovering a route to Asia. The second was the ideology of imperial justification that developed rapidly during the sixteenth century to portray the Conquest as divine intention and Spaniards as agents of providence. Despite these claims, the Conquest remained incomplete for centuries after the initial Spanish invasions; the chapter's second half presents seven aspects of this incompleteness.

"The New World is a disaster!" remarks Queen Isabella in the 1992 movie *1492: Conquest of Paradise*, to which Christopher Columbus replies, "And the old one an achievement?" Vital to the success of all conquistadors was their ability to portray their endeavors as anything but a disaster. While the Spanish monarchy neither dispatched would-be conquerors as members of a royal army nor did it conceive, organize, and finance Conquest expeditions, it did nonetheless exercise some control over the consequences of discoveries and conquests through the granting of licenses or contracts to explore or conquer. In return for the title of *adelantado* (captain-general or, more literally, invader) up front, and gubernatorial titles and privileges after a conquest, the recipient of the license had to bear most or all of the costs of the expedition, as well as plan and execute it. Such contracts were thus of great benefit to the crown in an era when centralized state power was a fraction of what it would become in modern times. They were a mechanism for the dispensing of royal patronage, both when the license was granted and when its terms were deemed to have been fulfilled—or not. Equally important, such agreements were also sources of revenue, as the monarchy often sold them and could claim contracts were unfulfilled if the crown's customary *quinto* (fifth of all Conquest spoils and taxes) had not materialized. In time, the crown added to typical *adelantado* contract provisions various laws regarding Conquest procedure, making it easier to imprison conquistadors for contractual violations (as Sebastian de Benalcázar and Hernando Pizarro were imprisoned in the 1540s) or fine them (as Juan de Oñate was fined in 1614, to the tune of 6,000 Castilian ducats).[1]

The challenge for the leaders of Conquest companies was thus considerable. Not only did they need to avoid the disasters of shipwreck, disease, and capture or death at the hands of invaded natives, but their enterprises needed to meet royal definitions of colonial success. Simply finding and claiming lands was not enough. Putative colonies needed immediate economic viability, preferably in the form of gold and silver mines and sedentary native societies to locate and work the mines and provide other goods and labor. The point here is not that it was tough to be a conquistador, but that it was tough to convince the crown that one was a successful conquistador.

As a result, expedition leaders were quick to claim that regions were overflowing with precious metals and compliant native peoples. Such claims began with Columbus, who from the outset was keen to convince the crown that he had fulfilled the terms laid out in his contract (known as the *Capitulaciones de Santa Fe*, after the garrison town near Granada where the agreement was drawn up in April 1492). Early in 1493 Columbus explained to Ferdinand and Isabella that setting out on his voyage "I took the route to Your Highnesses' Canary Islands, which are in the said Ocean Sea, in order from there to take my course and sail so far that I would reach the Indies and give Your Highnesses' message to those princes and thus fulfill that which you had commanded me to do."[2]

These assertions of fulfillment or compliance were crucial to Columbus's being able to take his third of all trade revenues from the discovered lands, as well as to administer them as "Admiral of the Ocean Sea, Viceroy and Governor"—as guaranteed in the *Capitulaciones*. Columbus's insistence that he had both reached Asia and found new lands was disputed as soon as he returned to Spain from his first voyage. His claims were increasingly contested as further voyages by Columbus and others revealed more and more about the Atlantic and the Americas. Afraid of losing his contract-based privileges (as he eventually would), Columbus averred ever more stridently that "I have found and continue to find nothing less in any respect than what I wrote and said and affirmed to their Highnesses in days gone by."[3]

The Spaniards who crossed the Atlantic in growing numbers in the early sixteenth century developed a similar concern over contractual approval and fulfillment. The letters of Cortés to the king are the best-known series of contract-related documents, but they are unusual only in that Cortés wrote them in part as petitions for a license and in part on the assumption that he had been granted one. Like Cortés, Francisco de Orellana drew up a series of documents during his treacherous journey of 1542 down the Amazon in anticipation of finding native lands that could be conquered (in which case, like Cortés, he would need a retroactive license in order to become governor). Orellana's letters to the king correctly anticipated accusations by his patron Gonzalo Pizarro that he had illegally abandoned Pizarro in Amazonia, just as Cortés's letters anticipated the anger of his own betrayed patron, Velázquez. Similarly, Juan de Oñate took considerable pains over his 1595 license to conquer New Mexico. He then submitted numerous petitions regarding contractual fulfillment in 1597, when the license was temporarily withdrawn, and between 1606 and 1624, when he underwent a protracted royal investigation, condemnation for use of excessive violence, and partial rehabilitation.[4]

The *adelantado* Francisco de Montejo wrote a series of letters to the king designed to reassure him that Yucatan was both worth conquering and conquerable. Indeed, these two themes of contract-related Spanish writing were so commonplace that the language of discovery and fulfillment came close to being formulaic. The following example, a description of Yucatan by Montejo in his letter to the king of 1529, could have come from any one of dozens of conquistadors: "The land is heavily peopled and has very large and beautiful cities and towns. All the towns are a [veritable] fruit orchard. . . . I have found many signs of gold. . . . I went over a great part of the land and I heard many reports of the gold and [precious] stones that are in it."[5]

This was one-half of the formula—the suitability of the region for colonization. The other half was the supposed degree of control over the region that Spaniards had already established. A decade before Montejo prematurely waxed lyrical over Yucatan, Cortés had written to the king that before setting out for central Mexico he had conquered a vast coastal region.

> I left all that province of Cempoala [*Cempoal*] and all the mountains surrounding the town, which contain as many as fifty thousand warriors and fifty towns and fortresses, very secure and peaceful; and all of these natives have been and still are faithful vassals of Your Majesty, for they were subjects of Moctezuma [*Mutezuma*] and, according to what I was told, had been subdued by force not long previously. When they heard through me of Your Highness and of Your very great Royal power, they said they wished to become vassals of Your Majesty and my allies and asked me to protect them from that great lord who held them by tyranny and by force, and took their children to sacrifice to his idols; and they made many other complaints about him. Because of this, they have been very loyal and true in the service of Your Highness, and I believe that they will always be so, as they are now free of his tyranny, and because they have always been honored and well treated by me.[6]

The reader needs virtually no additional or contextual information to see how the situation has been misrepresented in order to fit the requirements that fed the myth of completion during the sixteenth century. The claim to a completed conquest is too unlikely to stand on its own, so Cortés resorts to spinning one of the submyths of the myth of completion—that of willing native submission. Here Cortés gives support to the assertion of willing submission using the tried and true juxtaposition of a benevolent and powerful king, and his honorable representative, with a cruel native tyrant. The physical implausibility of completion claims are overridden by the evocation of a process that is both physical and metaphysical, the triumph of civilization over barbarism.

Thus if the system of royal patronage encouraged rapid claims of success in exploration and conquest, conquistadors were soon able to draw upon an ideology of imperial justification that offered tools for making such claims plausible to their compatriots. The ideology of the Spanish empire was rooted in medieval jurisprudence and the mythology of the Christian *reconquista* (reconquest) of the Iberian peninsula, in Judeo-Christian concepts of time as progressive and providential, and in recycled Roman notions of universal empire.[7] From the 1490s on, an additional factor was added to this potent mix: the experience of the Discovery and Conquest. The result was an ideology of empire that made the Discovery and Conquest not only noble and justified endeavors but also the duty of the faithful. This ideology consisted not just of abstract ideas concocted for the benefit of the crown; it was supported by official statements that came both from the papacy and the Spanish monarchy. In the wake of Columbus's first voyage, the pope presided over a Castilian-Portuguese treaty that divided the Americas, still a largely imagined region, between the two kingdoms. Thus, in effect, Spaniards were the recipients of a divine grant of lands and peoples they had yet to find and see, let alone subdue. This permitted claims of possession to be seen as synonymous with possession itself. Through the simple acts of arrival and declaration, Spaniards placed lands "under the lordship" of the Spanish crown. Everything that followed, the entire business of Conquest and colonization, was the consolidation of that possession.[8]

By extension, native peoples were Spanish subjects waiting to be located and informed of their new status. As Queen Isabel stated in 1501, when the vast majority of Native Americans were still unknown to Europeans, these "Indians" were the queen's "subjects and vassals" and thus as soon as they were found were "to pay us our tributes and rights."[9] Such sentiments, repeated by the crown to Cortés in 1523, to Ponce de León in 1525, and to other conquistadors on many occasions, were at the heart of an assumption of rightful acquisition that made the Conquest seem half-complete before it had even begun. Furthermore, because native peoples were royal "subjects and vassals" before the fact, their resistance to conquest made them rebels. This category conveniently cast native resistance to invasion as the unjustifiably violent and illegal disruption of the *pax colonial* (colonial peace). Spanish military activities were then framed as campaigns of "pacification" rather than conquest, and resistance leaders could be tried and executed for treason. Long after the crown banned the enslaving of natives in the Americas, a persistent loophole regarding "rebels" permitted captured natives to be sold as slaves.

This pattern can be seen in the Yucatan as well as in virtually every region of Spanish America. Having founded a new colonial capital in 1542, named Mérida, the Spaniards in Yucatan declared the Conquest achieved and set about "pacifying" the peninsula. But as they controlled only a small corner of it, they were obliged to engage in major military hostilities with one Maya group after another, encountering particularly strong resistance in the northeast in the late 1540s. This was clearly an episode in a conquest war now in its third decade, but just as the Spaniards had already declared the Conquest complete so did they now classify this resistance as a rebellion—"the rebellion that took place in this recently conquered province," as one Spanish colonist put it.[10] This was used to justify the execution of captives, the use of display violence (notably the hanging of women), and the enslaving of 2,000 Mayas of the region.[11] Four centuries later, historians were still calling this "The Great Maya Revolt."[12]

By insisting on the completeness of the Conquest in the face of massive evidence to the contrary, Spanish colonists bequeathed an identity crisis to their Mexican descendents. In 1862 Lord Acton wrote that Mexican national identity was unattainable. Because Mexico was made up of "races divided by blood . . . fluid, shapeless, unconnected" it was "therefore neither possible to unite them nor convert them into the elements of an organized State."[13]

Time would seem to have proved the Englishman wrong, but nineteenth-century Mexicans were almost as pessimistic and divided themselves over how to interpret the Mexican past with a view to forging a national identity. The conservative position was simply to apply the term "nation" to the sixteenth-century Spanish view of the Conquest. Thus 1521 saw the providential dawn of civilization in Mexico, with Cortés as founding father, and the spiritual conquest symbolized by the apparition of the Virgin of Guadalupe a decade later. The political opponents of the conservatives placed more emphasis on the Virgin of Guadalupe and less on Cortés. Indeed, many liberals demonized the conqueror as a symbol of colonial tyranny and idolized as "national" heroes the last Mexica emperor, Cuauhtémoc, and early friars such as Las Casas and Motolinía, along with iconic Independence figures such as Hidalgo and Morelos.[14]

The evolution of Mexican nationalism, and the debate over it in the nineteenth century, was of course more complex. Anticlericalism and hispanophobia would wax and wane, a love-hate relationship would develop with the United States and its culture, and few of the (in)famous figures of the

Mexican past would be left undisputed through the nineteenth and twentieth centuries. But one element remained constant throughout, one rooted in the sixteenth century and still showing remarkable vitality—the assumption that 1521 was a monumental turning point in Mexican history, the end of one era and the beginning of another. Had such assumptions been questioned, Mexicans might have found solutions to the riddle of national identity.

Similar debates over national and regional identity were waged in all the new republics of nineteenth-century Latin America. The debaters seldom questioned the accuracy or implications of using dates such as 1492, 1521, 1535 (the founding of Lima), 1541 (the founding of Santiago de Chile), or 1542 (the founding of Mérida) as milestones that marked the completion of the Conquest and the start of colonial rule. In doing so they perpetuated the perspectives of the conquistadors for their own political and practical reasons, and helped lead modern historians into the same traps.[15]

A classic statement along these lines is Prescott's comment that "the history of the Conquest of Mexico terminates with the surrender of the capital."[16] While such a statement conforms with the vast majority of what has been written on the Conquest, from the sixteenth century to the present, in the wake of the destruction of Tenochtitlán the Spaniards had not conquered Mexico; they had simply dismembered the Mexica empire. In a note appended to Cortés's second letter to the king, an official in Spain, despite his optimistic tone, revealed the precariousness of the situation in 1522: "They found little treasure . . . but the Spaniards, of whom there are at present fifteen hundred men on foot and five hundred men on horseback, are very well fortified in that city, and they have more than a hundred thousand Indian allies in the countryside."[17]

Here we have the conquistadors, a year after the supposed completion of the Conquest, still searching for war booty, needing to be fortified in the ruins of the city they had destroyed, and dependent upon vast numbers of native allies. Meanwhile, the Spanish presence in the rest of the region covered by the Mexica empire was minimal, and Spanish control over the larger area that would become modern Mexico was virtually nonexistent. Indeed, Spaniards had yet to even set foot in most of the regions of what would become colonial New Spain (roughly the civilizational area called Mesoamerica). In the early 1520s, Cortés apparently believed the Spanish assertion that Michoacán was conquered and under Spanish rule. Yet the native Tarascan government remained intact and the Tarascans viewed their empire as the region's dominant power.[18] Twenty years later the wars of conquest in northern Mexico were still sufficiently extensive to warrant the viceroy of New Spain himself leading Spanish-native forces into battle.[19] So while 1521 was the end of the two-year war against the Mexica empire, it was the beginning of the wars of conquest in most of greater Mexico and Mesoamerica, wars that would persist into the twentieth century.

The incompleteness of the military conquest of Mexico in 1522 is, of course, merely one piece of the puzzle. The full picture of incompleteness features seven dimensions, each one corresponding to one aspect of the myth of completion. The first dimension of incompleteness is that of the rapidity of the Conquest in the core areas of native and subsequent colonial settlement. #1 In addition to the tenuous Spanish grip on central Mexico in 1521, Spanish control over Peru was almost nonexistent in 1532, despite Atahuallpa's capture and execution, and tenuous in 1536, after the lifting of the Inca siege of Cuzco. An independent Inca state persisted until its ruler, Túpac Amaru, was executed by the Spanish in 1572, and significant portions of the Andes remained outside direct colonial rule even after that.[20] Similarly, when the Spaniards founded Mérida in 1542, Mayas continued to rule the vast majority of the Yucatan peninsula. Independent Yucatec Maya polities still existed in 1880, when Bishop Crescencio Carrillo y Ancona asserted that "the conquest [of Yucatan] was completed entirely with the victory gained in the battle of San Bernabé of June 11, 1541, against the army of Cocom, king of Sotuta, who was the only one who had not offered obedience."[21]

The second dimension of incompleteness relates to the protracted nature of the military conquest of the so-called fringe or marginal regions of what #2 gradually became Spanish America. Above all else Spaniards sought native settlements upon which to construct their colonies. But outside Mesoamerica and the Andes, they found sparse populations of semisedentary and nomadic natives who were not amenable to colony building. In such regions it took decades to establish toeholds and these remained unstable, poor, and attractive to few colonists. Writing in 1701, Juan de Villagutierre Soto-Mayor, author of the official account of the Spanish conquest of the Itzá Maya in the previous decade, admitted that Spanish expansion had left "great portions" of the Americas partially or entirely unconquered—and he recognized that this was due to the intractability of some natives and to the difficult terrain in some regions. But most of all, argued Villagutierre, it was because God was saving some natives for subsequent generations of Spaniards. So much for secular explanation![22] As Villagutierre predicted, the colonial frontiers of northern New Spain, Yucatan, Peru, and other regions would gradually expand, but that process included periodic contractions of frontiers and frequent military activity.

For example, early attempts at conquest and settlement at two ends of Spanish America—Florida and the River Plate basin—were disastrous. At least six expeditions to Florida failed dismally between 1513 and the 1560s, when a permanent Spanish settlement was finally established. The first founders of Buenos Aires in the late 1520s were reduced to cannibalism and the town was not permanently refounded until the 1580s, while lasting Iberian settlement on the northern bank of the River Plate (now Uruguay) did not come until a century later. New Mexico was conquered at the turn of the seventeenth century, but was then lost to the Spanish empire in 1680 and had to be reconquered in the 1690s. The Sambos-Mosquitos were able to push back the colonial frontier in Nicaragua during the seventeenth century. The seventeenth-century subjugation of the Tule of Panamá was never consolidated and then reversed in a revolt in the 1720s, necessitating a protracted reconquest beginning in 1735. Chocó and Petén were not conquered at all until the 1680s and 1690s, respectively, but the Spanish presence in Petén declined rather than grew in the early eighteenth century.[23]

Looking at Spanish America in its entirety, the Conquest as a series of armed expeditions and military actions against Native Americans never ended. Florida's Seminoles were still fighting Spaniards when the colony was taken over by the United States (to whom they have never formally surrendered either). The Araucanians of Chile—who fought for decades and eventually killed the black conquistador Juan Valiente—resisted conquest into the nineteenth century, when they continued to fight the Chilean republic in the name of the monarchy they had previously defied. The Charrúa of Uruguay were not finally subdued until the new nation's president organized their massacre in the 1830s.[24] Argentines also faced—and eventually slaughtered with machine guns—unconquered native peoples in the nineteenth and early twentieth centuries. The Guatusos-Malekus of Central America were enslaved and slaughtered in the late nineteenth century. Yaqui resistance in northern Mexico also lasted into the modern period, while at Mexico's southern end, the Maya of Yucatan pushed the colonial frontier back in 1847 to its sixteenth-century limits, and a string of Maya polities persisted there into the early twentieth century.[25]

The third aspect of the myth of completion is that of the *pax colonial*, the peace among natives and between them and the Spanish colonists that supposedly came in the Conquest's wake. The flip side to this—the corresponding dimension of incompleteness—is the fact that Spanish America was rife with native revolts against colonial rule. As one prominent historian has observed, "then and now the colonial era has typically been thought of as a peaceful time," despite "apparent endemic violence."[26]

There is a pair of possible reasons for this. One is the localized nature of colonial revolts, which made them relatively easy to put down and therefore appeared to colonial and modern observers insignificant compared to the kinds of wars that swept Europe during the same centuries and would ravage much of modern Latin America. The other relates more closely to the myth of completion. Despite periodic Spanish hysteria over real or imagined revolts by natives and enslaved Africans, Spaniards believed that their empire was God's way of civilizing natives and Africans in the Americas. Colonial rule was thus seen as peaceful and benevolent, an interpretation that relied upon the Conquest's being complete. Ironically, although the native perception was almost the opposite—that the Spanish presence was a protracted invasion that required a mixed response of accommodation and resistance—it also contributed to the illusion that the *pax colonial* was real. The willingness on the part of native leaders to compromise, to find a middle course between overt confrontation and complete capitulation, helped give the impression of a colonial peace.

The impression of a colonial peace overlooks the ubiquity of everyday forms of resistance—the fourth dimension of incompleteness. Historians tend to look for dramatic revolts and miss less obvious patterns of resistance, even if they are more pervasive and often as violent.[27] Everyday resistance manifested itself in numerous ways, ranging from individual acts of violence by natives against Spaniards to workplace ploys such as footdragging, sabotage of equipment, and theft. The ongoing existence of unconquered regions—often referred to by the Spaniards as *despoblados* (uninhabited areas)—and shifting colonial frontiers gave natives a further option. As individuals, families, or entire communities, they could resist Spanish rule by temporarily fleeing or permanently migrating out of the empire. #4

The fifth dimension of the Conquest's incompleteness was the degree to which native peoples maintained a degree of autonomy within the Spanish empire. This was in part an autonomy permitted and sanctioned by Spanish officials, and it was nurtured by native leaders through illegal means and legal negotiations. As a general rule, Spaniards did not seek to rule natives directly and take over their lands. Rather they hoped to preserve native communities as self-governing sources of labor and producers of agricultural products. This practice had precedent in Islamic-Iberian custom, as it developed in the eighth-century Muslim invasion of the Iberian peninsula and during the subsequent centuries of the *reconquista*.[28] But it was also a practical response to Spanish-American realities. The new settlers were not farmers, but artisans and professionals dependent upon the work and food provided by native peoples who greatly outnumbered them. #5

This colonial system worked best where organized, sedentary agricultural communities already existed—that is, well-fed city-states—and it was in such areas, primarily in Mesoamerica and the Andes, that Spaniards concentrated their conquest and colonization efforts. Although it is unlikely that any native community escaped the ravages of epidemic diseases brought across the Atlantic, native regions unevenly experienced direct conquest violence. For centuries after the arrival of Spaniards, the majority of natives subject to colonial rule continued to live in their own communities, speak their own languages, work their own fields, and be judged and ruled by their own elders. These elders wrote their own languages alphabetically (or, in the Andes, learned to write Spanish) and engaged the colonial legal system in defense of community interests skillfully and often successfully. The native town, or municipal community, continued to be called the *altepetl* by the Nahuas of central Mexico, the *ñuu* by the Mixtecs, the *cah* by the Yucatec Mayas, and the *ayllu* by Quechua-speaking Andeans.[29]

Only very gradually did community autonomy erode under demographic and political pressures from non-native populations. From the native perspective, therefore, the Conquest was not a dramatic singular event, symbolized by any one incident or moment, as it was for Spaniards. Rather, the Spanish invasion and colonial rule were part of a larger, protracted process of negotiation and accommodation. From such a perspective, as long as the *altepetl* and *ayllu* still existed, the Conquest could never be complete.

#6

The sixth dimension of incompleteness is that of the spiritual conquest. Amidst the complex sixteenth-century debates among Spanish priests and friars regarding the efficacy of different conversion methods and the spiritual state of native peoples, there emerged a myth regarding their Christianization. This myth held that while native people remained superstitious and prone to recidivism, they had essentially been converted in the early days of evangelization. As the vanguards of that process, the Franciscans were the greatest proponents of its myth; their perspective fared well over the centuries and was given renewed vigor in the early twentieth century by Robert Ricard, whose *La Conquête Spirituelle du Mexique* (The Spiritual Conquest of Mexico) was a widely read paean to the success of Franciscan conversion campaigns.[30]

In recent decades, scholars have painted a more complex picture of native reaction to Christianity. While some have argued that native religion survived behind a veneer of Christianity, and others have proposed that native and European religions blended into a set of unique regional American variants on Catholicism, the most sophisticated interpretations recognize that a combination of both processes occurred. With variations right down to the level of the individual Andean, Chibcha, Muisca, Maya, and Nahua, natives accommodated and understood Christianity and its place in their world in ways that we are only just beginning to grasp.[31]

Franciscans and other Spanish friars and clergy hoped to utterly destroy all traces of native religions, to wipe the slate clean and establish a new church free of the pagan accretions of both sides of the Atlantic. They certainly succeeded in bringing Catholicism to native America, but if the purpose of the spiritual conquest was to install a Christianity free of local cultural variation, that conquest was not completed in the sixteenth century. In 1598 the Archbishop of New Granada (colonial Colombia) lamented in a letter to the king that six decades of Christianization efforts had left the native Muisca as "idolatrous" as ever.[32] Nobody would accuse Latin Americans of being idolatrous today, but few would disagree that the spiritual conquest, as conceived almost five centuries ago, remains very much incomplete.

#7

The final dimension of incompleteness concerns the persistence of native cultures. The aspect of native culture of greatest concern to Spaniards was religion, as Christianization provided the empire with a rationale and justification that transcended and was supposed to disguise the mundanely self-serving realities of colonial expansion. Other aspects of native culture were of secondary importance. There was no campaign to force natives to learn Spanish, for example. In fact, Spanish priests were encouraged and periodically required to preach in native tongues, while the church generated an extensive religious literature in local languages. And although the lack of a preconquest writing tradition in the Andes meant that Quechua-speaking lords and other local Andean rulers learned to write legal documents in Spanish, Mesoamerica community leaders learned to write their own languages alphabetically.[33]

Another example of native cultural persistence is dress. Where native clothing was deemed overly scant by the church, a change was imposed. Men's loincloths were replaced by loose cotton trousers, for example. But by and large, native dress remained unaltered by the Conquest, changing only gradually over the centuries. Some of the more practical styles of native dress were even adopted by Spaniards, especially at home. Like other aspects of native culture, native dress survived, not in any "pure" form, but by very gradually absorbing European influences, and to some extent influencing the evolving culture of the colonists.

Beyond aspects of culture with religious implications, Spaniards were not concerned with the wholesale Hispanization of native peoples. Not until the nineteenth century did such issues become a major governmental concern and the subject of debates among the dominant classes. This underscores once more that the cultural conquest, if we can talk of such a thing, was so incomplete that three centuries after the Spanish invasion the descendents of the conquistadors, from Mexico to Argentina, were debating ways in which their nations's "Indians" could be made into true citizens of the republics—that is, less "Indian" and more European.[34]

Thus the Conquest of the core areas of the Andes and Mesoamerica was more protracted than Spaniards initially claimed and later believed, and when warfare did end in these areas it was simply displaced out to the ever-widening and never-peaceful frontiers of Spanish America. Conquest violence was also displaced internally, taking on myriad forms of domination and repression, but met continually by an equally diverse set of methods of native resistance. The spiritual and cultural conquests were equally complex and protracted, defying completion to the point of rendering the very concept of completion irrelevant.

Spaniards insisted on the Conquest's completion not only for reasons of political expediency or because it conformed to a developing imperial ideology to which they were increasingly exposed; they also presumed that events

were unfolding in a way that was familiar to them within their own traditions. They doggedly insisted the Conquest was complete until it looked to
them as though it was. And they were unaware of native perspectives that
blurred the division between conquest and colonization, seeing the two as a
single, interminable negotiation and likewise presuming to find familiar
forms and concepts.

Historian James Lockhart has called the process of cultural interaction in
colonial Mexico one of Double Mistaken Identity. According to his interpretation of this process, "each side of the cultural exchange presumes that a
given form or concept is functioning in the way familiar within its own tradition and is unaware of or unimpressed by the other side's interpretation."[35]
Lockhart's focus is the Nahuas of central Mexico, but Double Mistaken Identity as an analytical tool is broadly applicable to the Conquest and its aftermath in the Spanish colonies—and specifically relevant to the myth of
completion. Spaniards thought natives were all firmly "under the lordship
of the king." Natives saw themselves as much subject to their own lords as
any distant Spaniards. In their own ways, they were both correct and both
mistaken.

5

The Lost Words of La Malinche
The Myth of (Mis)Communication

When the friar reached [Atahuallpa], he told him . . . that he was a priest of God who preached His law and strove wherever possible for peace rather than war because that pleased God very much. While he was saying this, he held his breviary in his hands. Atahuallpa listened to this as something of a mockery. Through the interpreter he understood everything well.

—Pedro de Cieza de León (1550)

Sir, as I understand it, they are not contrary, nor do they behave badly on purpose, but it is because they cannot comprehend you, which they earnestly strive to do.

—The Calusa ruler in Florida,
to Hernando de Escalante Fontaneda (1575)

They were all groping in the darkness, because they did not understand what the Indians were saying.

—Fray Bartolomé de Las Casas (1559)

It was absurd, unwieldy, a translator's nightmare, an epistemological maze which we can only wonder at as we recall that each time Cortés said this, or Moctezuma said that, their words were conveyed through this trilingual chain of voices.

—Anna Lanyon (1999)

On the morning of 8 November 1519, on a causeway crossing Lake Texcoco in the Valley of Mexico, a unique encounter in world history occurred. Moctezuma met Cortés.

For centuries this meeting has been taken as symbolic of the great encounter of continents that was now in its third decade. And with good reason. For the very first time, a Native American emperor greeted a representative of the Europeans who had come to conquer and settle in his lands. The meeting was friendly, with both sides keen to display an unswerving commitment to diplomacy. Yet a clash of cultures was also immediately apparent. Within

Fig. 9. "The Encounter of Cortés and Moctezuma." Attributed to Juan Correa, c.1683. Oil on canvas, on a folding screen or biombo *(from the Japanese,* byobu, *"protection from the wind"), a popular Mexican artform introduced by the Japanese ambassador to Mexico City in 1614. The portrait of Cortés (second panel from the right) appears to be a reasonable likeness, compared to sixteenth renderings, but Malinche*

(first panel on the right) and Moctezuma (second panel on the left) are both highly Europeanized. The reverse of the screen is a painting of four sets of royal families, titled "The Four Continents"; that of "Europa" is Spanish king Charles II and his wife Marie-Louise d'Orléans (who married in 1683), and that of "America" is a monarch who appears, by comparison with the obverse painting, to be Moctezuma.

months the two sides would be locked in a bloody war that would lead to Moctezuma's death and Cortés's succeeding him as the most powerful man in central Mexico.

At first, Moctezuma was aloft on a litter, and Cortés on horseback—as depicted in the highly stylized screen painting of the encounter by Juan Correa (see Figure 9). When the Mexica monarch descended onto the causeway and walked with his entourage toward the Spaniards, Cortés likewise dismounted and approached Moctezuma.

At this point, accounts diverge a little, but the tension is tangible in all versions. According to Bernal Díaz, "Cortés, I think, offered Moctezuma his right hand, but Moctezuma refused it and extended his own." Gómara glosses over the awkward moment by stating simply that "the two men saluted each other." Cortés himself makes no mention of hands, but confesses that he "stepped forward to embrace [Moctezuma], but the two lords who were with him stopped me with their hands so that I should not touch him." Díaz and Gómara also mention the aborted hug (that would have been, in Mexica eyes, "an indignity," wrote the former, and "a sin," according to the latter), albeit in a different sequence to the aborted handshake and an exchange of necklaces. Díaz also states that the two leaders "bowed deeply" to each other, but Gómara and Cortés omit this detail.[1] An illustration that appeared in various European publications during the colonial period (Figure 10 is one example) attempted to portray the Gómara-Díaz version of the encounter.

A pair of other sixteenth-century versions of the encounter are worth mentioning—the Nahuatl and Spanish texts in Sahagún's *Florentine Codex*. In these texts, there are no attempted embraces or hand clasps, and the giving of necklaces to Cortés by Moctezuma is not reciprocated by the Spaniard. Nor is the bow reciprocal. In the Nahuatl text, the Mexica emperor "bowed deeply to" Cortés; "thereupon he stood up straight, he stood up with their faces meeting . . . he stretched as far as he could, standing stiffly." As it was forbidden to look the emperor in the face, the text suggests that Moctezuma took the initiative in breaking the taboo, permitting Cortés to look right at him, attempting to meet him at a cultural halfway point. The parallel Spanish text conveys the same impression, but in a way that subordinates Moctezuma, whose gracious bow becomes a submissive kowtow: "Then he prostrated himself before the captain, doing him great reverence, and then he raised himself face to face with the captain, very close to him."[2]

Facing page: *Fig. 10. "The Interview of Cortes and Motezuma in the City of Mexico," from* John Harris, Voyages and Travels, *Vol. 2 (1748), facing p. 97; "As soon as* Cortes *saw him he alighted off his Horse, at a small Distance with some Gentlemen, and drawing near saluted him after the Manner of* Spain. *Those that led* Motezuma *stopped* Cortes, *thinking it a grievous thing that any Man should touch him, being held as some Deity" (p. 97).*

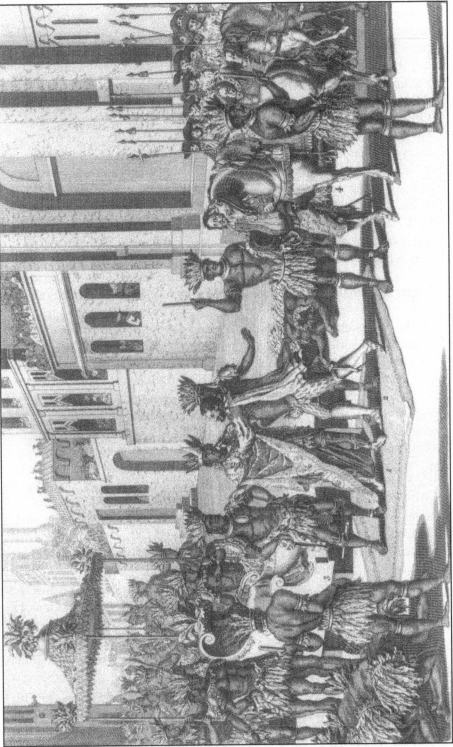

The Interview of *CORTES* and *MOTEZUMA* in the CITY of MEXICO.

These few minutes and these few gestures evoke much of the theme of communication and miscommunication that is the topic of this chapter. On the one hand there is communication; each leader successfully conveys to the other both his position of authority and his desire for their meeting to be friendly and imbued with mutual respect. On the other hand, there is miscommunication, as the two struggle to find common ground between two different cultures of lordly address and treatment. As if the confusion of gestures was not enough, there is further clutter added by the leanings and agendas of the authors of at least five different accounts of the event, each offering a different balance between emphasizing the regality of Moctezuma's diplomatic welcome and suggesting that the welcome contained the seeds of surrender.

The scene becomes more complicated still when what was said is considered. In the *Florentine Codex* accounts, Cortés asks if the lord placing necklaces around his neck is really the emperor, to which the reply is *yo soy Motecuçoma* (in the Spanish text, "I am Moctezuma") or *ca quemaca ca nehoatl* (in the Nahuatl text, "Yes, it is me"). Moctezuma then delivers a splendid speech, to which Cortés replies with some brief reassurances of friendship. In the accounts by Gómara, Díaz, and Cortés, the leaders exchange no more than brief greetings on the causeway, and the Mexica emperor's greeting is then repeated by the senior Mexica lords. Moctezuma's great speech and Cortés's reply are not delivered until the Spaniards have been led to their accommodations in Tenochtitlán and left to eat and rest a while.

How is all this dialogue achieved? Díaz mentions once during the whole episode that Cortés was "speaking through doña Marina," and Gómara remarks once that Moctezuma made his speech by "speaking through Marina and Aguilar" (Cortés's interpreters). Cortés makes no mention of an interpreter, as though he and the Mexica emperor spoke the same language. One is reminded of old Hollywood movies, in which different languages are reduced to English spoken in different accents.[3] The *Florentine Codex* is clearer, stating that after Moctezuma's speech to Cortés, "Marina [*Malintzin*] reported it to him, interpreting it for him. And when the Marqués [Cortés] had heard what Moteucçoma [Moctezuma] had said, he spoke to Marina in return, babbling back to them, replying in his babbling tongue" (from the Nahuatl version). To illustrate this process, one of the drawings that accompanied the texts of the *Codex* depicts a native woman standing between a group of Spaniards and a group of Mexica, headed by the emperor (see Figure 9).[4]

Who was this native Nahuatl-speaker who also spoke the Spanish "babble?" Why was she called "doña Marina," a Spanish noblewoman's name? Doña Marina was Malinche, or La Malinche, a Nahua noblewoman from the eastern edge of Nahuatl-speaking central Mexico. As a child she was either stolen by slave traders or sold into slavery, and ended up among the Chontal Mayas whose small kingdom lay a little further east on the Gulf coast.[5] In 1519 she was given by the Chontals along with 19 other native women to

Cortés and his colleagues as part of a peace agreement, an inducement to the Spaniards to keep traveling west. Still a teenager, she was baptized Marina and assigned to one of the captains of the expedition, Alonso Hernández de Puertocarrero.

Within a month Cortés had taken Marina back. It was discovered that she was able to converse with the "Indians" through whose territory the Spaniards were now moving, whereas their language, Nahuatl, was unknown to Gerónimo de Aguilar—the Maya-speaking Spaniard shipwrecked off the coast of Yucatan in 1511, rescued by Cortés earlier in 1519, and then serving as the expedition's interpreter. After just a few weeks as Puertocarrero's servant and perhaps his involuntary mistress, Marina knew little or no Spanish. But, like Aguilar, she had learned Yucatec as a slave among Mayas, and so Cortés could now communicate with Nahuatl-speaking lords and Mexica emissaries through the Maya of Aguilar and Marina.

Marina appears to have risen to the occasion, seizing the opportunity to improve her grim situation by making herself an invaluable member of the expedition. She soon learned Spanish, making Aguilar redundant as an interpreter probably sooner than Gómara recognized. Cortés gave Marina little credit, mentioning her in his letters to the king only twice, in 1520 as "my interpreter, who is an Indian woman," and in 1526 as "Marina, who traveled always in my company after she had been given to me as a present." Díaz was more accurate in according her the "doña" title, in recognition not just of her noble native origins but of the respect she earned among the Spaniards for her loyalty, tenacity, and intelligence—that Díaz claimed saved the expedition on a number of occasions. The Mexica and other Nahuas also recognized her status, giving her name the Nahuatl honorific suffix of *–tzin* that turned "Marina" into *Malintzin*, which the Spaniards heard as "Malinche."

The Nahuas soon dubbed Cortés himself with the name of Malinche, as though captain and interpreter were one. Indeed, Cortés never seems to have let Malinche out of his sight, according to Díaz and judging from contemporary illustrations (Figures 9 and 11 are examples). It also seems likely that she was not required to be his mistress during the march to Tenochtitlán and subsequent Spanish-Mexica war; she was too valuable to Cortés for him to risk her becoming pregnant. Significantly, she bore him a son ten months after the fall of Tenochtitlán, suggesting their relationship became sexual as soon as her role as interpreter ceased to be crucial to Spanish success.

Had Malinche earned Cortés's respect as she did Bernal Díaz's? Perhaps, as he named their son after his father, Martín, had him legitimized, and seemed to favor him. For the remainder of Malinche's short life (she died in 1527 or 1528, still in her twenties), Cortés never seemed to cast her aside. She lived in his house in the new Mexico City (albeit with other women, including for a brief time his Spanish wife and three of Moctezuma's daughters, one of whom also bore Cortés a child). And in 1524 he took her with him on

Fig. 11. Malinche acting as interpreter from fray Bernardino de Sahagún's
General History of the Things of New Span *or* Florentine Codex *(1579).*
The symbols coming from and to Malinche's mouth are speech glyphs.

an expedition to Honduras and en route arranged for her to marry a fairly
high-ranking Spaniard and close associate of his, Juan de Jaramillo, bringing into the marriage a dowry of an *encomienda* provided by Cortés.[6]

Malinche was a godsend for Cortés, as he urgently needed to be able to
communicate with native leaders. But the communication system offered by
Malinche and Aguilar was imperfect. The system embodied the same para-
dox of simultaneous communication and failure to communicate that was
illustrated by the gestures made by Cortés and Moctezuma at their first encounter. For much of the long journey from the coast to the Valley of Mexico,
Spaniards and natives played a version of the childhood game of telephone.
For one simple piece of dialogue to be achieved, Cortés spoke in Spanish to
Aguilar, Aguilar translated into Yucatec Maya, which Malinche then trans-

lated into Nahuatl, before repeating the process in reverse. Even once Malinche learned Spanish, how much must have been lost in the translation, in the reading of meaning into her words, in on-the-spot attempts to cross the cultural divide? What indeed were her actual words? They are, of course, lost to us, buried within the artifice of interpretation as reported in Spanish and Nahua accounts of the Conquest, hidden within the speech glyphs that emanate from her mouth in the illustrations of the *Florentine Codex*.

The myth of this chapter is therefore the paradoxical myth of communication/miscommunication. Historically, the myth of communication was constructed by the conquistadors and predominated during Conquest and colonial times. The myth was convenient to Spaniards in that claims of communication with native peoples bolstered claims that natives were subjugated, co-opted, and converted. The questioning of that myth by modern scholars also has sixteenth-century roots, most notably in the writings of the Dominican friar Bartolomé de Las Casas, but has become so common in recent decades as to constitute its own countermyth. Perhaps the best-known articulation of the modern myth of miscommunication is by Tzvetan Todorov. The semiotics scholar contrasts Cortés, as a master reader of signs and information, with Columbus, who has no interest in communicating with Caribbean natives, and the Mexica, whose failure to read signs results in their downfall—conquest by (mis)communication. In other words, the invaders are either disinterested in communication, or they are so good at it that their skill defeats the natives.[7]

The themes of communication and miscommunication have therefore been misused as explanations of the Conquest. Through such usage they have become myths, and neither adequately explains Conquest outcomes. The remainder of this chapter details how the conquistadors generated the myth of communication, examines the arguments of the countermyth of miscommunication, and finally looks at several Conquest moments to suggest how a middle ground between the two extremes allows us to understand better how Spaniards and natives came to read each other's intentions.

Malinche's lost words lie not only between the lines of sixteenth-century texts or in the speech glyphs of the *Florentine Codex*. According to one traveler to Mexico City in the 1990s, Malinche's ghost still walks the corridors of a house where she once lived. Located on a street now named Republica de Cuba, the house has become a school, some of whose children say they have heard Malinche "weeping as she walks along the balcony and through the rooms," as one little girl told the visitor.[8]

The old house on Republica de Cuba is not the only place in Mexico City, or even in Mexico, where Malinche's ghost is heard. Her spirit, it seems, at some point in the past became intertwined with a Mexica legend that predates the Conquest and that in colonial times became known as *La Llorona* (The Weeping Woman).[9] The conventions of the legend state that Malinche/ La Llorona is lamenting her children, but her actual words go unreported. Like those of the real Malinche, they are lost in the wind.

Malinche herself would have been completely lost to the siroccos of history were it not for her speech; her historical identity is based upon what she said. Yet because she spoke the words of others, as their interpreter, she is also strangely silent. This has allowed her to become many things to many people: a symbol of betrayal; an opportunistic sexual siren; a feminist icon; an Aztec goddess in disguise; the mother of the first *mestizo*, and thus of the Mexican nation; the ultimate rape victim of the Conquest. Almost all of this tells us much about modern Mexican history but little about the Conquest, especially as most of these interpretations, including all the negative ones, date from the dawn of Mexican Independence in the early nineteenth century.[10]

In the sixteenth century Malinche was portrayed neither as victim nor as immoral, but as powerful. In the half a dozen or so illustrations of her in the *Florentine Codex* she always appears with the hairstyle and clothes of a noblewoman, and her name is always Malintzin, with reverential suffix (an honor likewise accorded to Cuauhtémoc but not always to Moctezuma).[11] Bernal Díaz gave her high praise for her time. "Although a native woman," he wrote, doña Marina "possessed such manly valor . . . [and] betrayed no weakness but a courage greater than that of a woman."[12]

Nevertheless, the seeds of a more derogatory view of Malinche can be found in the early sixteenth century, most obviously in Cortés's failure to detail her role in his letters to the king. This apparent contradiction—Malinche both ignored and respected—can best be understood in the context of the broader Spanish attitude toward interpreters, and the way in which that attitude generated a myth of communication.

On the one hand, as natives, interpreters were unreliable. "We thought the interpreter was deceiving us," one Spaniard remarks, "for he was a native of this island and town."[13] Gómara was highly dismissive of Melchor, the Maya captured by Hernández de Córdoba in 1517, who as a native "fisherman" was "uncouth" and "knew neither how to speak nor to answer." In the end, claims Gómara, only Malinche and Aguilar were "trustworthy interpreters."[14] As natives, interpreters were also destined to be given second billing, or none at all, in Conquest accounts by Spaniards. The tendency to ignore or dismiss interpreter roles is thus a corollary to the myths discussed in Chapters 3 and 4, whereby Spaniards complete the Conquest rapidly and alone.[15] The impression is frequently given in Spanish narratives of the invaders speaking directly to native rulers. Cortés, Gómara, and Díaz sometimes insert a phrase such as "through our interpreters" but more often than not this detail is omitted. At the first meeting of Cortés and Moctezuma, for example, Cortés tells the king that the Mexica lord "addressed me in the following way," quotes the speech as though verbatim, and then states that "I replied to all he said." There is no mention of interpreters or language barriers.[16]

On some level, Spaniards believed that there was no real language barrier between them and Native Americans, a belief that underpinned the 1513 edict that required conquistadors to read a statement—in Spanish—to natives before attacking them.[17] The document, known as the *Requerimiento* (Requirement) informed natives of a sort of chain of command from God to pope to king to conquistadors, with the latter merely putting into effect the divinely sanctioned donation of all American lands and peoples by the pope to the Spanish monarch. Native leaders were asked, therefore, to recognize papal and royal authority (that is, to surrender without resistance), and if they did so, the expedition leader was to tell them,

> His Majesty and I, in his name, will receive you . . . and will leave your women and children free, without servitude so that with them and with yourselves you can freely do what you wish . . . and we will not compel you to turn Christians. But if you do not do it . . . with the help of God I will forcefully enter against you, and I will make war everywhere and however I can, and I will subject you to the yoke and obedience of the Church and His Majesty, and I will take your wives and children, and I will make them slaves . . . and I will take your goods, and I will do to you all the evil and damages that a lord may do to vassals who do not obey or receive him. And I solemnly declare that the deaths and damages received from such will be your fault and not that of His Majesty, nor mine, nor of the gentlemen who came with me.[18]

The text makes no mention of interpreters, nor is there any evidence of the Requirement being translated into native languages. The document is patently contradictory; the comment by Las Casas, that one did not know "whether to laugh or cry at the absurdity of" the Requirement, is oft quoted.[19] The Requirement symbolizes the Spanish conviction in their ability to communicate with natives—at least to the extent that they deemed necessary. On the other hand, Spaniards were also aware that on occasion there were language barriers that needed to be surmounted. As often as they were ignored, interpreters were valued and recognized as efficacious and exigent. According to the physician with Columbus's first expedition, the Admiral brought seven Tainos back to Spain from his voyage and used the two who survived as interpreters on his second voyage.[20] If such interpreters were able to rapidly acquire the necessary skills, survive exposure to Old World diseases, and outlive the wars of Conquest, they were often able to attain the kind of status in colonial society otherwise denied to all but the most privileged native nobles. Ironically, it was Spanish ethnocentrism that partly prompted admiration for native interpreters. Europeans tended to be surprised when Native Americans showed themselves able to learn European languages, and thus for a native to become fully bilingual was a notable achievement.[21] Just as Bernal Díaz complimented Malinche by saying that she behaved like a man, so were native interpreters granted status by the invaders because they behaved more like Spaniards.

The transformation of Malinche's status and the reverential image of her projected in many Spanish and native sources in subsequent decades, were significant, but because she was a woman and she died young, she is not the best example of the long-term status granted to native interpreters. Better examples can be found in the Andes and Yucatan.

In 1528 Pizarro acquired a pair of native boys on the northern Peruvian coast. They were taken back to Spain in 1529, taught Spanish, then brought on the Conquest expedition of 1531, and acted as interpreters at Cajamarca in 1532, when Atahuallpa was captured. Like Malinche in Mexico, these two became well known, even famous, among Spaniards and natives. Christened, diminutively, Felipillo and Martinillo, the latter was later able to style himself don Martín Pizarro. This impressive-sounding name partly reflected don Martín's status as a native noble, but also his value to the Spaniards and crucial role at Cajamarca. He was granted a share of the Cajamarca spoils (although Pizarro cheated him of it) and, later, an *encomienda*. He lived in Lima for many years, acquiring the prestigious title of Interpreter General as well as a second *encomienda*, before being caught up in the Gonzalo Pizarro revolt. He traveled to Seville to appeal the sentence against him, where shortly afterward, around 1550, he died. In 1567 his half-Spanish daughter, doña Francisca Pizarro, was at court in Madrid petitioning the king for a pension as did so many of the descendents of conquistadors.[22]

The other example is Gaspar Antonio Chi, a Maya nobleman who, like the Andean don Martín, found bilinguality in the Conquest era to be a medium of mobility into colonial society. Spaniards invaded Yucatan when Chi was a boy, and as a teenager he was taken to be educated and raised by Franciscans in Mérida, the capital of the colony of Yucatan. There he rose to become Interpreter General. Chi's career was in many ways extraordinary (it lasted until his death, at the age of 80, in 1610), but also notably comparable to that of don Martín Pizarro and other prominent native interpreters in Conquest times. Such men bridged the native and Spanish worlds. Chi served as interpreter to both the colony's first two bishops and to several of its governors, as well as holding important political positions in Maya communities, such as that of town governor.[23] Chi seems to have been exceptionally gifted, but it was not exceptional for Spaniards to seek and nurture native interpreters and to some extent admit them into colonial society.

During one of his many encounters with the natives of the Caribbean islands, Columbus found himself in a small boat with a number of his men preparing to land on the shore of a river, where a party of local men awaited them. According to Columbus's own account, as later summarized by Las Casas:

> One of the Indians advanced into the river near the prow of the boat, and delivered a long speech which the Admiral failed to understand. But he observed that the other Indians from time to time raised their hands toward the sky and uttered a great shout. The Admiral surmised that they were assuring him that his coming was a welcome event, but he saw the face of the Indian whom he had taken with him, and who understands the language, change color, turn yellow as wax, and tremble mightily while saying by signs that the Admiral should leave the river because they sought to kill him.[24]

Moments like these illustrate the "crude pantomime" to which Europeans and natives in the Americas were often reduced by language barriers.[25] Miscommunication was hardly unusual, but examples like the one above have also fostered a myth of miscommunication, rooted not directly in Columbus's experiences and diaries, but indirectly through the commentary of Las Casas. The Dominican is generally scathing about Columbus's treatment of Caribbean natives, and his "ignorance" and failure to understand them.[26] Modern commentators have picked up and expanded this theme considerably.

In Todorov's view, "Columbus does not succeed in his human communications because he is not interested in them." Margarita Zamora, a scholar of Spanish literature, uses the term "aphasia"—literally loss of understanding due to brain damage—to describe this failure. Zamora does not mean to imply that Columbus suffered from a "personal shortcoming" but that he was handicapped by the "essential incapacity of the discourses at his disposal" to help him comprehend what he saw and heard. Another prominent literary scholar, Stephen Greenblatt, gives the Genoese more communicative credit than do Todorov and Zamora, but he still observes that Columbus tended to see what he wanted to see, to read the familiar into the new; Columbus's narratives thus become "a fantasmatic representation of authoritative certainty in the face of spectacular ignorance."[27]

In Todorov's discussion of the Conquest of Mexico, Cortés becomes the great communicator, in contrast to Moctezuma and the Mexica, whose inability to read human signs condemns them to defeat. The historian Inga Clendinnen has argued that miscommunication went in all directions during Mexico's Conquest, explaining not so much native defeat but rather the deterioration of Spanish-Mexica relations into a brutal and destructive war.[28] J. H. Elliott, in a classic study written over 30 years ago, detailed the difficulties that sixteenth-century Europeans had in comprehending the Americas and making according adjustments to their world view. He was able to find plenty of instances of Europeans struggling to describe and comprehend Native America. "Everything is very different," wrote fray Tomás de Mercado, for example. And Juan de Betanzos, in the dedication to his *History of the Incas* of 1551, observed

> how differently the conquistadors speak about these things, and how far removed they are from Indian practice. And this I believe to be due to the fact that at that time they were not so much concerned with finding things out as with subjecting and acquiring the land. It was also because, coming new to the Indians, they did not know how to ask questions and find things out, for they lacked knowledge of the language; while the Indians, for their part, were too frightened to give them a full account.[29]

Here, in a nutshell, would appear to be an anecdotal antidote to the conquistadors's myth of communication—colonial evidence of the miscommunication that derived from Spanish ignorance, from the Spanish preoccupation with conquest, and from consequent native terror. So why is the myth of miscommunication a myth, and not simply an analysis that corrects the conquerors' myth of communication?

Betanzos's observation that Spaniards were initially more interested in subjugating natives than "finding things out" about them is insightful. The problem lies in the use by modern scholars of this kind of observation to explain the Conquest. Todorov's argument that Mexica's defeat stemmed from a failure to master "interhuman communication" is presented in starker terms by the French writer, Le Clézio, who depicts Cortés as achieving conquest less with his sword than with his words, with "his most formidable, most efficacious weapon: speech," and with "his most fearsome instrument of domination: speech."[30] This interpretation has several dimensions to it. The vaguest one refers to signs and speech as part of a larger process of communication. A more specific dimension refers to interpreters, drawing upon evidence regarding the role played by bilingual natives and "the importance of language as a tool of conquest" (in the words of one editor of Bernal Díaz's account).[31]

The most specific dimension of the argument refers to writing. "There is a 'technology' of symbolism," asserts Todorov, "which is as capable of evolution as the technology of tools, and, in this perspective, the Spaniards are more 'advanced' than the Aztecs (or to generalize: societies possessing writing are more advanced than societies without writing), even if we are here concerned only with a difference of degree." Despite Todorov's use of "scare quotes," the argument is clear—that the Spaniards conquered because they were more advanced—and it is one that the conquistadors, and Prescott and his nineteenth-century contemporaries, would have liked and understood. Greenblatt refers to this passage too, and his pithy response is worth quoting: "There seems to me no convincing evidence that writing functioned in the early encounter of European and New World peoples as a superior tool for the accurate perception or effective manipulation of the other."[32]

Jared Diamond's *Guns, Germs, and Steel* also argues for writing as a hallmark of European superiority, specifically in his depiction of the initial meeting of Pizarro and Atahuallpa in 1532, in the central plaza of the northern Peruvian Inca city of Cajamarca. Pizarro had less than 200 men, all heavily armed. Atahuallpa had an entourage of 5,000, but most were unarmed and the rest lightly armed (his army waited on the plains outside the city). The first Spaniard to approach the emperor was not Pizarro, but a Dominican friar, holding a cross and a Bible or missal. Within minutes the book was on the ground, and shortly after that Atahuallpa was pulled from his litter and taken captive, while the Spaniards cut down thousands of his servants, killing about a third of his entourage. Diamond's assertion is that literacy explains the nature and outcome of the meeting between the Spanish captain and the Inca emperor. "Spain possessed it, while the Inca Empire did not." Spanish writing transmitted information that brought Spaniards to Peru in the first place. Writing then gave the invaders a cognitive advantage over Atahuallpa—whose access to "scant information" thus led him to make "naïve" and "fatal miscalculations."[33]

There are a number of problems with this argument. First, there is no evidence that Pizarro and his colleagues were any better informed about the Inca empire and Andean culture than Atahuallpa was about the Spaniards; both leaders had sent out spies and questioned northern Andean natives before the meeting. Second, it is highly debatable whether writing would have been a better system of communicating information than the oral techniques and *quipu* devices (complex sets of colored, knotted strings attached to rods) developed over centuries by Andeans. Even if we concede writing to be marginally more efficient, under the specific circumstances of Pizarro's invasion, its possible advantage hardly explains the entire outcome of the Conquest of Peru. Third, Diamond's assertion that "literacy made the Spaniards heirs to a huge body of knowledge about human behavior and history" that was denied to Andeans is a highly problematic generalization that is better explained by the geographic factors articulated by Diamond elsewhere in his book.[34]

Fourth, as it is not clear how much or little Atahuallpa knew of Pizarro's expedition, we might accept Diamond's premise, but it is still not at all clear what difference it could have made. The Spaniards, allegedly better informed, followed the predictable patterns of the Conquest. During the initial encounter this included using legalistic measures to validate their actions (the reading of the Requirement), the use of display violence (the massacre of unarmed retainers), and the capture of the native ruler. In the encounter's immediate aftermath, this included a dependence upon native interpreters, the use of native allies, and the emphasis on acquiring precious metals. It seems unreasonable to deem Atahuallpa naïve for not attempting to have the Spaniards all killed before they could get near to him, and unrealistic to expect that any amount of information would have inspired such a brutal and draconian decision. It is doubtful that knowledge of the Mexica empire and its collapse would have deterred the Inca ruler from engaging—rather than simply slaughtering—the invaders. Had the circumstances been reversed, and unknown foreigners landed on Iberian shores, curiosity would certainly have gotten the better of the Spaniards too.

Finally, the argument is further undermined by the parallel case of the Cortés-Moctezuma encounter. Mesoamericans did have writing, forcing Diamond to dispense with the literacy argument and resort to another myth (to be refuted in the next chapter), that "Montezuma miscalculated even more grossly when he took Cortés for a returning god and admitted him and his tiny army into the Aztec capital of Tenochtitlán."[35]

Diamond's argument about writing is part of a well-entrenched myth going back at least to the Middle Ages and Thomas Aquinas's assertion that alphabetic writing distinguished civilized people from barbarians. Las Casas claimed that Aristotle had made the same distinction. While the Dominican was wrong, his claim illustrates the deep-rooted validity of the distinction in the European mind. In the late twentieth century, scholars dedicated to rejecting ethnocentrism were still unable to shake completely the belief that alphabetic writing indicates superiority in some sense. Examples are the influential anthropologist Claude Lévi-Strauss—who wrote in 1955 that "of all the criteria by which people habitually distinguish civilization from barbarism, this one should at least be retained: that certain peoples write and others do not"—and more recently, Todorov and Diamond.[36]

The Pizarro-Atahuallpa encounter is thus an example of how the myth of miscommunication has been perpetuated and used by scholars to explain the Conquest in colonialist terms—terms that would have made sense to the conquistadors themselves. Yet the differences between Spanish and Andean communicative technologies do not adequately explain the Conquest of Peru. But what of the actual point of contact, that between the Dominican friar, Vicente Valverde, and the Inca emperor? Was that not a symbolic moment of miscommunication, one that articulated the culture clash in gestures just as the awkward gestures of Cortés and Moctezuma did at their first meeting?

The conquistador-chronicler, Francisco de Jerez, who was present at Cajamarca, wrote that Atahuallpa deliberately threw the Bible to the ground out of pride, because he was unable to read its writing. When the friar told Pizarro this, the captain grabbed the emperor and let out the war cry, "Santiago!" as the signal for the general attack. Thus although Jerez details how the attack was planned all along, it is also a response to Atahuallpa's blasphemous act—and thus further justified. In contrast is the account dictated in 1570 by Titu

Cusi Yupanqui, a nephew of the emperor, in which: "My uncle Atahuallpa . . . received them very well. He gave one of them a drink of the kind we use from a golden vessel, [but] as the Spaniard took it from his hand, he poured it on the ground. And because of this my uncle became very angry." In the Inca version, then, the initial insult and blasphemy is committed by the invaders, and the hurling down of the book is a justifiable quid pro quo.[37] The theme of the Jerez and Titu Cusi accounts is not directly that of miscommunication, as in each version one ruler clearly signals his disdain for the other. But what actually happened was sufficiently unclear to permit highly contrasting narratives.

In two additional accounts of the incident, miscommunication is placed at the center of the encounter. One is by a seventeenth-century *mestizo* of mixed Inca-Spanish descent, Garcilaso de la Vega, the other by a sixteenth-century conquistador, Pedro de Cieza de León. Each offers still further variation on the details, and each takes a rather predictable position on Atahuallpa, but both blame a third party (other than the emperor or Pizarro) for a breakdown in communication leading to the Spanish attack. Garcilaso has Atahuallpa taking the initiative in proposing the meeting, but his friendly, even deferential intentions are inadequately conveyed by interpreters both before the meeting and during it. He is especially derisive of Felipillo, whom he characterizes as a low-class Andean whose Spanish was coarse and whose grasp of Christian dogma was virtually nonexistent. For all Felipillo's failings, he is not ultimately to blame. Garcilaso instead calls the real culprit "the Indian language" of Quechua, which he derides as the inferior tongue of an ignorant people.[38] Garcilaso's final verdict anticipates the argument that the natives were defeated by their communicative disadvantages—be it lack of writing, inability to read "signs," or, in Garcilaso's crude version, the inferiority of their language. In his view of events, the friar's book falls from his lap by accident and is not the immediate cause of hostilities, which break out because the Spaniards become impatient with the lengthy discussion between the friar and the emperor and begin to harass Atahuallpa's servants.

Fray Valverde comes off well in Garcilaso's version, but in Cieza de León's account he is the villain of the piece. Like most narrators of the meeting, Cieza de León places the fallen book at the center of the encounter, but he adds a unique twist: "Annoyed with so many pages, [Atahuallpa] flung it into the air without knowing what it was, because to have understood it, they should have told him in another way, but the friars never preach around here, except where there is no danger of raised lances." Not only does the friar fail to open up a dialogue between the emperor and the Spaniards, but he also attempts to cover up his inadequacies by running back to Pizarro to tell him that Atahuallpa was a "tyrant" and "wounded dog" and "that they should attack him."[39] Thus miscommunication, albeit with a clerical face, causes the collapse of diplomacy and the outbreak of open hostilities.

The differences between these accounts—and other versions offering yet further variations—vividly illustrate the difficulties historians have in deducing what "really" happened, in finding "something true" about an event.[40] They also show how fertile Conquest history is as ground for the blooming, and cutting down, of myths about the past. But what these narrative differences do not do is clearly demonstrate the applicability of either the analytical theme of communication or that of miscommunication, for both themes, and their myths, are tangled up within those differences.

In her interpretation of events, historian Patricia Seed proposes (in part following Garcilaso) that the text read by the friar to Atahuallpa was "presumably" the Requirement, which she describes as exemplifying "an imperialism of speech."[41] The Requirement is usually viewed as a paragon of miscommunication or, in Las Casas's words, communicational "absurdity." Equally absurd were the circumstances under which the text was delivered. According to intellectual historian Lewis Hanke: "It was read to trees and empty huts.... Captains muttered its theological phrases into their beards on the edge of sleeping Indian settlements, or even a league away before starting the formal attack.... Ship captains would sometimes have the document read from the deck as they approached an island."[42] In addition to Las Casas, other sixteenth-century Spaniards denounced the delivery of the Requirement in terms ranging from the wry to the scathing. For example, Charles V's official court historian, Gonzalo Fernández de Oviedo, described how the text was delivered during the early decades of the Caribbean conquest, when natives were still routinely enslaved: "After [the captured Indians] had been put in chains, someone read the Requirement without knowing their language and without any interpreters, and without either the reader or the Indians understanding the language they had no opportunity to reply, being immediately carried away prisoners, the Spaniards not failing to use the stick on those who did not go fast enough."[43] Here the wielding of the "stick" suggests that even if the content of the Requirement could not be communicated, the violent context of its delivery communicated its broader message of menace and hostility.

In another study, Seed persuasively showed how the message of the Requirement was rooted in Iberian Islamic tradition, specifically in the summons to acknowledge the superiority of Islam or be attacked. Part of the Requirement's apparent absurdity is that it seems to demand that natives will not be forced to convert, provided that they convert. Like its Islamic antecedent, it leaves matters of conversion for later, demanding only a formal recognition of the religious and political superiority of the invader. This acknowledgment in the Islamic world was expressed in the form of a head tax, essentially the same manifestation of conquest as the tribute first claimed by Queen Isabella in 1501 and levied on every individual Native American in the Spanish empire for over three centuries. The Requirement's assertion that acceptance of papal and royal authority would bring protection and privilege seems absurd in the context of conquest violence and colonial exploitation, but the concern of Spanish officials for native population levels (expressed in numerous colonial laws) was genuine, albeit based on economic interests. From the crown to local Spanish community leaders, the empire depended upon native tribute, whether paid in cash, goods, or labor. The Requirement's offer of privilege seems risible because the document also appears to promise destruction. In fact, Spanish colonial rule confirmed and relied upon the integrity of native communities, for it was there that tribute was generated and collected.[44]

Seen in this light, the Requirement becomes less absurd. In fact, in the context of open and blatant conquistador hostilities, it becomes irrelevant. More than that, it becomes an invader's ritual less potentially confusing to the invaded precisely because it cannot be understood. As "babble" it can more easily be ignored and the nature of the Spanish threat be more clearly contemplated.[45]

We cannot be sure whether the Requirement was indeed read or explained to Atahuallpa by fray Valverde, nor can we be sure of the emperor's words, or even his tone—whether welcoming and deferential, haughty and hostile, or arrogant and dismissive. But we can ponder the similarities and differences between narratives of the event, place them in larger cultural and historical contexts, and come to a reasonable speculation as to the friar's words—a basic explanation of Christian dogma and its immediate political relevance, as expressed in a summary of the Requirement—and Atahuallpa's reply—a recognition both of the absurdity of the friar's speech and of its irrelevance to the immediate political situation. Within all this there was miscommunication, to be sure, but also a threat successfully communicated.

An illuminating parallel is offered by the speeches made by Cortés and Moctezuma on the day of their first meeting. As with the details of the encounter in Cajamarca, there are different versions and many possible interpretations of what Moctezuma said and meant. But in contrast to the Atahuallpa incident, in which a message was successfully conveyed through apparent miscommunication, Moctezuma's speech was an act of apparently successful communication that contained within it the seeds of miscommunication, seeds that would germinate a deep-rooted myth.

Cortés recorded the Mexica emperor's speech in a letter to the Spanish king, and although other Spanish chroniclers wrote down very similar versions, the speech shows signs of evolving as it passed through Spanish hands. From the very start, with the version reported by Cortés, the speech seems to have been spun in a way that turned the emperor's words of welcome into a statement of submission. Most improbably, Cortés has Moctezuma telling the Spaniards that his people had always awaited the arrival from overseas of a lord descended from their original ruler, and that they now believed the king of Spain to be that lord.

> So be assured that we will obey you and hold you as our lord in place of that great sovereign of whom you speak; and in this there shall be no betrayal or offense whatsoever. And in all the land that lies in my domain, you may command as you will, for you shall be obeyed; and all that we own is for you to dispose of as you choose. Thus, as you are in your own country and your own house, rest now from the hardships of your journey and the battles which you have fought.[46]

The emperor then denied that "my houses are made of gold," or that he "was, or claimed to be, a god," exposing his torso to show that he was made of flesh and blood.

In Gómara's version, written three decades later, the same speech is recorded (probably drawn from Cortés's letter) with the addition of a preamble that introduces the notion that Mexico's natives at first took the Spaniards to be gods. The added paragraph gave the speech a new symmetry, with Moctezuma recognizing that Cortés is not a god and affirming that neither is he, Moctezuma, that he is "mortal . . . like you."[47] But it also built upon the theme introduced by Cortés, that the Spaniards represented the return of an ancestral lord or his descendent, and was thus a step closer to the full-blown myth of Cortés as the returning Mexica god, Quetzalcoatl.

The version by Bernal Díaz, although written down later in the sixteenth century, is closer to that of Cortés, and emphasizes Moctezuma's alleged claim that his ancestors had said that "men . . . would come from the direction of the sunrise to rule over these lands." Díaz makes no mention of gods, Spanish or Mexica, but the tale of the prodigal returning lord still smacks too much of biblical themes (the Prodigal Son, the Second Coming of Christ) and of the classic conquistador claim of completion to be viewed without suspicion.[48]

How does the Nahuatl version of this speech, recorded in the *Florentine Codex*, compare to the Spanish ones? The Conquest narrative in the *Codex* was written down several generations after the events described, and was the product of a Franciscan-Nahua collaboration. In addition, Moctezuma's reputation had suffered in the decades between his death and the compilation of the *Codex*, and this may be reflected in this version of the speech. Still, the *Codex* version is close enough to the Cortés-Díaz versions to suggest that the Spanish accounts were interpretations of what Moctezuma actually said. The Nahuatl version read:

> O our lord, be doubly welcomed on your arrival in this land; you have come to satisfy your curiosity about your *altepetl* [city-state] of Mexico, you have come to sit on your seat of authority, which I have kept a while for you, where I have been in charge for you, for your agents the rulers—Itzcoatzin, the elder Moteucçoma, Axayacatl, Tiçocic, and Ahuitzotl—have gone, who for a very short time came to be in charge for you, to

govern the *altepetl* of Mexico. It is after them that your poor vassal [myself] came. Will they come back to the place of their absence? If only one of them could see and behold what has now happened in my time, what I now see after our lords are gone! For I am not just dreaming, not just sleepwalking, not just seeing it in my sleep. I am not just dreaming that I have seen you, have looked upon your face. For a time I have been concerned, looking toward the mysterious place from which you have come, among clouds and mist. It is so that the rulers on departing said that you would come in order to acquaint yourself with your *altepetl* and sit upon your seat of authority. And now it has come true, you have come. Be doubly welcome, enter the land, go to enjoy your palace; rest your body. May our lords be arrived in the land.[49]

The theme of a long-anticipated returning lord is not only clearly present, but is the device upon which the speech is constructed. It is easy to imagine how these words could become in Spanish minds a declaration of submission, especially if one takes into account the filter of Malinche's translation, Spanish ignorance of the Mexica cultural context, and Spanish wishful thinking on the day of the meeting for a friendly reception. Furthermore, Cortés was concerned to project to the king a positive scenario at the time he wrote down the speech (that was the following year, when the Spaniards had been defeated in the first battle in Tenochtitlán and expelled from the city). He makes no mention of the speech of surrender made by the Iberian peninsula's last Muslim lord to King Ferdinand outside the gates of Granada in 1492, but the Granada speech was a famous one and the Muslim surrender seen as a great milestone in Spanish history. Cortés might have imagined he was witnessing a similar event and expected Charles V likewise to hear an echo of that moment in Moctezuma's "surrender."[50]

However, this does not explain why Moctezuma's speech was so seemingly deferential. In Mexica culture—as indeed in most Mesoamerican cultures—the language of polite speech was highly developed. Élite children were taught the skill of address appropriate to the age, gender, and social standing of the addressee, and the circumstances of the meeting. This type of elaborate Nahuatl is usually called *huehuehtlahtolli* (ancient discourse or sayings of the elders) and a considerable amount is known about such speech and its model dialogues because many were written down in the late sixteenth century (60 alone in the *Florentine Codex*).[51]

Within the larger genre of *huehuehtlahtolli*, the only style of address that could be used in Moctezuma's presence would have been *tecpillahtolli* (lordly speech), in which Nahuatl words are heavily laden with reverential prefixes and suffixes and sentences are built upon the principles of indirection and reversal. In other words, to be polite and courteous one must avoid speaking bluntly or directly, which requires saying the opposite of what one means. Thus Moctezuma's assertion that he and his predecessors were just safeguarding the rulership of the Mexica empire in anticipation of Cortés's arrival is not to be taken literally. It is a rhetorical artifice meant to convey the opposite—Moctezuma's stature and multigenerational legitimacy—and to function as a courteous welcome to an important guest. It is a royal *mi casa, su casa* welcome whose offer of courtly hospitality would be utterly undermined if taken as a literal handing over of the keys to the kingdom. Even the claim to be poor and as mortal as any man, not included in the Nahuatl or Spanish texts of the *Codex* but in the Cortés-Gómara versions, was very possibly delivered by Moctezuma as a piece of contrived humility intended to underscore his imperial status.

Malinche was able to understand *tecpillahtolli*, a legacy of her noble birth, and she had been translating it into Spanish for months leading up to the Cortés-Moctezuma meeting. Otherwise, Moctezuma's speech could not have been conveyed to Cortés and his colleagues with any degree of fidelity.[52] But even with the benefit of Malinche's education, when rendered in Spanish, with the polite adornments of Nahuatl prefixes and suffixes gone, and the principle of courteous reversal lost by the lack of a genuine equivalent in Iberian culture, the speech does indeed seem to be one of surrender.

Unlike the Atahuallpa-Pizarro encounter, there was that first day the Spaniards entered Tenochtitlán no fallen or hurled book to symbolize or make blatant the failure of cross-cultural communication. Moctezuma delivered a speech that Malinche seemed to understand, and thus translate faithfully, and that clearly pleased the Spaniards. Successful communication took place. Or did it?

Something of the theme of Double Mistaken Identity appears in the contrasting accounts of the Moctezuma-Cortés and Pizarro-Atahuallpa first encounters. Each side saw the meetings as displays of dignity by their leaders and crudeness or weakness by the other leader, even interpreting in this way the very same exchanges and moments. This would seem to suggest that communication between the invaders and the invaded did indeed amount to little more than a "groping in the darkness," to use Las Casas's phrase.

However, these interpretations followed the events they describe, some immediately and others decades later. Certainly there was plenty of miscommunication during the Conquest, but to argue that such miscommunication was so imbalanced and benefited the Spaniards to such an extent that it explains the Conquest ignores the complexity of Spanish-native interaction.

Furthermore, forms and moments of miscommunication were more than equaled by more or less successful readings of the statements and intentions of the foreigners. Eventually, Columbus understood that the Native Americans on the river bank were hostile toward him. It made no difference to the natives in the plundered village or in the wooden cage that the Requirement was incomprehensible to them—Spanish actions conveyed their purposes more clearly than the text did anyway. Atahuallpa and Moctezuma learned of Spanish intentions and methods too late to save their own lives, but their successors led campaigns of resistance hampered not by lack of information but by crippling epidemics, native disunity, differences in weaponry, and other factors. Sooner or later, one way or the other, Spaniards understood what they needed to, and natives understood what that meant. As Betanzos observed in 1551, at first the invaders "were not so much concerned with finding things out as with subjecting and acquiring." As the conquistador Bernardo de Vargas Machuca indicated in the frontispiece to his 1599 book on the "Indies," Spaniards had acquired "By the sword and the compass / More and more and more and more" (see Figure 12). The word—the instrument by which Vargas Machuca wrote his book—would ultimately be almost as important, maybe more so. As one of the prefatory sonnets to Vargas Machuca's book declared, the Conquest was a theme that only "arms and the pen could develop."[53] But in the early decades of the Conquest it was by the sword and the compass that the Spaniards most successfully communicated.

Fig. 12. Frontispiece to Milicia y Descripción de las Indias
("Soldiery and Description of the Indies"), by Bernardo de Vargas Machuca (1599).

6

The Indians Are Coming to an End
The Myth of Native Desolation

The history of Mexico [contrasts] a noble, valiant Cortés, with a timorous, cowardly Moctezuma, whose people by their iniquitous desertion of their natural leader demonstrated their indifference to the good of the commonwealth.

—Juan Ginés de Sepúlveda (1543)

These mysteries cannot be understood unless one accepts the fulfillment of the prophecy made by the blessed father fray Domingo de Betanzos, that before many ages the Indians as such would disappear, that those who came to this land would ask what color they had been.

—Agustín Dávila Padilla (1595)

The Indian Monarch [the Tarascan Cazonci] gazed with silent awe on the scene of desolation, and eagerly craved the protection of the invincible beings who has caused it.

—William Prescott (1843)

Enough-enough, submissive to my fate
I now return to my distressful fate.

—the native ruler in Mrs. Edward Jemingham's
The Fall of Mexico (1775)

There is no remedy, and the Indians are coming to an end.

—don Felipe Huaman Poma de Ayala (1615)

Early in the seventeenth century, a descendent of the imperial dynasty of the Incas, don Felipe Huaman Poma de Ayala, wrote a book-length letter to the king of Spain, describing all that was wrong with the colony of Peru. His denunciations of the practices of corrupt colonial officials were particularly vivid, periodically punctuated by the declaration that the situation was beyond remedy and by an apparent prediction of native Andean extinction.[1]

An echo of Huaman Poma's lament can be found in French historian Nathan Wachtel's 1971 study of the Conquest of Peru, *La vision des vaincus* (*The Vision of the Vanquished*). Wachtel quotes an Andean lament, written in Spanish, probably in the sixteenth century, in which the sounds of an earthquake become a funeral chant, the foam of river rapids becomes tears, the sun is darkened, the moon shrinks, and

> All things hide, all vanish
> in suffering
>
> (*Y todo y todos se esconden, desaparecen padeciendo*).

According to Wachtel, the elegy, written for the death of Atahuallpa, describes "the birth of a kind of chaos . . . an abyss of emptiness in which the universe is swallowed up. Suffering alone remains." This, he argues, was the nature of "the trauma of the Conquest" for Andean peoples, whose sense of purpose and harmony with the world were inconsolably lost in the destruction of the Spanish invasion.[2]

In fact, the elegy that Wachtel quotes was specific to Atahuallpa's death and exemplifies the pre-Conquest rhetorical tradition of formal mourning for a recently deceased Inca. It is neither evidence nor symbolic of the traumatic impact of the Conquest on Andeans. Likewise, Huaman Poma's lament was a rhetorical device designed to bring the king's attention to the declining numbers and increasing poverty of native Andeans. However, his words, and those of others who denounced colonial practices, such as Las Casas, represented a thread of critical thinking about the impact of conquest and colonization upon Native Americans.

Over the centuries, this has developed into a myth about the nature of native civilizations before the Conquest, native reactions to the Conquest, and the long-term impact of colonization on native societies. The threads of this myth include the lament for native peoples, as introduced above by Huaman Poma and Wachtel, and its perpetuation today in *The Broken Spears*, a compilation of translations of Nahua accounts of the Conquest of Mexico. This book is now four decades old, but is still widely read and assigned in classrooms. In his introduction to it, Miguel León-Portilla refers to the Conquest as "the tragic loss that resulted from the destruction of indigenous culture," a sentence that is quoted in the syllabus of a course developed in 1992 at the Yale-New Haven Teachers Institute for use in public high schools (and still posted on the Institute's web site). The course, entitled "The Indians' Discovery of Columbus," intends, in the spirit of "multi-cultural . . . awareness," to view the Conquest from "the perspective of the Aztecs themselves." But by emphasizing "loss" and "destruction" it unwittingly perpetuates a myth that does little favor to the native cultures with which students are supposed to sympathize.[3]

Another thread of the myth is the notion that native civilization was some kind of Arcadia, as deftly illustrated by the title of Kirkpatrick Sale's book, *The Conquest of Paradise*. According to this perspective, the perfection of native societies and the innocence of their inhabitants could not possibly survive the experience of European invasion, depredation, and cultural imperialism. Another thread comes from the opposite direction, being grounded in an often-racist disdain for Native American cultures, rather than their romanticization. This approach holds that the Americas before Europeans arrived were largely "unused and undeveloped," and "life was nasty, brutish, and short" (in the words of Michael Berliner, at the time executive director of the Ayn Rand Institute, a right-wing think tank). Berliner's and Sale's positions on the Conquest are diametrically opposed in that Berliner views the Conquest's outcome as favorable for both natives and Europeans, because the latter brought "an objectively superior culture" to the Americas.[4] But both of the perspectives they represent contribute to this myth because they take it for granted that native cultures were destroyed, unable to withstand the onslaught of European invasion.

I have dubbed this the myth of native desolation. Over the centuries Europeans have imagined and invented the cultural and social breakdown of Native American societies. In its most extreme form, this perspective not only emphasizes depopulation and destruction, but perceives a more profound desolation amounting to a state of anomie. When a society is in a state of anomie, its individuals are suffering from a sense of futility, emotional emptiness, psychological despair, and a confusion over the apparent breakdown of previous systems of value and meaning.[5] This is precisely the state of mind that Le Clézio imagines pervaded Native American communities in the sixteenth century, where the Conquest left in its wake a "silence [that] was immense, terrifying. It engulfed the Indian world . . . reduced it to a void. Those indigenous cultures, living, diverse, heirs to knowledge and myths as ancient as the history of man, in the span of one generation were sentenced and reduced to dust, to ashes."[6]

This chapter will trace the development of this myth of native desolation, beginning with Columbus, and looking first at early colonial views of pre-Columbian native cultures, then at European perceptions of native reactions to invasion and colonization. I will argue that native cultures were neither barbarous nor idyllic, but as civilized and imperfect as European cultures of the time. Native responses to invasion were based on appraisals of self-interest similar to Spanish decisions, and their responses were highly varied, not homogeneous. Native cultures proved resilient and adaptive, and many natives, especially élites, found opportunity in the Conquest-era transition.

One of the native groups of South America's northern coast, according to six-teenth-century English explorer Sir Walter Ralegh, was called Ewaipanoma: "They are reported to have their eyes in their shoulders, and their mouths in the middle of their breasts, and that a long train of haire groweth backward betwen their shoulders." Ralegh is skeptical of such a report, admitting that "I saw them not." But he seems reluctant to condemn completely the notion that acephali, or headless men, existed in the Americas, citing European and native sources, as well as a Spaniard who told Ralegh he had seen such a creature.[7]

Indeed, the larger context of Ralegh's elusive acephali is a large body of references to these and other human, semihuman, or subhuman beings, in-cluding Amazons (women-only "tribes") and cannibals. Tales of such aber-rant peoples had existed both among Europeans and Native Americans for centuries before Contact, making the Conquest period a fertile time for the convergence, spread, and discussion of these "monsters."[8] Even when they did not personally sight them, Europeans commented on their absence, as Ralegh did. Columbus wrote to the king and queen in 1493 that one Carib-bean island was inhabited by Amazons, one by cannibals, another by people with tails, and yet another by bald people. But these were islands Columbus had yet to explore, and he would soon admit that, with the exception of cannibals, "I found not a trace of monsters, nor did I hear of any."[9]

As Europeans became more familiar with Native Americans, the more fantastic tales became less frequent. But Contact and the Conquest stimu-lated the medieval European idea that there existed creatures in a category between animals and true human beings. Native Americans turned out not to be headless, but they were perceived as many other things that more or less placed them in this intermediary category. One such perception charac-terized natives as less than fully human because they lacked the attributes of human cultures and communities. An oft-quoted example of this is Columbus's initial reaction to the Guanahaní natives he encountered on his first voyage: "I believe that they would become Christians very easily, for it seemed to me that they had no religion. Our Lord pleasing, at the time of my departure I will take six of them to Your Highnesses in order that they may learn to speak."[10] By this Columbus did not mean that the natives were mute, but that their language was so primitive as not to rise to the level of true speech. Likewise he commented on the political organization of the Arawaks, whom he describes as living "without order or government." Caribbean natives were not capable of using real weapons, because "they are hopeless cowards," and in all respects "their deeds are like children's."[11] Native Americans are thus a blank slate upon which "civilization" can be easily inscribed.

In the first decades of Contact, Europeans encountered only the semi-sedentary peoples of the Caribbean and its borders. Semisedentary peoples subsisted on hunting as much as agriculture. Their communities were smaller and their social structure less complex than those of the sedentary societies of Mesoamerica and the Andes. Thus the notion of native societies being virtual nonsocieties can most commonly be found in this early period. In 1503, for example, Vespucci wrote that natives "have no property; instead all things are held in community. . . . They live without king and without any form of authority, and each one is his own master."¹²

At first this kind of primal anarchy tended to be seen as a utopian innocence. Like Adam and Eve in the Garden of Eden, "<u>Indians" lived "in agreement with nature</u>," claimed Vespucci. "The innocence of Adam himself," wrote Brazil's first chronicler, Pedro Vaz de Caminha, in a letter to the king of Portugal in 1500, "was no greater than that of these people." This characterization of natives thus emphasized "their goodness and gentleness" (in the words of Las Casas), thereby highlighting their consequent vulnerability. As Las Casas puts it, in his summary of Columbus's *Diario*: "It should be noted here that the natural docileness, simple, benign, and humble condition of the Indians, and their lack of weapons, together with their going naked, gave the Spaniards the audacity to hold them in low esteem, and put them to such harsh labor as they put them to, and to be relentless in their oppression and destruction of them."¹³ Such a view was anticipated by fray Antonio de Montesinos as far back as 1511, when the Dominican, in his famous sermon to the Hispaniola colonists, asked them: "On what authority have you waged a detestable war against these people, who dwelt quietly and peacefully on their own land? . . . <u>Are these not men?</u>"¹⁴

The combination of these views of natives as blank slates and naturally innocent, with the general perception that colonial brutality had caused the dramatic decline in native Caribbean populations, inspired various attempts to build utopian Christian communities upon the natural foundation of native simplicity. The mystic Franciscan Gerónimo de Mendieta proposed that all native peoples be administered by friars under a modified version of monastic rule. Mendieta's plans challenged the authority of the secular church and seemed incompatible with royal and settler extraction of native tribute and labor, and were thus blocked by the crown. However, Vasco de Quiroga, a colonial judge, went ahead without royal approval and built two utopian "hospital-republics" in Mexico in the 1530s. Based consciously on the fictional community in Sir Thomas More's *Utopia*, such experiments could take place in the paternalistic colonial setting of early Spanish America only because of the degree to which Native Americans were seen as malleable. "<u>The Indians are not good as teachers, but as disciples</u>," proclaimed Mendieta, "<u>nor as preachers, but as subjects, and for this the best in the world.</u>"¹⁵

Of course, natives were no more naturally malleable than were Spaniards. The Spanish colonial enterprise worked relatively well when it coincided with native practices, patterns, and structures, but otherwise it met with the same level of tenacious resistance that all peoples tend to display to outsiders radically interfering in their lives. Manifestations of this resistance con-

tributed to the development of a European perception of natives as funda-
mentally wicked rather than essentially innocent. At one end of the spectrum, Europeans blamed the culture clash on native failings. Exasperated by
the frequent flight of Tainos, for example, Columbus remarked (in an echo
of the Requirement) that "it is not the result of any harm that we might have
done them, for on the contrary, everywhere I have been and have been able
to speak to the natives, I have given them everything I had . . . without receiv-
ing anything in return."[16]

At the other end of the spectrum, the view was downright hostile and
often venomously racist. One Dominican friar, in a letter to colonial officials
in Spain, described Native Americans as stupid, silly, disrespectful of the
truth, unstable, lacking foresight, ungrateful, changeable, brutal, disobedient, and incapable of learning. Such a judgement could be used to justify
any Conquest act. Indeed, the conquistador-chronicler Oviedo, refusing to
lament the extinction of the natives of Hispaniola, asked "Who can deny
that the use of gunpowder against pagans is the burning of incense to Our
Lord?" Vargas Machuca concluded that "Indians . . . are a people without any
kind of virtue when they are not in fear, but when fearful they are completely meek." Other Spaniards may not have viewed mere paganism as justifying the use of gunpowder or terror tactics, but there were plenty of pagan
stereotypes to provide additional justification—natives had a supposed pro-
clivity for sodomy, for example, or were committed cannibals, or were in-
fected with diabolism. Even Bernal Díaz, usually seen as more evenhanded
than most Spanish chroniclers, harps repeatedly on native tendencies toward sodomy, human sacrifice, cannibalism, and larceny.[17]

All three of these stereotyped perceptions of natives (as cultureless, as
innocents, as nefarious) are illustrated in an engraving by Jan van der Straet
around 1575 (Figure 13). The image's combination of detail and ambiguity have
encouraged numerous and varied interpretations, some of which have emphasized its erotic content, others its depiction of Contact as overtly gendered,
others its illustration of how Europeans "invented" America.[18] Van der Straet's
engraving illustrates the notion that native peoples lacked culture and society through the absence in the picture of native clothing or evidence of permanent settlements. There are a few native-made items—a hammock, a club,
the woman's hat, a roasting spit. But otherwise the natives seem more akin
to the animals whose land they share than to the civilized man, represented
by Vespucci, with his elaborate dress, astrolabe and bannered cross in hand,
and the state-of-the-art ship from which he has just disembarked.

The position of the native woman seems to represent an innocence and
naiveté that is both hesitant and welcoming, childlike and sexually charged;
she seems to be inviting Vespucci to both protect and possess her. The success
of this image in the sixteenth and seventeenth centuries lies in the fact that it
would have resonated in viewers' minds regarding the appropriate nature of

Americen Americus retexit, & AMERICA. Semel vocauit inde semper excitam.

Ioan. Stradanus invent.
Theodor Galle sculp.

male-female and European-native relations. This included the notion of native "gentleness" (Las Casas's term), here rendered visually both in terms of female sexuality and childish innocence.

The scene in the background depicts that emblematic monstrous activity, cannibalism, illustrating the perception of natives as wickedly subhuman. The caption to the scene could almost be the following passage taken from the sixteenth-century jurist Ginés de Sepúlveda: "Here is the proof of their savage life, like that of wild beasts: their execrable and prodigious immolations of human victims to demons; the fact of devouring human flesh; . . . and other similar crimes."[19] Spaniards ascribed cannibalism to natives because it was the classic marker of barbarianism. Sepúlveda and van der Straet do the same, then taking this as proof of that "savage" barbarianism. This kind of circular argument is fundamental to the myth of native desolation.

Sepúlveda's phrase "like that of wild beasts" evokes another aspect of this negative view of natives. By comparing natives to animals, they thereby acquire a range of supposed animal attributes, including dangerousness. Thus hostile natives are, along with hostile fauna, tropical diseases, difficult terrain, and a harsh climate, part of what makes the Americas a challenging environment for Europeans. In his descriptions of early Spanish encounters with Yucatan and its Maya population, the Franciscan bishop Diego de Landa emphasized the treacherous shores that shipwrecked Spaniards, dangerous animals (from the crab that bit off one Spaniard's thumb to lions and tigers), and the fate of those captured by Mayas. Spanish captives, Landa suggests, met one of three ends: they were "fattened up," sacrificed, and "given to the people" to be eaten; they were "used as slaves"; or they went native, "becoming an idolater like them" (as did Gonzalo Guerrero, a legendary figure in colonial-era histories and in Mexico today).[20]

Finding somewhat contrasting perceptions of natives together in one drawing is not surprising. Examples of all three attitudes can be found in Columbus's writings, for example, and Cortés too variously sees Mexico's natives as innocent or savage, childlike or barbarous. Though the phrase "noble savage" was not coined until 1609 (by a French chronicler named Lescarbot), and did not become a full-fledged and complex myth until the 1850s, the roots of that construct and its attempt to reconcile two otherwise contradictory strains of ethnocentric perception can be found in the attitudes of Columbus and Conquest-era Spaniards.[21] Furthermore, perceptions of the nature of Native Americans at the time of Contact served as the basis for perceptions of how natives reacted to conquest and colonization.

Facing page: *Fig. 13. "America," by Theodore Galle, engraving after a drawing from* Nova Reperta *by Jan van der Straet (Stradanus) (ca.1575).*

"If they say that I'm a god, that's what I am," sing the two Spaniards washed up on Native American shores in the recent animated movie, *The Road to El Dorado.* The rulers of El Dorado, the king and high priest of the film's imaginary natives, who seem based mostly on Mayas but who embody various native and Latin American stereotypes, appear to take the Spanish visitors for gods. It turns out that the local lords are actually manipulating the occasion of the sudden arrival of the two Spaniards for their own ends, but the film has the city's populace accepting the notion as a fulfillment of an ancient prophesy. The Spaniards, meanwhile, embrace their sudden apotheosis. In the words to the soundtrack song, "It's Tough to Be a God:" "Listen if we don't comply / With the locals' wishes I / Can see us being sacrificed or stuffed / Let's be gods, the perks are great / El Dorado on a plate / Local feeling should not be rebuffed."[22] This song and the accompanying portion of the plot evoke various stereotypes—native lords who are seemingly submissive but are actually duplicitous and untrustworthy, natives who do not merely kill strangers but "sacrifice" and eat them (although this is not depicted in the movie). Among them is a key element of the myth of native desolation—the myth that Native Americans believed Spanish invaders to be gods. In an echo of a study of a similar phenomenon in eighteenth-century Hawaii, this myth might be labeled "the apotheosis of Captain Cortés."[23]

The apotheosis myth—part of the larger myth of native desolation—is central to the way Europeans perceived the native reaction to the Conquest. That connection is made explicit by Todorov, when he refers to "the paralyzing belief that the Spaniards are gods."[24] Todorov is not alone in taking the apotheosis myth for granted; it is more a part of the Western understanding of the Conquest today than it was in the sixteenth century. Larson's lampooning of the myth (Figure 14) works only because it is still such common currency in popular histories and textbooks. But there was no apotheosis, no "belief that the Spaniards are gods," and no resulting native paralysis.

Like so much of Conquest mythology, the apotheosis of the conquistadors seems to be rooted in the voluminous writings of Columbus. Or at least so it appears. In Dunn and Kelley's translation of the diary of the first voyage, the natives "are credulous and aware that there is a God in heaven and convinced that we come from the heavens." In Zamora's translation of the 1493 letter to the king and queen, Columbus states that "generally, in whatever lands I traveled, they believed and believe that I, together with these ships and people, came from heaven, and they greeted me with such veneration." But here is Morison's translation of the parallel passage in another letter written by Columbus in 1493:

THE FAR SIDE® By GARY LARSON

"With a little luck, they may revere us as gods."

Fig. 14. "With a little luck, they may revere us as gods,"
from Gary Larson's, The Far Side (1981).

And they are still of the opinion that I come from the sky, in spite of all the intercourse which they have had with me, and they were the first to announce this wherever I went, and the others went running from house to house and to the neighboring
towns with loud cries of, 'Come! Come! See the people from the sky!' They all came,
men and women alike, as soon as they had confidence in us, so that not one, big or
little, remained behind, and all brought something to eat and drink which they gave
us with marvelous love.[25]

The key word in these passages is *cielo*, glossed as "heaven" in the first two
translations above, and as "sky" in the third. *Cielo* means either, or both, so
accurate translation hinges on context. Zamora states clearly that she disagrees
with Morison's gloss because both of the 1493 letters "imply that the Indians
took the Spaniards for divine beings, venerating them and making offerings to
them as such."[26]

In fact, the passages are ambiguous, at best. Columbus never uses the word
"gods," nor are we are given any idea as to what native word he has taken to
mean *cielo*. In light of the inexact nature of Columbus's so-called conversations (*conversación*, "intercourse" in Morison's translation) with Caribbean
natives, his interpretations of native statements and actions must be taken with
more than a pinch of salt. Furthermore, there remains not even circumstantial
evidence that the provision of food and drink and other gestures of friendship—made to Europeans by natives all over the Americas for various practical reasons—constituted "offerings" of a religious nature.

Zamora accepts the apotheosis myth tentatively, but others have embraced
it fully. Swiss historian Urs Bitterli, for example, spins the scant "evidence" in
Columbus's writings into a full-blown acceptance of the myth, summarizing his reasoning with the question, "Was it not the most obvious conclusion to regard these beings, so unfamiliar in their appearance, their behavior
and their powers, as supernatural?" Surely the most obvious conclusion was
to see Europeans as human beings, as they looked and acted like them, and
as in fact they were taken to be by natives throughout the Americas. Bitterli's
question is related to his discussion of the Tainos of Hispaniola, but he goes
further still, asserting that "the civilized peoples of the Central and South
American mainland, the Aztecs, Mayas, and Incas, saw the advancing conquistadors as gods." Upon first seeing Europeans, claims Bitterli, natives felt
"a sensation of trembling awe, which is present in all acts of divine worship."
The colonialist nature of Bitterli's perspective is illustrated by a drawing in
John Ogilby's *America* (1670), depicting Mexica lords prostrate before Cortés
(see Figure 15).[27]

Facing page: *Fig. 15. Mexica lords prostrate before Cortés, from John Ogilby's* America
(1670), *p. 85.*

If Mexico's Nahuas and other natives did indeed take Cortés to be a god, a good place to look for evidence would be the conquistador's hagiographer, Gómara. But Gómara makes no direct mention of the captain's apotheosis, referring vaguely to the topic only a few times. He alleges that the natives of Tabasco (Totonacs) initially "thought that man and horse were one," a probable Spanish invention that had grown in proportion by late colonial times. Gómara states that as the Spaniards passed through Valley of Mexico towns on their approach to Tenochtitlán, locals came out to marvel at their "attire, arms, and horses, and they said, 'These men are gods!'"—an exclamation of wonder at something new, rather than a statement of belief in the divinity of the invaders. He also reports that "Teudilli," a regional Tabascan lord allied to the Mexica, wondered if the Spaniards' ships meant that "the god Quetzalcoatl had come, bearing his temples on his shoulders." However, Gómara's other references to Quetzalcoatl are as the patron deity of Cholula, and to native concerns over Quetzalcoatl's displeasure as a background cause of the massacre of Cholulans instigated by Cortés. Were the Spanish captain deemed to be this god, one would imagine that Gómara, always keen to seize on anything that glorified the conquistador, would mention it. He does not. Gómara does have Cholulan lords saying, in reponse to Cortés confronting them with knowledge of their plot to ambush the Spaniards, that "this man is like one of our gods, for he knows everything; it is useless to deny it [the plot]." This is not the same as natives believing Spaniards actually to be gods. The entire exchange is also called into question by evidence that Cortés and/or the Tlaxcalans invented the plot as a pretext for the massacre.[28]

Similarly, Bernal Díaz's account contains no consistent evidence of Spaniards being taken for gods. According to Díaz, some Cempoalans (Gulf coast natives) exclaim upon learning of guns, "Surely they [the Spaniards] must be *teules!*" *Teules* is usually translated as "gods," but the term is a more ambiguous than that. The Nahuatl for "god" is *teotl*, *teteoh* in the plural, but it has a less restricted meaning than the English "god" or Spanish *dios*. It could be combined with other words, for example, to qualify them not as specifically godly or godlike, but as fine, fancy, large, powerful, and so on.[29] Thus, without the substantiating support of other evidence, the casual nicknaming of Spaniards as *teules* suggests a recognition not of divine status but of their political and military significance in the region. Furthermore, there is no follow-up to this moment to show that Cempoalans really did adopt the notion of Spanish apotheosis.[30]

Like Gómara, Díaz tells of the same Mexica lord (whom he calls "Tendile") expressing wonder at the Spaniards and their technology. But instead of the Quetzalcoatl reference, he tells an odd Cinderella-as-conquistador tale of matching helmets. One of the Spaniards has a rusty old helmet that resembles the headgear on an image of Huitzilopochtli, the patron deity of Tenochtitlán. Tendile is given the helmet to send or take to Moctezuma, who is supposedly so struck by the similarity he is "convinced that [the Spaniards] were of those whom his ancestors had said would come to be lords of that land."[31] This is an echo of the speech that Moctezuma allegedly delivered to Cortés upon their meeting. This does not mean that Spaniards were seen as gods, merely as descendants of men who once ruled Mexico, but it is one of the threads of invention and misunderstanding that became woven into the myth of Spanish apotheosis. Shortly after the Spanish-Mexica war, the Cortés-Huitzilopochtli connection evolved into a story that Moctezuma had welcomed Cortés because he believed the Spaniard to be Huitzilopochtli. But the royal chronicler Oviedo, who found the story in a letter written by colonial Mexico's first viceroy, stated it to be untrue.[32]

As for Cortés himself, he neither names Teudilli/Tendile nor mentions any tales of wonder, referring to him as a local lord who offered gold and provisions to the Spaniards (as native rulers often did to avoid hostilities and encourage the invaders to move on). In his letters to the king Cortés makes no claims to having been taken either as Huitzilopochtli or Quetzalcoatl (whom he never mentions at all) or any kind of god. His concern is more to establish the political legitimacy of his invasion and, in letters written before Tenochtitlán has fallen, to convince the king that despite ongoing hostilities the Mexica empire had already in some sense been ceded to Spain.

Perhaps it is not surprising that we find overt references to the apotheosis of the Spaniards in accounts by Franciscans, whose concerns were more religious than political, and whose emphasis was on the legitimacy and divine approval of Christianization campaigns. Writing in the 1530s, fray Toribio de Benavente, who took the name Motolinía, claimed that the Nahuas "called the Castilians *teteuh*, which is to say gods, and the Castilians, corrupting the word, said *teules*."[33] Whereas Díaz omits discussion of the origins or implications of the term *teules*, Motolinía seizes upon it as supposed evidence that Mexico's natives somehow anticipated the arrival of the Spaniards—an anticipation that proved the Conquest was part of God's plan for the Americas. For this reason, Franciscans such as Motolinía appear to have invented the Cortés-Quetzalcoatl identification after the Conquest.[34]

The most fully developed version of the Quetzalcoatl aspect of the myth is found in Sahagún's *Florentine Codex*. Because the text was written in Nahuatl as well as Spanish and was compiled using native informants, it has mistakenly been taken as gospel evidence of native reactions to the invasion. In fact, the *Codex* is a native *and* Franciscan source, as Sahagún conceived, compiled, and formulated the questionnaires for all 12 volumes between about 1547 and 1579. Book XII (on the Conquest) was first drafted about 1555, 35 years after Moctezuma's death, when the *Codex*'s informants would not have been old enough to know what went on before and during the war, or would not have been directly privy to the emperor's thoughts, words, and deeds. The informants were from Tlatelolco, the original Mexica island city that in the fifteenth century had become subsumed into Tenochtitlán but retained some semblance of separate identity. Its people usually called themselves Tlatelolca, rarely Mexica, and as Tlatelolco was the last part of the island to fall to the Spaniards, Tlatelolcans blamed the Mexica-Tenochca for the defeat. As a result, Moctezuma receives harsh treatment in the *Codex*, which portrays him as vacillating, inert with anxiety, terrorized by omens predicting his downfall, and ingratiating to the Spaniards.[35]

This depiction of Moctezuma has him shaken by a series of portents predicting the arrival of the Spaniards before and during their advance on Tenochtitlán. Some of these omens were phenomena that can easily be explained and probably occurred—a comet, an eclipse, an especially rough storm on the lake surrounding Tenochtitlán, the birth of Siamese twins. But whether these and others occurred or not, there is no evidence that they determined Moctezuma's response to Cortés. The same Franciscans who spread the Quetzalcoatl myth also spread the story of the omens to further promote the idea that the Conquest was providential. Motolinía wrote of the portents in the 1540s and by the time of the *Florentine Codex* they seem to have become common currency among Nahuas and Spaniards, having evolved into a set of eight, complete with details drawn from medieval European literature. Omens were a part of both European and Native American cultures in the fifteenth and sixteenth centuries, so it is not surprising that the story was readily accepted. This acceptance was part of the spread of the myth of native desolation and the myth of Moctezuma's psychological collapse, but it is not evidence of that supposed collapse.[36]

By the mid-sixteenth century this derogatory portrait of Moctezuma had already been circulating among Spaniards and had clearly become convenient as a native explanation for a complex series of developments. Already there had been a historical convergence of the Tlatelolcan scapegoating of Moctezuma, with the Cortés invention of Moctezuma's willing submission to Spain, and with the Franciscan campaign to present the Conquest as divine intention. The legend of the returning lords—originated during the Spanish-Mexica war with Cortés's reworking of Moctezuma's welcome speech—had by the 1550s merged with the Cortés-as-Quetzalcoatl legend that the Franciscans had started spreading in the 1530s.[37]

The myth of native desolation was thus personified in Moctezuma. Given a famous face, the myth became increasingly entrenched as the centuries passed. Moctezuma's image has remained tarnished ever since. In her best-seller, *The March of Folly*, a study of foolish decisions made by leaders in history, Barbara Tuchman blames the entire Conquest of Mexico on Moctezuma's being paralyzed by superstition or "delusion," by a sense of impending doom. Similarly, Todorov both blames Moctezuma and credits Cortés with embracing and encouraging the legend of the return of Quetzalcoatl and his identification as that god, so as to gain "control over the ancient Mexican empire."[38]

The rest of the Mexica, as Le Clézio puts it, were "naively led by the myth of the return of their ancestors" and of Quetzalcoatl, "blinded ... incapable of seeing the true motives of those whom they already named *teules*, or gods." By the time they had understood, "it was too late. The Spaniards had taken advantage of the Indians' hesitation to penetrate into the very heart of their empire."[39]

Because of the argument's potentially broad applicability, it has also been used to explain the Conquest in regions beyond central Mexico. For example, in the Cakchiquel Maya account of the Spanish invasion of highland Guatemala (part of the *Annals of the Cakchiquels*), there is a line that is usually translated as "the lords took them for gods" and interpreted literally as an "admission" by native chroniclers that their rulers initially saw the Spaniards as divine beings.[40] But the original Cakchiquel phrase could as easily be read as "the lords looked at them as though they were gods" and, set into context, it suggests that a figurative meaning was intended. The Maya passage was intended to convince the reader that at first Alvarado and the Cakchiquels were at peace, with the Spanish leader well disposed to the Mayas and the Mayas fearful and respectful. This spin on initial relations is a setup for the subsequent presentation of Spanish-Cakchiquel hostilities as entirely the fault of Alvarado. Because the account was written down at the end of the sixteenth century, it cannot be taken as a direct and unfiltered representation of native attitudes—or even basic events—in 1524. Finally, nowhere else in the Cakchiquel account is there mention of Maya rulers taking Spaniards for gods, nor is there evidence of such a perspective in this or any account. On the contrary, from the sending of ambassadors to Mexico in 1522 to the end of the Cakchiquel-Spanish war in 1530, the Cakchiquels consistently sought to manipulate the Spaniards and preserve, if not improve, their status with respect to other Maya groups in highland Guatemala.[41] The Cakchiquels were no different in this respect from other native peoples.

Another example of the appearance of the apotheosis argument is in the *Relación de Michoacán* (Account of Michoacán), a 1540 narrative of the Conquest of that Mesoamerican region written by a Franciscan friar using Tarascan noble sources. In the *Relación* the Tarascan king or Cazonci fails to resist the Spaniards because he believes them to be gods, an unlikely explanation that has been accepted by historians from Prescott to Todorov. As James Krippner-Martínez points out in a new appraisal of the *Relación* and of the Conquest of Michoacán, "this deeply rooted yet false image of Indian passivity" is part of a larger "bias."[42]

The apotheosis myth also surfaced in accounts of the Conquest of Peru, perhaps not coincidentally in a form similar to that of the Cortés-Quetzalcoatl legend. The myth was not mentioned in the earliest "eyewitness" accounts, but by the 1550s it was reported in several sources. Cieza de León remarked that the Spaniards acquired the name "Viracocha," because, as some say, "they were believed to be [the god] Ticsi Viracocha's children," or, as others say, because "they came by sea like foam." As with parallel Mexican accounts, the reference is a brief, vague, and half-hearted attempt to convince the reader that native Andeans really viewed Spaniards as divine.[43]

However, other accounts soon showed signs of the creative imagination of colonial chroniclers, the possible influence of stories about Cortés and Moctezuma, and the desire of proselytizers to "prove" that the Conquest was preordained and divinely sanctioned. "When Atahuallpa heard of this," wrote Pedro de Sarmiento, referring to the Spanish arrival in northern Peru, "he was delighted, believing that it was Viracocha who had come, just as he had promised them when he went away. . . . And he gave thanks to Viracocha because he was coming at the appointed time." Aside from its improbability, Atahuallpa's apparent "delight" runs contrary to all evidence of his attitude toward the Pizarro-led invasion.[44]

The intrusion of biblical tropes into the story is made even more transparent by the Jesuit chronicler José de Acosta, who explains that native Andeans "called the Spaniards *viracochas* because they thought they were children of heaven and as it were divine, just as others attributed divine status to Paul and Barnabas, calling one Jupiter and the other Mercury and trying to offer them sacrifices as though they were gods."[45] The Peruvian version of the apotheosis of the conquistadors thus turns largely on the legend and meaning of Viracocha. Although Viracocha's Mexican equivalent, with respect to this myth, is Quetzalcoatl, the parallel misunderstood Nahuatl term is *teteoh* (rendered as *teules* in Spanish). Christianity's sharp division between humanity and God was found neither in Mesoamerican nor in Andean religions, which recognized gradations of natural and supernatural, with some of those gradations consisting of mortal humans of high status. Thus Andeans nicknamed Spaniards *viracochas* for the same reason Nahuas called them *teules*—in recognition of their status. The term *viracocha* is still used today in Quechua as a reference not to the divine in the European sense but to the privileged and powerful.[46]

Another Quechua term applied to Spaniards and altered in meaning in the course of its translation was *supay*, which originally meant a morally neutral spirit that could be evil or benevolent. However, the Santo Tomás dictionary of 1560—that has *viracocha* glossed as "Christian"—shows the early accommodation of *supay* to the spiritual concepts of Spanish culture. It is entered as meaning "angel," with the qualifiers of *alliçupa* (*ángel bueno* or good angel) or *manaalliçupa* (*ángel malo* or bad angel). But as Spaniards could not find in Quechua a good term for "devil," one of these meanings soon came to dominate *supay*, while at the same time it became a more appropriately derogatory nickname for Spaniards. As Cieza de León observed in the 1550s, "the Indians . . . later said that these people [Spaniards] were not the sons of God, but worse than *supays*, which is the name of the devil."[47]

Interestingly, the Andean chronicler Titu Cusi Yupanqui, the nephew of Atahuallpa whose account was written about 1570 when Titu Cusi himself was Inca, says almost the same thing: "I thought that they were kindly beings sent (as they claimed) by Tecsi Viracocha, that is to say, by God; but it seems to me that all has turned out the very opposite from what I believed: for let me tell you, brothers, from proofs they have given me since their arrival in our country, they are the sons not of Viracocha, but of the Devil."[48] Within this passage three things undermine the notion that this is evidence of Spanish apotheosis in Andean minds. One is that the passage has the Spanish not as Viracocha(s) but merely sent by Viracocha, and as his sons, meant not in a literal sense but in the way Spaniards called themselves and other Christians "sons of God." Another important detail is the reference to the Spanish claim to have been sent by God. This reflects both the way in which the use of religious language was so easily misunderstood in translation, and the Spanish expectation that natives might view them as gods.[49]

The degree to which Andean beliefs and Quechua phrases could be misunderstood by Spaniards, and the degree to which Spaniards bandied about vague tales of prophesy and apotheosis, is illustrated well by the following passage by colonial Peruvian official Agustín de Zárate:

> When they afterwards saw Atahuallpa killed, the Indians believed that Huascar was truly a son of the sun since he had prophesied his brother's death. And Huascar also said that his father, on his deathbed, had commanded him to make friends with a white and bearded people who would one day come to the land, since these men would become lords of the kingdom. This may well have been a trick of the devil, since before Huayna Capac's death the Governor [Pizarro] was already travelling down the coast of Peru, conquering the country.[50]

A "trick of the devil" is certainly a succinct way of explaining the spread of rumors about omens, predictions, and native deification of Spaniards. As the colonial period progressed, the subordinated status of natives in the Spanish colonies seemed to confirm that these were the kinds of people "in whose minds superstition and credulity go hand in hand," as a governor of Yucatan in the 1840s described the Mayas. The supposed substitution of sympathy for prejudice has not stopped modern-day commentators from likewise seeing natives as likely to have been "paralyzed by terror" as the invaders approached, and desperately hoping "for support from the 'gods' or 'divine emissaries.'"[51]

Two brief examples illustrate the state of the myth by the eighteenth century. One is the following comment by Ilarione da Bergamo, an Italian friar who learned of Mexican history from local Spanish settlers while traveling in the colony in the eighteenth century: "At the beginning of the war, that race [the Spaniards] had the reputation of being immortal, because they [the Indians] had not seen a single dead Spaniard, whether from natural or violent causes. They also said that Spaniards were children of the sun, and they thought the cavalryman was a single body of both horse and rider."[52] Eighteenth-century Spanish notions of the sixteenth-century native mentality cannot be taken as good evidence of that mentality. It seems unlikely for natives to assume that men on horses were a new type of creature when the riders were accompanied by other men who looked the same but were on foot. Indeed, Mesoamericans had never seen horses, but they had seen deer, and indeed immediately began to call horses a type of deer.[53] Delight, not fear, was the reaction of the Chontal Maya king, Paxbolonacha, when invited by Cortés on the occasion of their initial meeting to ride for the first time on horseback into the Chontal capital.[54]

Similarly, it seems unlikely that natives would assume a man was a god pending his death as evidence of his mortality. The human experience leads us to assume, from a very young age, that people (in fact, all living creatures) are mortal, an assumption that would only logically be overturned by repeated acts of invincibility or resurrection. But the myth has no tales of such acts. Nor can we speculate on some sort of cultural exceptionalism on the part of Mesoamericans. There is plenty of evidence that they took death for granted much as other cultures do. One of the most important deities in Mesoamerica, the rain god and Earth god called Tlaloc by the Nahuas, was also a death god.[55] Furthermore, deification in Mesoamerica was postmortem, not premortem. The ruler Quetzalcoatl became a god, or became associated with the god of the same name, only after he died.[56] Finally, there are many more logical explanations for Spaniards being called "children of the sun." For example, a lieutenant of Cortés, Pedro de Alvarado, was nicknamed Tonatiuh, "the sun," by the Mexica because of his shock of blonde hair—no doubt his most notable feature from the perspective of the dark-haired natives. As we have seen, in the Andes the designator "son of the sun" was one of high status originally reserved for the Incas.

But the desolation myth, in all its various forms, fitted well with the perception of native peoples by eighteenth-century Europeans—and perhaps too with eighteenth-century native perceptions of their own pagan ancestors. It helped explain the Conquest and suggested a relationship of inequality and deference that was reflected in the structure of colonial society. Even when, a century and a half later, the Mexican Revolution gave rise to a new discourse on the nation's past, the myth of Spanish apotheosis persisted under the misguided belief (or pretense) that it was a part of the native perspective on the Conquest.[57]

The other illustration of the state of the myth in the eighteenth century is found in a powerful parallel English myth known as the Black Legend. It originated in the rise of England as a world power in the late sixteenth century, in the global Catholic-Protestant conflict stemming from the Reformation, and in the consolidation of English-Spanish hostility in the decades after the Armada affair of 1588. The legend depicted the Spaniards as brutal and bloody colonists who systematically victimized their native subjects. It was perpetuated primarily by the English, later the British, drawing upon such sources as Las Casas, but by the late eighteenth century it was also conventional wisdom among other Protestants, such as the Dutch, the Prussians, and the Anglo population of the new United States. While the Black Legend can be found in numerous sources over the centuries, an infrequently cited one efficiently evokes its relevance here. An epic poem published in 1775 by Mrs. Edward Jemingham, *The Fall of Mexico*, portrays Cortés as a diabolical genius and the Spanish as cold-blooded killers, with their native victims resigned to their fate but permitted by God to take revenge by cursing the Spanish Armada of 1588. Jemingham's poem thus unwittingly articulates a clear connection between the Black Legend and the myth of native desolation, with Mexico's natives "submissive" to their "fate" and able only to strike back at the conquistadors through the divine agency of the English.[58]

In the twentieth century the myth has received not only the support of many historians and writers, but also an indirect boost—and, in response, an assault—from an unexpected source. In contrast to examples from Latin America (that tend to take the myth's historical basis for granted), the case from eighteenth-century Hawaii has taken the form of a fierce debate between two highly articulate anthropologists. Marshall Sahlins has argued that the native Hawaiians took Captain Cook and his fellow British seamen to be gods, with the commoner women seeking—with the connivance of their husbands—to become pregnant by these "gods" in order to have children of high status and good fortune. Although the Hawaiian chiefs objected to this behavior and later redefined Cook as a mere human (for Cook, a fatal development), when the British captain first stepped ashore the Hawaiian lords and their subjects prostrated themselves before the *akua* (god), who had come from the Kahiki, the mythical homeland of divine and sacred chiefs.[59] Gananath Obeyesekere took issue with this interpretation, arguing that Westerners have tended to take literally and uncritically the sources that allegedly prove that natives did view Europeans as gods. Obeyesekere's principal concern is Sahlin's view of the apotheosis of Cook, but he also takes aim at Todorov and the myth of Cortés's apotheosis, arguing that the notion of "the European as a god to savages" is not a native tradition but one rooted in "European culture and consciousness."[60]

The interpretations by Sahlins and Obeyesekere of Hawaiian reactions to Cook, as different as they are, are arguably compatible explanations of adjacent aspects of a very complex encounter. Sahlins reminds us of the function of cultural consistency in human societies; how people tend to accommodate the new to the old, something we have seen with respect to Columbus and the Spaniards. Obeyesekere shows that political considerations are always relevant, in part because decisions made by the powerful have political motivations that are universally comprehensible. In colonial encounters, native peoples were not innately prone to esoteric thinking, but were as likely as Europeans to make choices based on "the pragmatics of common sense."[61]

Although Obeyesekere does not frame his argument in terms of a myth of native desolation or anomie, he does expose the way in which Western historians have tended to juxtapose a progressive and pragmatic Europe with a tradition-bound native world. In doing so, he connects the apotheosis myth to larger problems of European perceptions of Native Americans. The Spaniards-as-gods myth evolved over the centuries to take various forms, but all of them share a vision of Native Americans as so superstitious, credulous, and primitive in their reactions to the invaders as to be beneath reason or logic—and Spaniards as so superior in their technology and its manipulation as to be psychologically overwhelming. In a sense, the juxtaposition is between the subhuman and superhuman. But despite superficial differences of appearance, Spaniards looked and acted like human beings, and there is overwhelming evidence of myriad ways in which natives treated the invaders as such. The Spaniards-as-gods myth makes sense only if natives are assumed to be "primitive," childlike, or half-witted.

In 1539, Jerusalem was attacked by three Christian armies at once. One was an imperial force led by Charles V, Holy Roman Emperor and king of Spain, accompanied by his brother, the king of Hungary, and French king Francis I. This army had come as reinforcements for a separate Spanish army led by the Count of Benavente. The third attacking force was the army of New Spain, led by Viceroy Mendoza. The battle raged for hours, until the Muslim defenders of Jerusalem finally capitulated. Their leader, "the Great Sultan of Babylon and Tetrarch of Jerusalem," was none other than "the Marqués del Valle, Hernando Cortés."

This battle did not actually take place in the Middle East, but in the vast central plaza of Tlaxcala, the Nahua city-state whose alliance with Cortés had proved crucial to his defeat of the Mexica empire almost two decades earlier. The mock battle, part of a day-long series of plays and battles, was staged on Corpus Christi day by the Tlaxcalans, with the possible assistance of Franciscan friars. One of the friars witnessed the spectacle and wrote an account of it, published soon after in Motolinía's *History of the Indians of New Spain.*[62]

While a mock battle in which the victorious armies are led by the Spanish king, the colonial Mexican viceroy, and a Spanish count prominent in colonial Mexican affairs might seem to be a celebration of the Spanish Conquest of Mexico, Tlaxcala's theatrical "Conquest of Jerusalem" was hardly that. Cortés (played by a native Tlaxcalan actor) was not the victor in the drama, but the Sultan, doomed to defeat—and the captain general of the Moors was Pedro de Alvarado, the second most prominent Spaniard in the fall of Tenochtitlán and the subsequent conqueror of highland Guatemala. As the losers, Cortés and Alvarado requested mercy and baptism, and admitted that they were the "natural vassals" of the Tlaxcalan-played Charles V—an interesting inversion of the conquistadors' claim that natives were naturally subject to Spaniards.[63] As possible insurance against Cortés's reacting negatively to his role in the play, the Tlaxcalans had the army of New Spain led by a Tlaxcalan playing the viceroy, don Antonio de Mendoza, with whom Cortés was in dispute in 1539 (resulting in Cortés's sailing to Spain later that year).[64]

The parts in the play were all played by Tlaxcalans. It was Tlaxcalan warriors, in their thousands, who took Jerusalem, just as 18 years earlier thousands of them had taken Tenochtitlán. And whereas the Tlaxcalans playing soldiers in the European armies all wore the same bland uniforms, the Tlaxcalans of the army of New Spain dressed as themselves—in the traditional multicolored costumes of the city-state's warriors, complete with feathered headdresses, "their richest plumage, emblems, and shields" (in the words of the Franciscan observer). The setting for the play was Tlaxcala's impressive new plaza, the size of four football fields, whose buildings, still under construction, became part of the elaborate scenery. An important aspect of the festival's political context was Tlaxcala's age-old rivalry with the Mexica, as the play was put on in part to trump a similar spectacle staged four months earlier in Mexico City and centered on an imaginary Spanish "Conquest of Rhodes" that was a thinly disguised Mexica reconquest of Mexico.[65] The "Conquest of Jerusalem" was thus a Tlaxcalan creation intended to glorify Tlaxcala's recent triumphs and current status as an important, if not the most important, *altepetl* or central Mexican city-state.

Called "the most spectacular and intellectually sophisticated theatrical event" of its time, Tlaxcala's 1539 Corpus Christi celebration is an especially rich illustration of the genre.[66] But it was by no means the only such festival in sixteenth-century Mexico, or indeed in colonial Spanish America. Throughout the colonies in Mesoamerica and the Andes, plays, dances, and mock battles were staged by native communities. Many persist to this day. All placed complex local spins on a mix of traditional native ritual performance and various elements of Spanish theatrical tradition. The effect, if not the purpose, of such festivals was to reconstruct the Conquest not as a historical moment of defeat and trauma, but as a phenomenon that transcended any particular historical moment and was transcended in turn by that local native community. These festivals were not commemorations of something lost, but celebrations of community survival, micropatriotic integrity, and cultural vitality.[67] Festivals of reconquest therefore represent the first of the seven indicators of Conquest-era and post-Conquest native vitality.

The second such indicator consists of other expressions of native denial or inversion of defeat. An extraordinarily rich body of sources illustrating this phenomenon with respect to Mesoamerica is contained within the genre referred to by scholars as the primordial title, or *título*. The *título* was a community history that promoted local interests, particularly related to land ownership, often those of the local dynasty or dominant noble families. Such documents were written down alphabetically, in native languages, all over Mesoamerica during the colonial period—but especially in the eighteenth century when land pressures mounted due to population growth among Spaniards and natives alike. Late-colonial *títulos* drew upon earlier sources, both written and oral, representing continuities from pre-Conquest histories and often including accounts of the Spanish invasion.[68] Maya accounts of the Conquest contained in *títulos* from Yucatan reveal that there was no single, homogeneous native view; perspectives were determined largely by differences of class, family, and region. Most of the Maya elite, however, tended to downplay the significance of the Conquest by emphasizing continuities of status, residency, and occupation from pre-Conquest times. Mayas placed the Spanish invasion, and the violence and epidemics it brought, within the larger context of history's cycles of calamity and recovery, relegating the Conquest to a mere blip in their long-term local experience.[69]

Another example of the localized nature of native responses to the Conquest come from the Valley of Oaxaca, in southern Mexico. In the 1690s a legal dispute over land erupted between two native communities in the valley, one Nahua, the other Mixtec. In court, both submitted *títulos* to prove their cases, each complete with a brief Conquest account. The Nahua version of events of the 1520s asserted that Nahua warriors had come down to Oaxaca from central Mexico in response to a plea from the Zapotecs, who needed help defending themselves from the cannibalistic Mixtecs. Cortés approved the mission, but when he came to Oaxaca in the wake of Nahua victory, he and the Nahuas fell out and fought. The Nahuas won this battle too, and after this, the "original conquest," they settled in the valley on land granted to them.

In contrast, the Mixtec version claimed that Cortés came to the valley first, where he was welcomed by the Mixtecs, who gave Spaniards some land on which to settle. The trouble began when Cortés returned with a group of Nahuas, who started a fight and were soundly defeated by the Mixtecs. With Cortés as peace broker, the Mixtecs graciously allowed the Nahuas to settle in the valley. The boundaries of the land they were given were not surprisingly less generous in the Mixtec *título* than in the Nahua version.

In both versions, local community—or micropatriotic—identities remain paramount. There is no acceptance of the colonial division of peoples into Spaniards and "Indians," nor is there an acceptance of the Conquest as either a Spanish initiative or a primarily Spanish triumph. Native defeat is not only denied, but inverted. Even the phrase "native defeat" is meaningless from a community perspective that views all outsiders in more or less the same way, whether they be Spaniards, Mixtecs, Nahuas, or Zapotecs—or even people of the same language group who live in a separate town.[70]

The third indicator of native vitality during the Conquest was the role played by natives as allies in the campaigns that followed the major wars of invasion. Although in the long run these campaigns usually (but not always) resulted in the spread of Spanish colonial rule, in the short run they often constituted local native exploitation of the Spanish presence to advance regional interests. For example, the armies of Nahua warriors who waged campaigns in what is now northern Mexico, southern Mexico, Yucatan, Guatemala, and Honduras helped create the colonial kingdom of New Spain and were led by Spanish captains. But the vast majority of those who fought were Nahuatl-speakers under their own officers. Many of them remained as colonists in new colonial towns such as Oaxaca, Santiago (Guatemala), Mérida, and Campeche, and their culture and language made a permanent mark on these regions. As symbolized by place-names in highland Guatemala to this day, Nahuatl became a lingua franca in New Spain. In many ways, these campaigns were a continuation of the Mexica expansionism that had gone almost unchecked for a century before the Spanish invasion.[71]

A slightly different type of example is that of the Chontal Maya expansion of the late sixteenth century under their king, Paxbolonacha. His simultaneous colonial identity was as don Pablo Paxbolon, the region's governor. Although the Chontal Mayas's first major contact with Spaniards was as early as 1525, not until the 1550s did the region become fully incorporated into the nearest Spanish colony, Yucatan. Beginning in the 1560s, and running continuously until his death in 1614, Paxbolon engaged in campaigns against neighboring Maya communities that had yet to be incorporated into the colony or that had slipped out of colonial control. The Spanish presence on most of these expeditions was minimal or nonexistent. Although Paxbolon had a license from Mérida permitting him to round up refugees and "idolaters," a Chontal Maya *título* written during his rule recorded such campaigns before and after the Spanish invasion, revealing the colonial ones to be little more than continuations of age-old slaving raids.[72]

Paxbolon's expansionism was a localized phenomenon, but so were all cases of native military activity after the Spanish invasion—from Nahua campaigns after the fall of the Mexica empire to campaigns by Andean warriors for decades after the capture and execution of Atahuallpa. Local circumstances produced regional variations, but the general pattern reveals considerable native military activity during the Conquest and after it was supposedly over, not always directed against Spaniards but often pursued to advance local native interests.

The historian Charles Gibson, in his seminal study of colonial Tlaxcala, remarked that there were times when "Indians accepted one aspect of Spanish colonization in order to facilitate their rejection of another."[73] This situation is illustrated by the role often played by native élites, whose partial and complex collaboration in Conquest and colonial agendas represents the fourth antidesolation indicator. At the highest level of native leadership, that of the Mexica and Inca emperors, such collaboration served only to buy time. But while Moctezuma and Atahuallpa lived, even as captives, their policies of collaboration and appeasement served to save native lives and prevent full-scale wars. The Moctezuma of myth—invented by Franciscans and Tlatelolcans and perpetuated by modern historians from Prescott to Tuchman—was no artful collaborator. But the real Moctezuma was the most successful ruler the Mexica empire had known; "the most dynamic, the most aggressive, the most triumphantly self-confident of all," in Fernández-Armesto's words, Moctezuma "outstripped all predecessors" with campaigns that ranged over some 150,000 square miles and continued even after Cortés had taken up residence in Tenochtitlán. Cortés later claimed to have captured Moctezuma soon after reaching the city, but it is clear from descriptions of the emperor's activities in other Spanish and native sources that his arrest did not take place for months. Meanwhile, the Mexica ruler spun a web of confusion around the Spaniards, who remained unsure right up to their disastrous and bloody escape from Tenochtitlán whether to expect submission, deadly duplicity, or open hostility.[74] Atahuallpa's capture was more immediate, but even as a captive he was able to plot and strategize, temporarily containing the Spaniards and using them to win his own war against his brother.

The high status of Moctezuma and Atahuallpa made them unsuited in the long run for the roles of puppet rulers and condemned them to death at the hands of Spaniards. Lesser native rulers, however, were able to negotiate their way out of captivity and execution, or avoid imprisonment altogether, and be confirmed in office by the colonial authorities. Don Pablo Paxbolon is a good example of such a ruler who was able to maintain this dual status throughout his long reign/rule, partly because his small kingdom was of relatively little interest to Spaniards. In contrast, Manco Inca Yupanqui's kingdom attracted so much Spanish attention that he soon rebelled against his dual status. As well as being Inca (meaning "emperor") by right of succession, Manco was confirmed in office as regent of Peru by the Spaniards in 1534 and was supposed to function as a puppet of the colonial régime (see Figure 16). But by 1536 the conditions of compromise had become too onerous, and the abuse of the Inca's family and retainers by the Pizarros and their associates had become intolerable. Manco fled the capital of Cuzco, raised an army, and laid siege to the city for a year before retreating into the Andes, where an independent Inca kingdom lasted until 1572. Meanwhile, in 1560,

Fig. 16. "Manco Inca, raised up as Inca king," in Nueva corónica y buen gobierno, by don Felipe Huaman Poma de Ayala (1615).

Fig. 17. "The Xiu Family Tree," probably by Gaspar Antonio Chi (c. 1557),
updated by don Juan Xiu (c. 1685).

Manco's son Titu Cusi became Inca, later becoming baptized and negotiating a rapprochement with the Spanish. Although his brother, Tupac Amaru, and other family members were executed in 1572 as rebels, Titu Cusi, his descendents, and other members of the Inca nobility were able to maintain considerable economic and political status within colonial Peru for centuries.[75]

Inca survival paralleled in many ways the perpetuation of status by Moctezuma's relatives and descendents. While they lacked their pre-Conquest political clout, their local social and economic significance was underpinned by confirmation of titles and honors by the Spanish crown.[76] Likewise, most of the highest-ranking noble Maya families, as a result of protracted negotiations through a Conquest decades long, succeeded in preserving their local status as community rulers in return for accepting Spanish political authority at a regional level. The Spanish governor of Yucatan became the *halach uinic* (provincial ruler) but the noblemen of dynasties such as the Cocom, Pech, and Xiu remained as *batabob* (local rulers or town governors) for the next three centuries.

The Xiu were among the most powerful noble families in Yucatan before and after the Conquest.[77] Figure 17 illustrates through the medium of a family tree the perpetuation of the Xiu dynasty's sense of historical legitimacy through the Conquest period. The semimythical founding couple are supposed to have lived centuries before the Conquest, while the named individuals run from the fifteenth to seventeenth centuries. Drawn in the 1550s by Gaspar Antonio Chi, and updated over a century later by a member of one branch of the family, the tree exhibits a complex mix of Maya, Nahua, and Spanish cultural elements. The image evocatively exhibits the blend of change and continuity, compromise and survival that underscored élite native adaptation to colonial rule.

Most of the Xiu noblemen named in Figure 17 served as *batabob*, illustrating the flourishing of the native municipal community from the sixteenth to eighteenth centuries—the fifth indicator of postinvasion native vitality. One of the native mechanisms of adaptation to colonial rule that fostered the golden age of the native town was the ready adoption of the Spanish *cabildo* (town council). The *cabildo*'s election, offices, and functions Spaniards imposed on native towns early in the colonial period—or at least, Spaniards assumed they did. In fact, native élites only appeared to create Spanish-style *cabildos*. Their "elections," if held at all, were but a veneer covering traditional factional maneuvers and cycles of power sharing. Spanish titles such as *alcalde* (judge) and *regidor* (councilman) were adopted, but the numbers, rankings, and functions of the officers followed local traditions, while many *cabildos* contained officers with pre-Conquest titles. In some cases municipal governors were Spanish appointed, but in many more instances native governors continued to function as they had before the Conquest, even keeping precolonial titles, ruling for life and passing the positions on to their sons.[78]

While Spaniards viewed native *cabildos* as products of colonialism, natives initially adopted the framework of the *cabildo* as a superficial change and then soon came to view it as a local institution rather than a colonial one. This double perception is another example of Double Mistaken Identity, whereby both Spaniards and natives viewed the same concept or way of doing something as rooted in their own culture. In this way, the native borrowing of Spanish cultural elements did not represent native culture loss or decline, but rather adaptability and vitality (the sixth indicator of post-Conquest native cultural vitality). Natives tended to view borrowings—be they Spanish words, concepts, ways of counting, of worship, of building houses, or of town planning—not as loans but as part of community practice and custom. They viewed them not as Spanish, nor even as native, but as local. And they were able to do this because of the integrity and flourishing of semi-autonomous municipal communities. By the end of the colonial period, there was little about native culture in most of Spanish America that (in James Lockhart's words) "could safely be declared to have been entirely European or entirely indigenous in origin. The stable forms that emerged in the long run often owed so much to both antecedents, with many elements having been similar from the beginning and others now interwoven and integrated, that identifying what belonged to which antecedent becomes to a large extent impossible, and even beside the point."[79]

Just as the violence and drama of the Spanish invasion gave way to gradual cultural change, so did the immediate tragedy of native population decline give way in the long run to opportunities of various kinds. The Andean chronicler Huaman Poma warned in 1615 that the "Indians are coming to an end," and in demographic terms, a century after Spaniards began their conquests on the American mainland, this almost seemed a real possibility. The rapid decline in the Native American population, beginning in 1492 and continuing well into the seventeenth century, has been called a holocaust. In terms of absolute numbers and the speed of demographic collapse—a drop of as many as 40 million people in about a century—it is probably the greatest demographic disaster in human history.[80]

But the decline was not a holocaust in the sense of being the product of a genocide campaign or a deliberate attempt to exterminate a population. Spanish settlers depended upon native communities to build and sustain their colonies with tribute, produce, and labor. Colonial officials were extremely concerned by the demographic tragedy of Caribbean colonization, where the native peoples of most islands became extinct within a few decades. That concern mounted with evidence of massive mortality on the mainland during—and even preceding—Spanish invasions. What Spaniards did not fully understand was the degree to which disease caused this disaster. The arguments of a vocal minority—of whom Las Casas remains the best known—that colonial brutality was the principal cause of the natives seeming to "come to an end" were taken seriously by the crown. As a result, edicts were regularly passed that were designed to protect natives from colonial excesses. Their impact was limited, but they reflected the important fact that Spaniards needed Native Americans to survive and proliferate, even if this was only so they could be exploited.

The combination of population decline and Spanish colonial dependence upon a shrinking—and then very slow growing—native population actually provided opportunities for the survivors. One type of opportunity was political. The relative stability of the ruling élite in Yucatan, and the few instances of upstart families acquiring power as a result, was not paralleled everywhere in Spanish America. In the Riobamba region of colonial Quito, for example, the pre-Inca élite and the surviving families among the local Inca nobility vied for power within the crucible of the Conquest and colonial rule. The situation was skillfully manipulated by the Duchiselas, a family that was prominent in the area before the Inca conquest but not a ruling dynasty. The family welcomed the 1534 Spanish expedition under Sebastián de Benalcázar and as a result was granted a local lordship. By the 1570s they parlayed this into the governorship of the town of Yaruquíes. Over the next two centuries the Duchiselas consolidated considerable regional political power, established a land-based family fortune, and largely succeeded in inventing the dynasty's deep-rooted historical legitimacy.[81]

The Duchisela family fortune was land based, and by the early seventeenth century its patriarch, don Juan, and his wife, doña Isabel Carrillo, owned almost a thousand hectares of land. Indeed, land was another arena of native opportunity in the Conquest's wake. Contrary to common belief, Spaniards did not come to the Americas to acquire land. The goal of conquistadors was to receive an *encomienda*, a grant of native tribute and labor—not land. The Spanish pressure on native communities to give up or sell land was not serious until later in the colonial period. In the sixteenth century there was a great deal more land available to natives than before the Conquest. And with the advent of iron and steel tools and a new array of crops and domesticated animals, there were new opportunities for working that land.[82]

To be sure native peoples in sixteenth-century Spanish America faced epidemics of lethal disease and onerous colonial demands. But they did not sink into depression and inactivity because of the Conquest. Instead they tenaciously sought ways to continue local ways of life and improve the quality of life even in the face of colonial changes and challenges. Furthermore, the decline in population did not mean that native culture declined in some or any sense. Native cultures evolved more rapidly and radically in the colonial period as a result of exposure to Spanish culture and the need to adapt to new technologies, demands, and ways of doing things. But as historians of late-medieval Europe have observed, when populations were periodically decimated by plagues and epidemics, this did not result in culture loss.

All of this is ignored by the myth of native desolation, which subsumes into "nothingness" the complex vitality of native cultures and societies during and after the Conquest.[83] As Inga Clendinnen puts it, the mythic or "conventional story of returning gods and unmanned autocrats, of an exotic world paralyzed by its encounter with Europe, for all its coherence and its just-so inevitabilities, is in view of the evidence like Eliza's progression across the ice floes: a matter of momentary sinking balances linked by desperate forward leaps."[84] The next chapter looks at those floes—specifically, the notion of Spanish superiority—and reveals that the ice is thin indeed.

7

Apes and Men
The Myth of Superiority

You would conquer this whole land, God giving us health, for Spaniards dare
face the greatest peril, consider fighting their glory, and have the habit of
winning.

—Hernán Cortés (1521)

The Spaniards are perfectly right to govern these barbarians of the New
World and adjacent islands; they are in prudence, ingenuity, virtue, and
humanity as inferior to the Spaniards as children are to adults and women
are to men, there being as much difference between them as that between
wild and cruel and very merciful persons, the prodigiously intemperate and
the continent and tempered, and I daresay from apes to men.

—Juan Ginés de Sepúlveda (1547)

Conquistador, there is no time, I must pay my respects.
And though I came to jeer at you, I leave now with regret.

—Procol Harum (1972)

Cortez: "Wild and untaught are Terms which we alone
Invent, for fashions differing from our own:
For all their customs are by Nature wrought,
But we, by Art, unteach what Nature taught."

—from John Dryden's *The Conquest of
Granada by the Spaniards* (1672)

Why is Conquest history so ridden with myths? According to the anthropologist Samuel Wilson, we seek to distance ourselves from the history of the Contact and Conquest because of the tragedy it contains. "It is politically safer and emotionally less taxing," suggests Wilson, "to blur history into myth and thereby confine it." This argument helps to explain not only the modern perpetuation of Conquest myths, but also their development in the Conquest period itself. That these myths can be found alive and well in both the sixteenth and twenty-first centuries should not surprise us; after all, as Wilson points out, we are still living in "the contact period."[1]

131

In colonial times, Spaniards sought to confine history by harnessing it to what may be the simplest trope ever invented to explain human behavior, differences between peoples, and the outcome of historical events—the trope of superiority. Colonial chroniclers and the modern historians who followed them found a satisfying simplicity and safety in the following circular argument: Spaniards conquered natives because they were superior, and they were superior because they conquered natives.

In its most extreme form, indigenous inferiority was expressed in terms that denied Native Americans their humanity. Juan Ginés de Sepúlveda's comment is often cited because it suggests this image so candidly. The Spanish jurist and philosopher openly stated that natives "hardly deserve the name of human beings." Even full conversion and subjection to the Spanish empire could only partially turn these "barbarians" into "civilized men."[2] While much opprobrium has been heaped upon Sepúlveda for his views, he merely articulated more vividly and directly what most Spaniards and other Europeans assumed at the time to be the case. Two centuries later, for example, the French anticolonialist and Enlightenment figure Denis Diderot characterized the Spanish explorers as "a handful of men surrounded by an innumerable multitude of natives." When anthropologist Michel-Rolph Trouillot quotes this sentence, he italicizes *men* and *natives* to emphasize their juxtaposition.[3]

This opposition of man and native, the civilized and the barbarous, the advanced and the primitive, is seen everywhere, not only in colonial and early modern sources. The more extreme views on the relative merits of the civilization that produced the Spanish Conquest were brought out by the public and highly politicized Quincentennial debate over Columbus and his legacy. Michael Berliner wrote in the *Los Angeles Times* that "Western civilization stands for man at his best" and should be honored (through the celebration of Columbus's discovery) "because it is the objectively superior culture." Berliner's juxtaposition of a barbarous pre-Columbian Native America ("sparsely inhabited, unused, undeveloped" but racked with "endless, bloody wars") with a Western Europe that defined civilization's virtues ("reason, science, self-reliance, individualism, ambition, productive achievement") is a version of the trope that Europeans used for centuries to justify the exploitation of Native Americans and the enslavement of West Africans.[4]

Not long ago, professional historians expressed similar views.[5] Although the language of civilization versus barbarism is nowadays more subtle and disguised in academic media, the words "superior" and "superiority" often crop up in modern texts and discussions of the Conquest. This chapter approaches the myth of superiority through a discussion of two sets of five explanations of the Conquest. The first set consists of mythic explanations, those based on the misunderstandings or misconceptions presented in this book. The second set are my antimythic explanations for the Conquest.

⌒

"We took this lord by a miracle of God," Gaspar Marquina wrote to his father in Spain, shortly after he had seen Atahuallpa seized at Cajamarca, "because our forces wouldn't be enough to take him nor to do what we did, but God gave us the victory miraculously over him and his forces."[6] Attributing to divine intervention an outcome that surprised or otherwise perplexed Spaniards was an easy option to which conquistadors often resorted. While he was governor of the colony of Tierra Firme, centered on the city of Panama, Pedrarias de Avila implied in a letter to the king in 1525 that both he and the local natives shared a view of epidemic disease as providential. He wrote,

> more than 400,000 souls have been converted to our holy Catholic faith of their own free will, and more continually come to request baptism, because the Indians in one town where a wooden cross had been set up tried to burn it and never succeeded, and then all the people of the town died of pestilence without an Indian remaining, and seeing this miracle and other miracles that have occurred, the Indians of the region around came to be baptized and request crosses.[7]

Sometimes the citing of miracles was specific, as in the claims that the Inca siege of Cuzco was lifted in 1537 by the appearance of the Virgin Mary, or by Santiago (St. James) riding his white horse into the Andean forces. In fact, early colonial accounts of the siege by both Spaniards and Andeans—Antonio de Herrera, Titu Cusi, Cristóbal de Molina, Garcilaso de la Vega, and fray Martín de Murúa—all credit the intervention of Santiago and the Virgin as important explanatory factors, if not the deciding factor.[8] On other occasions, the references to God by sixteenth-century Spaniards—to His will, blessing, and intervention—seem so much a part of the linguistic currency of the day that they can be seen as no more than convenient façades for complex explanations and understandings.

The most obvious question begged by the conquest-as-miracle explanation was *why* did God intervene on the side of the Spaniards? The answer was deceptively simple: because their endeavors were sanctioned by God. As Sahagún explained, "Many were the miracles which were performed in the conquest of this land." The sentence appears in Sahagún's 1585 revision of the Conquest account that is Book XII of the *Florentine Codex*, which the Franciscan friar felt gave insufficient credit to such factors as the role of providence. Before Sahagún, Las Casas and Motolinía had similarly argued that the Conquest was ordained by God in order to bring Christianity to natives. In general, the Franciscans and Dominicans worked hard to promote their evangelization efforts in the Americas not just as God's own work but as the very purpose and justification of the entire Conquest.[9]

#1

The message was easily transferred to the secular realm. Conquistadors such as Cortés laid claim to being agents of providence, and chroniclers such as Oviedo and Gómara constructed Conquest history around the notion that God's plan was to unite the world under Christendom and the Spanish monarchy. In a speech delivered in Tlaxcala to rally the Spaniards for the siege of the Mexica capital, as later reported to the king, Cortés used this idea to underpin his reasons for why the Conquest was a "just cause." "First, because we were fighting against a barbarian people to spread our Faith; second, in order to serve your Majesty; third, we had to protect our lives; and last, many of the natives were our allies and would assist."[10] This perspective allowed justification and explanation to be intertwined and mutually supportive. The Conquest had "good reason" because it was a civilizing mission against barbarians. It was successful because it was aided by God's will and the Spanish "habit of winning."[11] "As we had the flag of the cross and fought for our faith and service of our sacred majesty," Cortés explained on another occasion, "God gave us such a victory and we killed many persons."[12]

Conquistadors such as Marquina, Avila, and Cortés may have casually attributed events to God's will. But their understanding of what Spaniards were doing in the Americas and how they did it was nurtured by a culture that placed the conquest-as-miracle explanation within the ideological context of the Spanish claim to be the chosen people. For the unprecedented scope of their explorations, conquests, and conversions of "idolaters," proclaimed Gómara, "Spaniards are most worthy of praise in all parts of the world. Blessed be God who gave them such grace and power."[13] Even in attributing Conquest miracles, the concept of Spanish superiority was always transparent.

The second mythic explanation blames native peoples for their own defeat. It combines the notion that native resistance was hindered or forestalled by the belief that the Spaniards were (or may have been) gods, with the interrelated blaming of the Mexica and Inca emperors for the subsequent collapse of their empires. Spanish superiority is promoted through the contrast between native and Spanish leaders—the more that Moctezuma is condemned as "timorous and cowardly," in Sepúlveda's words, the more Cortés seems "noble and valiant"—and by the implication that the appearance, abilities, and actions of the conquistadors inspired natives to take them for gods.

The third myth-based explanation stems from the view of native cultures as inadequate to the task of fending off the Spanish invasion. Again, native inferiority serves to feed the myth of Spanish superiority. Early European views of Native Americans included the belief that they either lacked culture in any "real" sense, or that their cultures were weakened by naiveté or a rotten moral core. Such views also gave rise to explanations for the Conquest's outcome. That sixteenth-century Spaniards found such explanations convincing is not surprising, but these cultural explanations were also perpetuated in modern history books. For example, J. H. Elliott, the prominent English historian of Spain and its empire, argued that Spanish weaponry alone does not explain the Conquest.

> There must here have been a superiority that was more than merely technical, and perhaps it ultimately lay in the greater self-confidence of the civilization which produced the *conquistadores*. In the Inca empire they confronted a civilization that seems to have passed its peak and to have started already on its descent; in the Aztec [i.e. Mexica] empire, on the other hand, they successfully challenged a civilization still young and in the process of rapid evolution. Each of these empires was thus caught at a moment when it was least capable of offering effective resistance, and each lacked confidence in itself, and in its capacity for survival in a universe ruled by implacable deities, and for ever poised on the brink of destruction. The *conquistador*, hungry for fame and riches, and extremely confident of his capacity to obtain them, stood on the threshold of a fatalist world resigned to self-surrender; and in the sign of the cross he conquered it.[14]

This passage embraces much of Conquest mythology: the Conquest is achieved by a few gold-hungry exceptional men; native empires quickly collapse; natives are handicapped by fatalism and a lack of confidence; and Spaniards enjoy a double "superiority," technical and civilizational. Elliott does not explicitly blame native religion, but the idea is implicit in his phrase "fatalist world," which amounts to a modern version of the "superstition" of which colonial-era Spaniards accused natives. As Santiago Mendez, Yucatan's governor in the early 1840s, remarked, in "Indian" minds "superstition and credulity go hand in hand."[15]

In 1949 the Belgian illustrator Hergé vividly captured seemingly timeless attitudes toward natives in his *Prisoners of the Sun*, the illustrated adventure in the *Tintin* series in which the heroic reporter travels to Peru. On one level, the titular prisoners are Tintin and his friends (tied to stakes in Figure 18), but on another level it is the native Andeans who are imprisoned by a static, primitive culture.[16] Tintin's use of his knowledge of an imminent eclipse is wonderfully comic, but its theater works only because it plays upon European assumptions of Western ingenuity and native superstition.

Hergé's early Tintin strips portrayed a colonial world of civilized Europeans and barbarous others, while his later stories and his revisions of earlier work presented a postcolonial world imbued with neocolonialism. Tintin's adventures have been devoured by generations of European schoolboys, and have seen a resurgence among adults, with the books selling tens of millions of copies worldwide.[17] The representational legitimacy of *Tintin* thus lies in the dissemination of the series, but it is confirmed by the fact that less comic sources, from popular historians to revered scholars, have continued to articulate a comparative view of native culture not far removed from that illustrated by Hergé.[18]

Michael Wood, for example, suggests that the Mexica accepted their defeat because "the Aztec polity was, unquestionably, a moral order with a deep, if tormented, spirituality." Le Clézio goes further, stating that "the Maya, the

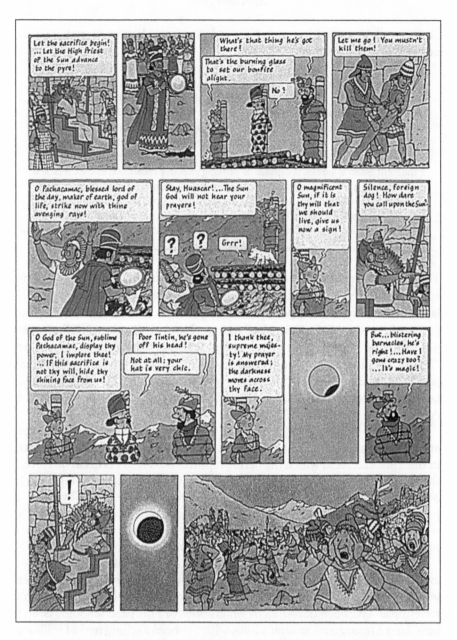

Fig. 18. Excerpt from Hergé's The Adventures of Tintin: Prisoners of the Sun
(1949; first English edition, 1962), p. 58. (© Hergé/Moulinsart 1962)

Totonacs, and the Mexica were profoundly religious tribes, completely sub-servient to the order of the gods and to the rule of their priest-kings."[19] Charles Dibble, misled by the *Florentine Codex* upon which he labored for decades, explained the Conquest of Mexico largely in terms of the Mexica cultural outlook as "omen-ridden" and "permeated with a resigned fatalism"; the Mexica were traumatized by the apparent "ineffectiveness of native religion and magic" and the realization that Cortés was Quetzalcoatl.[20]

Benjamin Keen, in his popular textbook on Latin American history, also contrasts European and Native American civilizations as one reason for the success of the Conquest. "The Spaniards were Renaissance men with a basi-cally secular outlook, while the Indians represented a much more archaic worldview in which ritual and magic played a large role." Spaniards viewed war as "a science or art," but "for the Aztecs and Incas, war had a large reli-gious component." Jacques Soustelle, in his classic study of the Mexica, first published in French a half century ago, made the same argument. Mexica civilization "went down above all because its religious and legal conception of war paralyzed it," argued Soustelle; "by reason of its material inadequacy or the rigidity of its mind, the civilization was defeated." The juxtaposition is thus between a progressive civilization and a traditional one. However the argument is articulated, the trope of civilization and barbarism always lurks in the background.[21]

One of the oldest definitions of the difference between civilization and barbarism is that of writing. The fourth myth-based explanation of the Con-quest assumes a Spanish superiority in language, literacy, and reading "signs." Columbus's comment, at first seemingly extraordinary, that he would bring Caribbean natives to Spain "in order that they may learn to speak," is echoed in Le Clézio's declaration that Mexico's Conquest "was achieved thanks to Cortés's chief weapon—his ability to speak." Columbus and Le Clézio mean to compare not the mute and the vocal, but superior and inferior communi-cators. Thus despite Todorov's claim that his explanation of the Conquest as a native defeat "by means of signs" is one that "has hitherto been neglected," the myth of the superior communication skills of Europeans is both deeply rooted and still alive.[22] Antonio de Nebrija's famous statement in his Intro-duction to the first published Spanish grammar that "language has always been the partner [*compañera*] of empire" is often quoted partly because of the symbolism of his book's presentation to Queen Isabella in 1492.[23] But it is also cited because it functions as a bumper-sticker slogan to support the idea that Spaniards enjoyed what Samuel Purchas termed "the litterall advan-tage." Purchas, an Englishman writing in the early seventeenth century, meant that literacy gave its possessors both a moral and technological advantage. Modern proponents of this idea have abandoned its moral dimension (al-most reversing it in their anticolonial sympathy for native peoples), but cling to its technological aspect.[24]

Fig. 19. The frontispiece to the first edition of Historia Verdadera de la Conquista de la Nueva España, *by Bernal Díaz (1632).*

The frontispiece drawing to the first published edition of Díaz's *True History* (Figure 19) depicts Cortés on the left, beneath a sign upon which is inscribed the Latin word *manu* (by hand, i.e., by deed), and a friar on the right beneath the word *ore* (by word). It seems to me that the intention of the Mercedarian friar who found and edited Díaz's manuscript, if indeed he designed the frontispiece, was to signal that the role of conversion and of the friars was as important as that of Cortés and the conquistadors. The symbolic significance of the images is their reflection of competing Spanish visions of the Conquest, its rationale, its importance, and the explanations for its success. It would probably be taking the symbolism too far to define the Conquest as "a conquest *of* language and a conquest *by* language."[25] Language was important in the Conquest, but trying to explain the Conquest in terms of signs, language, or writing comes far too close to Sepúlveda's blunt expression of what Purchas called "the litterall advantage." "The Indians," declared the Spaniard, were "little men in whom you will scarcely find traces of humanity, who not only lack culture but do not even know how to write."[26]

The final myth-based explanation is rooted in the notion that Spanish weaponry in and of itself explains the Conquest, something that not even the conquistadors believed. While weapons were clearly a factor in the Conquest's outcome, the extreme version of this explanation—whereby weaponry explains everything—has become a modern manifestation of the old superiority myth. As the once-dominant notion of civilizational superiority became unfashionable, the idea of Spanish technological superiority became a politically acceptable alternative.

Early expressions of this view in Cortés's letters to the king and in Díaz's account tend to mix the straightforward idea of differences in weapons with other explanations more clearly based in Conquest mythology. Later, Ilarione da Bergamo was given to understand from his travels in Mexico in the 1760s that the crucial moment of divine intervention in Cortés's campaign was the Spanish discovery of "saltpeter" at the mouth of the Orizaba volcano, with which gunpowder could be made. "For if there had not been powder," wrote Ilarione,

> to charge the field cannons with their cartridges and withstand the tremendous number of Indians who resisted their advance into their country, and (according to the history) nearly darkened the sky with the immense quality of arrows launched against the aggressors, they would not have been able to decimate them as they did. . . . These wretched Indians had all the more reason to claim that the Spaniards manipulated lightning when they heard the noise and saw the fire from the artillery and, at the same time, countless numbers of their own people dropping dead.[27]

There are recent versions of this colonial view, whereby superior Spanish weapons vanquish superstitious natives; Carlos Fuentes states that in both

Mexico and the Andes "two factors came together to defeat the Indian nation: myth and weaponry."[28] But modern versions of the explanation often focus exclusively on military matters, and thus become potentially pernicious because they can so easily be couched in material, rather than human, terms. The use of the word "superiority" to discuss the Conquest is thereby seemingly benign.[29]

The historians who have used the term "superiority" do not see natives as barbarians. Rather, the term tends to be used in the context of neutral discussions of the military specifics of a particular segment of the Conquest. But the heavy emphasis on so-called military superiority is *potentially* pernicious because of the way it can be read as an acceptable recycling of the old superiority myth. Web sites devoted to the Conquest often explain it in terms of European weaponry, but natives tend to be judged as primitive or unintelligent for not also having invented such weapons. Guns and steel are emphasized as the key factors, but natives, especially a scapegoated Moctezuma, still tend to be seen as "superstitious and weak."[30]

When the weapons factor is removed from context and privileged as the sole or overwhelming Spanish advantage, the entire Conquest comes down to the clash of superior and inferior weapons. But behind that clash lies the larger more problematic clash of civilization and barbarism. Whether the focus is on weapons, words, ideas, or the intervention of God, as long as the implication is that Spaniards were in some sense better than Native Americans, we are not moving any closer to better understanding the Conquest.

In this final section of the chapter I shall suggest five factors that, in combination, better explain, the Conquest's outcome. None of these explanations is entirely original; I have not found the lost key to the Pandora's Box of infallible Conquest explanations. But that means that all five—in particular the first three—are well evidenced, well documented, and easily pursued further in the historical record.

The conquistadors had two great allies, without which the Conquest would not have taken place. One of these was disease. For ten millennia the Americas had been isolated from the rest of the world. The greater numbers of people in the Old World, and the greater variety of domesticated animals from which such diseases as smallpox, measles, and flu originated, meant that Europeans and Africans arrived in the New World with a deadly array of germs. These germs still killed Old World peoples, but they had developed relatively high levels of immunity compared to Native Americans, who died rapidly and in staggeringly high numbers. During the century and a half after Columbus's first voyage, the Native American population fell by as much as 90 percent.[31]

Sudden epidemics had immediate impacts on the invasions of the Mexica and Inca empires. When Prescott put the fall of Tenochtitlán down to "causes more potent than those from human agency" he was in a way correct. The Mexica capital fell not by the force of Spanish arms, but to disease and plague. The siege of the island city cut off food supplies, but as starvation approached, defenders succumbed to plague or disease. Smallpox seems to have been the prime culprit. As Spaniards and their Nahua allies moved through the devastated city, they found pile after pile of corpses, and huddled groups of the dying, covered with telltale pustules. As the Franciscan chronicler Sahagún later put it, "the streets were so filled with the dead and sick people that our men walked over nothing but bodies."[32]

Diseases moved through the Americas faster than germ-carrying Europeans and Africans could. Moctezuma's successor, Cuitlahuac, was killed by smallpox during the siege of Tenochtitlán, but the Inca emperor Huayna Capac, and then his successor, both died of the disease before Pizarro and his colleagues had even reached the empire. A succession dispute arose as a result; Huayna Capac's two surviving sons, Atahuallpa and Huascar, attempted to share power, but the arrangement soon dissolved into a civil war that Pizarro was able to manipulate to his own benefit.[33]

The two great native empires in the early sixteenth century were not the only regions hit by Old World diseases. It is unlikely that any corner of the Americas escaped unscathed. The virus that killed Huayna Capac in the late 1520s was probably a continuation of the great pandemic that arrived in the Caribbean in 1518. It was brought to Mexico by the Narváez expedition of 1519, spread by the Spaniards and Africans led by Cortés and Alvarado through central and southern Mexico and into Guatemala, traveling rapidly through Central America in the early 1520s, before fanning out across South America. This smallpox pandemic, which alone killed millions of Native Americans, was followed in the 1530s by a lethal pandemic of measles that likewise ran from Mesoamerica to the Andes. These and successive waves of disease penetrated up into North America, decimating the densely populated lower Mississippi, and southwest into Amazonia, where large towns shrank to villages or became uninhabited. Whereas disease aided and accelerated the Conquest among Nahuas, Mayas, and Andeans, it averted invasion in regions such as the lower Mississippi and Amazon. Too few people were left to attract major expeditions and not until modern times were the population levels of the original native empires even realized.[34]

The second great ally of the conquistadors was native disunity in its many forms and manifestations. Native American identity was highly localized; native peoples saw themselves as members of particular communities or city-states, very seldom as members of larger ethnic groups and certainly not as anything even approaching the category of "Indians" or "natives." The nature of native identity was thus the root of a native disunity that the invaders encouraged to blossom. Natives allied to the Spanish cause were essential to the Conquest, almost always outnumbering many times over the Spanish and African members of an expedition. Their role in saving companies from disaster and turning the tide of Conquest wars can hardly be overstated. As Cortés himself admitted in a rare moment of candor, one of the factors in the Spanish favor was that "many of the natives were our allies and would assist."[35] Two further examples of how native disunity aided Spaniards were the roles played by native interpreters and the cooperation and collaboration of native rulers—the latter often stemming from their desire to advance their own dynasties and communities at the expense of neighboring ones.

#3

The third well-evidenced factor that helps to explain the Conquest's outcome is weaponry. Much has been made of five military advantages that Spaniards allegedly enjoyed: guns, steel, horses, war dogs, and the tactical skills needed to maximize the impact of these. But the advantages they offered faded during the Conquest period, as unconquered natives acquired the same technology; the Araucanian use of pikes and horses is a good example.[36] Furthermore, the theoretical tactical advantage of Spanish weapons was often very different from the actual possibilities for their application in the Americas. Arguably, the limited applicability of Spanish weapons such as guns and horses made the way in which they were used all the more important.[37] Nevertheless, it seems clear that guns, horses, and mastiffs were a minor factor.

Horses and dogs were in limited supply for most of the Conquest period, and both animals could only be used in battle under certain circumstances— horses on open ground, and dogs at close quarters, preferably against the unarmed. The insistence by the conquistador Vargas Machuca on the importance of dogs was based entirely on his opinion that "the Indian greatly fears the horse, and the harquebus, but he fears the dog more." Yet the general fearfulness of the "Indian" was mostly wishful thinking on the part of invaders. Another colonial writer, Herrera, details the gutting by a dog of an unarmed native chief on Hispaniola in 1502, but otherwise offers no evidence in his eight-volume Conquest history of the military utility of dogs.[38]

Conquistadors greatly prized horses, and during campaigns they exchanged hands for high prices. But this was not primarily because they offered a military advantage against native warriors. To some extent horses were valued because expeditions often traveled long distances over difficult ground, but they were only a rapid means of transportation if the whole company was mounted. Above all horses were prized because they were a status symbol; there were not enough to go around, they were expensive to buy and maintain, and their ownership placed one in a separate category that came with a larger share of the spoils. At the *fundición,* or meltdown of precious mineral booty, at such places as Cajamarca in 1533, larger shares were given to men with horses. Yet despite the enormous social importance of being a horseman, when it came to fighting, even Francisco Pizarro preferred to be on the ground.[39]

Guns, too, were of limited use. Cannons were few in number in the Americas, and without roads or navigable rivers, their transportation was a major challenge. Much of the Americas where Spaniards fought was tropical or subtropical, and in the humidity the powder became too wet to fire. Firearms, in the form of harquebuses, whose unwieldy barrels required the support of tripods, were likewise not plentiful and required dry powder. Vargas Machuca advocated Spaniards using harquebuses in the Americas, but his detailed exposition on how to avoid damaging the gun, getting it wet, or discharging it prematurely or by accident would surely have caused any conquistador to think twice about carrying such a weapon.[40] The more reliable and faster-loading musket was not invented until decades after Cortés and Pizarro invaded the American mainland. Nor had Europeans yet developed volley-fire techniques, in which soldiers formed banks of rows in order to provide continuous fire, although there were seldom enough firearms in a Conquest company to have made good use of such a technique. Those Spaniards who did have firearms were lucky to get a single shot off before reversing the weapon to use as a club or dropping it to concentrate on sword wielding.[41]

The one weapon, then, whose efficacy is indubitable was the steel sword. It alone was worth more than a horse, a gun, and a mastiff put together. Because a steel sword was longer and less brittle than the obsidian weapons of Mesoamerican warriors, and longer and sharper than Andean clubbing weapons or copper-tipped axes, a Spaniard could fight for hours and receive light flesh wounds and bruises while killing many natives. Spanish swords were just the right length for reaching an enemy who lacked a similar weapon. Pizarro preferred to fight on foot so he could better manipulate his sword. Descriptions of battles in which Spanish swordplay caused terrible slaughter among native forces pepper the Conquest accounts of Cieza de León, Cortés, Díaz, Gómara, Jerez, Oviedo y Baños, Zárate, and others. Military historian John Guilmartin deftly summarizes the point: "While Spanish success in combat cannot be attributed to a single factor, it is clear that the other elements of Spanish superiority took effect within a tactical matrix established by the effectiveness of Spanish hand-held slashing and piercing weapons."[42]

This trilogy of factors—disease, native disunity, and Spanish steel—goes most of the way toward explaining the Conquest's outcome. Remove just one and the likelihood of the failure of expeditions under Cortés, Pizarro, and others would have been very high. As Clendinnen has observed of the Spanish-Mexica war, both Spaniards and natives were aware that the Conquest was "a close-run thing," a point that applies broadly across the Conquest.[43] The failed expeditions outnumbered successful ones, and cautionary tales can be found by looking at the fate of Spanish expeditions such as Montejo's early attempts to conquer Yucatan, the early campaigns into Oaxaca's northern sierra, or the Pizarro-Orellana journey into Amazonia.[44] Spaniards would have suffered steady mortality from fatal wounds, starvation, disease, and so on, with survivors limping back to Spain or to colonial enclaves scattered along the coasts and islands. Time and again, this outcome was averted because Spanish steel weapons permitted them to hold out long enough for native allies to save them, while the next wave of epidemic disease disrupted native defenses.

#4   A fourth factor also played an important role—the culture of war. For example, the Mexica were hampered by certain battle conventions that the Spaniards ignored. Mexica methods of war emphasized the observation of prebattle ceremonies that eliminated the possibility of surprise attacks and the capture of Spaniards for ritual execution rather than killing them on the spot.[45] The conquistadors were outraged by the apparent native disdain for human life, as manifested in elaborate rituals of human "sacrifice." But from the Mexica perspective, it was the Spaniards who disrespected human life by slaughtering natives en masse, killing noncombatants, and killing from a distance.[46] Indeed, the pomp and ritual with which the Mexica—and to some extent all Mesoamericans—preferred to take a human life suggests profound respect, in contrast to Spanish practices, which seem indiscriminate and insufficiently ritualized.

But the culture of war must be considered along with other explanatory factors for several reasons. First, it is only one aspect of the combat that took place during the Spanish invasions of Mesoamerica. Both Spaniards and natives engaged at times in the killing of noncombatants, in mass slaughter, in killing from a distance (natives used arrows most effectively), and in ritual displays of public violence and ritualized executions—such as the Spanish burning alive of native lords in town plazas. Second, the point applies most to the Mexica, less to other Mesoamericans such as the Mixtecs and Mayas, and very little to Andeans and other Native Americans.[47] Third, the larger context of the point about different methods of war is not that of general cultural differences between Spaniards and natives, as it is usually presented, but that of the circumstances of war. Natives were fighting on their home ground; Spaniards were not. Spaniards had nothing more to lose than their lives. This may seem like everything—Cortés told the king that the conquistadors prevailed in part because "we had to protect our lives."[48] But Native Americans stood to lose their families and their homes and were thus quicker to compromise, to accommodate the invaders, to seek ways to avoid fullscale or protracted wars. While Dibble describes the "seasonal" Mexica view of war—"there was a time to plant, a time to harvest, and a time to fight"—as distinct to Mexica culture, this was a practical consideration that would have been made by all Native Americans—and by Spaniards, had they been fighting on their home ground.[49]

Finally, the Spanish Conquest can only be fully understood if placed in the larger historical context of the age of expansion. This larger story is not #5 one of Spanish superiority, or even of Western European superiority, but is instead a complex phenomenon in world history that transcends the particulars of the Spanish Conquest in the Americas. If we focus only on the century following Columbus's voyages we see Mexica and Inca warriors as losers, West Africans as fighting slaves, and Spaniards as quite reasonably contemplating a world empire. But the age of expansion began with the rise of empires outside Europe, with the Mexica fanning out across Mesoamerica and the Inca dominating the Andes, and in West Africa with the rising of the Songhay empire from the ashes of that of Mali. In Europe, the Ottomans and the Muscovites began empire building before the Spaniards, as did the Portuguese—who beat their Iberian neighbors in the race for a sea route to East Asia. And after the sixteenth century the Spanish empire was gradually eclipsed by the trading and colonial networks of the Dutch, English, and French.[50]

Looking at human history over thousands of years, the Spanish Conquest is a mere episode in the globalization of access to resources of food production. The plants and animals of certain Old World environments and regions have a greater potential as food, and the peoples of those regions have enjoyed advantages over others as a result. But eventually, through uneven encounters, those advantages have been introduced to the previously disadvantaged regions.

In the case of Europeans introducing new foods to Native Americans, the parallel introduction of Old World diseases made the encounter especially uneven, while colonialism hindered native access to these new resources. This process is too broad and complex to be understood in terms of the alleged and simple "superiority" of one group of people over another. It is also a process that is incomplete. We are still living through the long period of uneven encounters and the gradual globalization of resources.[51]

Epilogue
Cuauhtémoc's Betrayal

He who's been captured is crimson mudfish don Hernando [Cuauhtémoc].
And don Pedro [Tetlepanquetzal]! It's true! They're in a great ceiba tree!
We've bloodied ourselves on that reedy turf.

> —"The Fish Song," from
> *The Songs of the Aztecs* (late sixteenth century)

The equivocal conduct of Paxbolonacha during these fateful days does not
inspire admiration, and if he had any part in the sordid drama that culminated in Cuauhtémoc's death, he deserves severe condemnation.

> —France Scholes and Ralph Roys (1948)

Cuauhtémoc, not Cortés, triumphed in death and history as an important
symbol of Mexican nationalism.

> —Thomas Benjamin (2000)

Eventually, after the invaders were gone, he would reemerge into a new birth,
cleansed of the pollution of death and sacrilege to rule a new kingdom from
the embers of the old. History, however, would not remain the same.

> —Gananath Obeyesekere (1992)

It was the year 1525. The day was Mardi Gras, Shrove Tuesday, the last Tuesday in February. It was early in the morning, still relatively cool.

The place was Itzamkanac, called Acalan by Nahuatl speakers, meaning
"the place of canoes."[1] The canoe was the principal means of transportation
for the people of this city, located where the rivers that Spaniards later named
the Caribe and the San Pedro converge to create the Candelaria. Itzamkanac
was about 50 miles as the crow flies from the Gulf coast, further by canoe
down the Candelaria. Today the invisible border between Guatemala and the
Mexican state of Campeche lies 20 miles to the south of the forested, uninhabited site where Itzamkanac once thrived.

In 1525 several thousand Mayas lived in the city. It was the capital of the
kingdom of the Mactun people, as they called themselves—or Chontal Maya,

as we know them, from the Nahuatl term meaning "foreigner." Foreigners were very much on the minds of the Mactun Mayas that Shrove Tuesday morning. For the past fortnight, the city's natives had been outnumbered by over 200 Spaniards, several hundred Africans, and at least 3,000 Nahuas. These visitors had not come by canoe, but had struggled over land all the way from Tenochtitlán (still being rebuilt as the colonial capital city of Mexico). Some of the members of this expedition would be remembered well by history, including the expedition leader, Cortés, doña Marina or La Malinche, his interpreter and mother of his infant son Martín, and Bernal Díaz, who would become famous centuries after his death as a chronicler of the Conquest. Also present was Cuauhtémoc, the surviving Mexica emperor and now a puppet ruler under permanent guard. Rather than leave Cuauhtémoc in Tenochtitlán, where he might have fomented revolt, Cortés had brought the emperor with him, along with the rulers of the other major cities that had once been part of the Mexica empire.

Itzamkanac was not the ultimate destination of the foreign visitors—that was far-off Honduras—but they had arrived there greatly in need of rest and provisions after a nerve-racking crossing of the San Pedro Martír river and the swamps that formed Mactun's western border. There were no hostilities, no conquest in the conventional sense. Yet the presence of these uninvited guests was not especially welcome to the Mayas. As the expedition moved through Mactun's border towns, the king, Paxbolonacha, had sent his son to tell Cortés that he had died and that the foreigners would do best to move quickly through Mactun territory. This seems like a weak ruse, but Paxbolonacha was simply stalling, preparing a welcome that he knew would strain the resources of his kingdom but that he must have hoped would shorten the foreigners' visit.

If the strain on local resources was not enough, by the third Tuesday of his visit Cortés had overstayed his welcome by considerably raising the level of tension in Itzamkanac. Within five days the visitors would be gone. But they would leave behind them a gruesome reminder of the darker side of the Spanish presence in the Americas—the body of Cuauhtémoc, headless, hanging by his feet from a tree.

The circumstances of Cuauhtémoc's death have survived in sources that tell the story from four different perspectives. There are similar Spanish accounts written by Cortés and Gómara, and the somewhat different version by Díaz. There is an account by a Nahua nobleman, don Fernando de Alva Ixtlilxóchitl, a descendent of Coanacoch, the ruler of Texcoco who had been brought along on the expedition and was one of the lords hanged in Itzamkanac. Written the following century, Ixtlilxóchitl's account was based in part on the oral traditions of Texcoco. Finally, there is the Mactun Mayas's own account, written in Chontal Maya.[2]

Using and comparing the various source accounts, I will tell the tale of Cuauhtémoc's death in four stages, connecting the perspectives of these accounts to the seven myths of the Conquest. The first stage of the tale is the Spanish journey into Mactun territory, the second is the expedition's stay in Itzamkanac, the third is the discovery of an alleged plot, and the fourth is the violent dénouement at dawn on Shrove Tuesday.

The starting point for the Spanish accounts is the onset of the journey from Tenochtitlán. Cortés's narrative is part of the missive known to us as his fifth letter to the king, which begins with his departure from the new colonial capital in October 1524. The sojourn in Itzamkanac is thus merely an episode in the long, difficult journey from Mexico to Honduras, and it comes on gradually as the expedition moves slowly into Mactun territory. The Spaniards and their allies help themselves to local resources, despite which, according to Cortés, the people were "unafraid" and "very friendly." Gómara likewise portrays the natives as most accommodating and very impressed by the Spanish construction of a bridge across the San Pedro Martír river gorge. In Díaz's version, native hospitality is begrudging, several Spaniards are killed, and the expedition arrives in Itzamkanac in dire need of provisions.

Cortés and Gómara both report the ruse of Paxbolonacha's alleged death, and both claim that Cortés saw through it, persuading the king's son to bring his father to the small town where the expedition members had been spending the week. Paxbolonacha arrives, apologizes "shamefacedly" (Gómara's term), and brings Cortés and his vast company back to Itzamkanac. There the Maya ruler provides abundant supplies, and even "some gold and a few women, although I had not asked him for anything" (claims Cortés). Gómara numbers the women at 20, and adds that the Spaniards "were fed bountifully the whole time they were there."

None of this is mentioned by Díaz, who offers a different episode altogether, one whose slaving and plundering nature he seems to find embarrassing for the Spaniards (as opposed to the lie that supposedly embarrassed the Maya king). In return for Mactun Maya assistance during the next stage of the expedition's journey into the Itzá Maya kingdom of the Petén, in northern Guatemala, Cortés agrees to send a raiding party of 80 Spaniards (Díaz included) to a border region that had recently rebelled against Mactun authority. The raid benefits the Maya lords in Itzamkanac and helps provide Cortés's company with supplies.

In the Cortés account, the Cuauhtémoc affair begins late on Monday night (27 February 1525), when "an honored citizen" of Tenochtitlán (that is, a Mexica spy working for Cortés), named Mexicalcingo, comes to Cortés's tent (the third stage of the story). The spy informs the Spanish leader of a plot being hatched by the captive lords of the three principal cities of the Valley of Mexico—Cuauhtémoc of Tenochtitlán, Coanacoch of Texcoco, and Tetlepanquetzal of Tacuba. The report is a show-and-tell performance, with Mexicalcingo explaining to Cortés "a certain drawing on a piece of paper used in these parts" (that Gómara describes as "a paper with glyphs and names of the lords who were plotting his death"). The alleged plan is simple: "to kill me [Cortés] and all my company," and send messengers to Tenochtitlán "to incite the people to kill all the Spaniards in the city." Thereafter the rest of the empire would be regained and the invaders all put to death. Gómara's description of the plot is virtually identical to that of Cortés. In the Díaz version, there are two Mexica informers—whom he identifies by their adopted Spanish names of Tapia and Juan Velásquez—and the plot is simpler, consisting of killing the expedition's Spaniards, rather than reclaiming the whole empire.

In the Cortés and Gómara accounts, in the final stage of the story the Spanish leader moves swiftly, arresting the three lords, interrogating them separately, and using the old trick of telling each that the others had already confessed—until each in turn did confess. Supposedly, Cuauhtémoc and Tetlepanquetzal thereby emerge as the ringleaders. "These two were hanged," remarks Cortés casually. Gómara has three lords "tried" by Cortés "and forthwith sentenced to be hanged." Oddly the third lord is not Coanacoch, but one Tlacatlec—a variant repeated by Herrera, although the illustration in his *Historia General* shows one victim hanging from a gallows (see Figure 20). The other lords were released, under threat of like punishment (in Cortés's words) "if they ever relapse, but they are so frightened that I do not think that they will, for as they have never discovered from whom I learnt of their plot, they believe it was done by some magic art, and that nothing can be concealed from me."[3] This "magic art" was Cortés's compass and ship's chart, which he claimed the native lords viewed as some kind of crystal ball that revealed all things to him, a belief that "I encouraged." Gómara likewise gives credit to this story, and to the fear and credulity of the native lords—Paxbolonacha included.

As is generally characteristic of the Cortés and Gómara accounts of the Conquest, the version by the Spanish leader is self-justifying, while that of his biographer pushes the envelope a little further to glorify Cortés as bold, brilliant, and just. Even the hanging of the three lords is viewed as merciful, because they had "expected to be killed and burned." Díaz is considerably less charitable toward his former captain. In his version, there is not even a pretense of a trial, merely an interrogation that reveals Cuauhtémoc and Tetlepanquetzal to have merely heard disgruntled talk among the Nahuas, rather than plotted a revolt. Yet "without any more proofs whatever," Cortés has the two of them hanged "immediately."

To drive home his negative opinion of the whole affair, Díaz has Cuauhtémoc deliver a final damning speech: "Oh Malinche [i.e., Cortés]! Now I understand your false promises and the kind of death you have had in store for me. For you are killing me unjustly. May God demand justice from you,

Fig. 20. Title page to the third volume of Antonio de Herrera's
Historia General de los Hechos de los Castellanos (1615).
The illustrations include a depiction of the hanging of Cuauhtémoc.

151

as it was taken from me when I entrusted myself to you in my city of Mexico!" Díaz follows this up with a speech of his own to the reader, confessing how much he liked Cuauhtémoc personally, and how undeserved the deaths of the hanged lords seemed to him—and "to all of us who were there, to whom the death that they were given seemed most unjust and wicked [*mal*]." Díaz does not let Cuauhtémoc's parting curse rest. He depicts Cortés as so tormented by his conscience over the emperor's execution that he cannot sleep, and one night, "getting up out of bed and wandering into a room where there had been idols, part of the principal building of this settlement, he missed his step and fell down more than a dozen feet, giving himself a serious head wound."[4] Stumbling off a pyramid in his pajamas the great conquistador narrowly avoids an ignominious death. Thus did Cuauhtémoc take a little revenge.

How do the accounts by the Nahua nobleman and by the Mactun Mayas differ from the versions recorded by Spaniards? Ixtlilxóchitl's version is similar to Díaz's, only more sympathetic to the alleged plotters and centered on a unique defense of the condemned lords. The first two stages of the tale are highly truncated in the Texcoco version, with the main story beginning on the Monday evening, when Spaniards and Nahua warriors alike are celebrating the pre-Lenten festival of *carnestolendas* (that runs for three days from Sunday through Shrove Tuesday). The three Nahua kings are "engaged in pleasant conversation, jesting (or amusing themselves) with one another." Their morale uplifted by the (false) rumor that Cortés had decided to lead the expedition back to Mexico, their "jests" include arguing over which of them and their respective cities will be dominant in the valley after their return.

In Ixtlilxóchitl's version, the discovery of the plot is initiated by Cortés, who has his Mexica spy find out what the Nahua lords are talking about. The spy tells the truth, but that is not enough for Cortés, who sees an opportunity to manufacture a native plot and execute the royal conspirators, "so there would be no natural lord in the land." At dawn, Cortés hangs the lords, one at a time—not just the three kings, but also eight alleged plotters. The last to be strung up is Coanacoch. When the Texcocan ruler's brother begins to rally his warriors in response, Cortés cuts Coanacoch down. But, writes Ixtlilxóchitl, his royal ancestor died anyway, a few days later.[5]

The Mactun Mayas are invisible in the Spanish and Nahua accounts but are naturally at the center of their own history of the incident. Written down in the Chontal Maya language early in the seventeenth century, this account is part of a community history compiled during the previous century in Nahuatl and Chontal. The Maya version begins, not surprisingly, not with the departure of the expedition from Tenochtitlán, but with the arrival of the Spaniards at the edge of Mactun territory. The Maya response toward the Spanish presence is not the fawning welcome described by Cortés and Gómara, nor is it quite the initial hostility and then grudging hospitality depicted by Díaz. Instead, the story turns on Paxbolonacha's attempt to save face by obliging Cortés to come and see him (just as Moctezuma had lured Cortés into Tenochtitlán six years earlier). Cortés stands his ground, forcing the Mactun Maya king to leave Itzamkanac and meet the Spaniard in the smaller town where he waited. Once Paxbolonacha understands that the expedition will only be passing through his kingdom, he agrees that "it would be good if he [Cortés] left," but in the meantime, his hospitality is extended to the Spaniards. Of the tale's second stage, the expedition's stay in Itzamkanac, the Maya narrative consists of a single sentence: "Therefore they rested for twenty days."

At this point the Chontal Maya account mentions that Cuauhtémoc was accompanying the Spaniards. It describes the subsequent events as follows:

> And it happened that he [Cuauhtémoc] said to the ruler [*ahau*] Paxbolonacha, "My lord ruler, these Castilian men will one day give you much misery and kill your people. In my opinion we should kill them, for I bring many officers and you also are many." This is what Cuauhtémoc said to Paxbolonacha, ruler of the people of Mactun, who, upon hearing this speech of Cuauhtémoc's, replied that he would first think about what he wished to do about his speech. And, in considering his speech fully, he observed that the Castilian men behaved well, that they neither killed a single man nor beat a single man, and that they wished only to be given honey, turkey hens, maize, and various fruits, day after day. Thus he concluded, "I cannot therefore display two faces, two hearts, to the Castilian men." But Cuauhtémoc, the ruler from Mexico, continued to press him about it, for he wished to kill the Castilian men. Because of this, the ruler Paxbolonacha told the *Capitán del Valle* [Cortés], "My lord *Capitán del Valle*, this ruler Cuauhtémoc who is with you, observe him so that he does not revolt and betray you, for three or four times he talked to me about killing you." Upon hearing these words the *Capitán del Valle* seized him [Cuauhtémoc] and had him bound in chains. He was in chains for three days. Then they baptized him. It is not known what his baptismal name was; some say he was named don Juan and some say he was named don Hernando. After being named, his head was cut off, and it was impaled on a ceiba tree in front of the pagan temple [*otot ciçin*, devil's home] at Yaxdzan.[6]

The Maya account has a ring of verisimilitude to it because it is so devoid of stereotypes. The protagonists are not divided into the noble and the wicked, the brave and the feeble, or the civilized and the savage. There is neither a tone of judgement nor an obvious moral to the tale. Certainly the Maya narrative defends a partisan political position, as do the Spanish and Nahua accounts, but that defense is more subtly articulated.

⸺

Who is the chief protagonist in this drama, the character upon whom the tale turns? In the Spanish-language accounts it is Cortés, who discovers or invents the plot and orchestrates a rapid arrest, judgment, and execution. The degree to which Cortés is in control of the expedition and the outcome of events marks him as one of the mythical "exceptional men." Cortés's actions were not exceptional, however. Like other conquistadors, he followed predictable patterns of behavior and conformed to what in effect were Conquest procedures. One of these was the capture of native rulers, who would subsequently be ransomed, released, and confirmed in office as supposed puppets, or executed. The higher ranking the ruler, the lower his chance of surviving captivity. The circumstances of the deaths of Cuauhtémoc, Coanacoch, and Tetlepanquetzal, and Cortés's actions—regardless of whether he manufactured the plot, was responding to the reports of spies, or was tipped off by Paxbolonacha—likewise typified Conquest procedure.

The incident at Itzamkanac also reveals how misleading is the image of the conquistadors as soldiers sent by their king as part of a Spanish army that invades and conquers with little assistance and against great numerical odds. As was characteristic of Spanish accounts, the Spanish narratives of the expedition that passed through the Mactun Maya kingdom downplay the role of Nahua allies and almost completely ignore that of African slaves and auxiliaries. However, the crisis of discontent among the Nahua rulers, whatever form it may have taken, highlights the degree to which Nahua warriors and porters outnumbered Spaniards—by a factor of fifteen to one. These numbers served to make the expedition more intimidating to local rulers such as Paxbolonacha, but also necessitated the full cooperation of Nahua leaders. Spanish Conquest expeditions were private companies formed for profit, dependent on the Africans who were mostly purchased, and on the native warriors and porters who were recruited by co-opting native élites. The crucial context to Cuauhtémoc's execution—its very rationale—was the presence and significance of a large force of native allies. Cortés could not take a chance on Cuauhtémoc's alleged plot being genuine because the expedition included so many Nahua warriors.

The events at Itzamkanac four years after 1521, the date traditionally assigned to the Conquest of Mexico, illustrate the degree to which the Conquest was a far more complex and protracted affair than the myth of completion suggests. Cortés was still engaged in long expeditions of exploration and conquest. His ostensible motive for traveling to Honduras was to punish Cristóbal de Olid, a rebellious captain of Cortés's, but he also sought to explore the region between Mexico and Honduras. Indeed, the expedition marked the first time Europeans and Africans had ever set foot in Itzamkanac. Four years after the fall of Tenochtitlán most of Mesoamerica had yet to be touched directly by Old World feet, and the same was true of the Andes four years after Atahuallpa's execution. The Spanish control of even the core Conquest site, Tenochtitlán, four years after its capture, was tenuous enough that Cortés could be "really worried" (in Gómara's words) by the alleged plotters' understanding that the Spaniards in the capital were too few, too new to Mexico, lacking battle skills, and quarrelsome.

During those pre-Lenten days of 1525 in Itzamkanac there was much apparent communication across language barriers, with Cortés making use of Malinche to understand his spies and interrogate the arrested Nahua rulers—and Cuauhtémoc likewise delivering his last words through Malinche. Conquistadors often made bold claims of communication, asserting that their interpreters allowed them to express faithfully religious and political messages to native lords. Even in the Chontal-language version, Paxbolonacha converses both with Cuauhtémoc and Cortés. The dialogues seem clear within the context of each individual account.

But that clarity breaks down when the texts are compared. In the end, we cannot be sure there was a plot at all, or who knew of it or invented it, or whose initiative catalyzed the incident, or whether Paxbolonacha was central to events or completely out of the loop. Who betrayed Cuauhtémoc? Mexicalcingo, Paxbolonacha, or Cortés? The whole affair could easily be seen as a tragic mess of misunderstandings. Just as the conquistadors perpetuated a myth of verbal communication, so have some modern scholars argued that the communication barriers of language, interpretation, wishful thinking, and inflexible agendas characterized the Conquest and influenced its course. Yet the events surrounding Cuauhtémoc's death illustrate the fact that accurate translation between Spanish and native tongues was less important than the communication of intent and interest—that all the protagonists in Itzamkanac were able to convey, to the demise of the Nahua rulers, to the uneasy relief of the Maya king, and to the troubled conscience of Cortés.

Reflecting myths of native weakness and Spanish strength, the Cortés and Gómara versions of the events at Itzamkanac are full of conquistador stereotypes about "Indians." Natives are duplicitous, scheming, untrustworthy and yet also easily frightened, credulous, and superstitious. The Maya king and his son lie about the father's feigned demise, while the Nahua lords plot for days. The Mayas are so impressed by the bridge the Spaniards build (with African and Nahua labor, no doubt) that "they were convinced that nothing was impossible to the Spaniards," Gómara asserts. Nahuas and Mayas alike are certain that Cortés can see "all things" in his compass—from the road to the next town to the details of the plot against him. The wonder of the Spaniards at their own technology (the precursor to the emphasis by modern historians on Spanish technological "superiority") and their assumption of native "superstition" is a potent combination in the conquistador mind.

Yet the actions of the Nahua and Maya lords showed them to be far from the frightened, fatalistic, traumatized natives of the desolation myth. Although Díaz's picture of murmurs of discontent is more plausible than the full-scale conspiracy imagined by Cortés and Gómara, one still gets the impression that Cuauhtémoc and his fellow Nahua nobles were more than capable of seeking ways to improve their circumstances—even mounting an armed resistance like that organized by Manco Inca in Peru from 1536 on. As for Paxbolonacha, his decisions and actions were based on what he perceived to be in the best interests of his own status, of the stability of his dynastic position, of the security of Itzamkanac and its inhabitants, and of the general integrity of his kingdom. From the perspective of the Spaniards, and of the executed lords, the Itzamkanac affair was an episode in the Conquest. From the Mactun Maya perspective, it was a successful diplomatic manipulation of a situation that might otherwise have been a local tragedy.[7]

The Cortés and Gómara accounts have Cortés leaving Paxbolonacha trembling in his boots. But Díaz portrays him as having made a sound deal, offering guides and porters in return for Spaniards and Nahuas risking their lives in a punitive expedition to the margins of Mactun territory. And in the Mayas's own account, Paxbolonacha controls the outcome of the incident; he decides whether the uprising against the Spaniards takes place or not. The Maya account has a political purpose related to a later colonial context—to demonstrate Paxbolonacha's loyalty to the Spaniards—but it is couched in terms that preserve the Maya ruler's personal and political integrity.

All the elements of native cultural vitality during the Conquest period are here: the perception of the Conquest as in some sense a conquest *by* native lords; the use of political and military alliances with Spaniards to further local interests; the partial and complex collaboration of the élite; the flourishing of native municipal communities in colonial times (symbolized here by the Mactun Maya account, written alphabetically but in Nahuatl and Maya). Like so much of Conquest history, the Itzamkanac affair looks like one thing but is really many things, depending upon one's perspective and concerns. It both supports and undermines the myths of the Conquest. And as much as we might try to find out what "really" happened, we remain prisoners to the written accounts that have survived, as rich and as varied as they are.

The myths surrounding Cuauhtémoc's death, like the myths of the Conquest, are metaphors for all that happened and all that is said to have happened during the Spanish invasion of the Americas. If the particulars of a past event can be seen as "historical metaphors of a mythical reality,"[8] then the details discussed in this book are the mythical metaphors of historical reality—that is, the reality perceived by conquistadors and reconstructed and reified repeatedly over the centuries by colonial Spaniards and historians in the West who have studied colonialism. I have sought to offer a different perceived reality, one constructed through a cross-reading of multiple sources; one that, I believe, for all its own filters and biases, comes closer to telling us "something true" about the world of the Spanish Conquest.[9]

If myths dramatize the human world and its past "in a constellation of powerful metaphors," then our purpose as readers of history is to explore those metaphors, to journey behind them into the motives, methods, and mundane patterns of human behavior. Or, if "purpose" sounds too dutiful, perhaps we can turn to Bernal Díaz for a simpler reason for our reading; that the story has in it "much to ponder" and is, in the end, "a remarkable tale."[10]

Permissions

Fig. 1.   From Harris, *Voyages and Travels* (1744 [1705]), vol. 2, facing p. 114. Reproduced by permission of the John Carter Brown Library at Brown University.

Fig. 2.   Reproduced by permission of the Museo Nacional de Arte, Mexico City.

Figs. 3 and 4. Reproduced by permission of the John Carter Brown Library at Brown University.

Fig. 5.   Reproduced by permission of the John Carter Brown Library at Brown University.

Fig. 6.   Reproduced by permission of the Jay I. Kislak Foundation Inc.

Fig. 7.   Volume 3, Book XII, Folio 58v of Sahagún's *General History of the Things of New Spain*; reproduced by permission of the Archivo General de la Nación, Mexico City.

Fig. 8.   Plate 58 in fray Diego de Durán's *The History of the Indies of New Spain*; reproduced by permission of the Biblioteca Nacional, Madrid.

Fig. 9.   Reproduced by permission of the Banco Nacional de México.

Fig. 10. From Harris, *Voyages and Travels*, Vol. 2 (1748), facing p. 97; reproduced by permission of the John Carter Brown Library at Brown University.

Fig. 11. From Volume 3, Book XII, Folio 26r of Sahagún's *General History of the Things of New Spain*; reproduced by permission of the Archivo General de la Nación, Mexico City.

Fig. 12. Reproduced by permission of the John Carter Brown Library at Brown University.

Fig. 13. Reproduced by permission of the Smithsonian Institution.

Fig. 14. Reproduced by permission of the Creators Syndicate.

Fig. 15. Reproduced by permission of the John Carter Brown Library at Brown University.

Fig. 16. Reproduced by permission of The Royal Library, Copenhagen; p. 400 of the print edition by Adorno and Murra and on the Royal Library website (www.kb.dk/elib/mss/poma).

Fig. 17. Reproduced by permission of the Tozzer Library of the Harvard College Library, Harvard University.

Fig. 18. p. 58 of Hergé's *Prisoners of the Sun*; reproduced by permission of Moulinsart S. A.

Fig. 19. Reproduced by permission of the John Carter Brown Library at Brown University.

Fig. 20. Reproduced by permission of the John Carter Brown Library at Brown University.

Notes

Notes to the Acknowledgments

1. As vividly illustrated by Juan de Tovar in his sixteenth-century *Historia de la benida de los Yndios*: f. 85 (manuscript in JCBL as Codex Ind 2).
2. Motolinía wrote in 1541 that the region where the Seven Cities were being sought was where Álvar Núñez Cabeza de Vaca and his fellow survivors had been led on a journey of 700 leagues after seven years of captivity; Adorno and Pautz, *Cabeza de Vaca*, 2000, II: 30–31, 361, 428; III: 128, 142, 370–72. Mythical sevens can also be found in other parts of the Atlantic world that was created by European expansion; for example, the Dutch selected "seven of the boldest and ablest seamen" to explore Greenland in the 1630s; the seven kept a journal and acquired a semimythical status in European histories of exploration (Churchill, *Voyages and Travels*, 1704, II: 413–30).

Notes to the Introduction

1. Here, as throughout the book, I have made my own translations of Díaz (from Díaz, *Historia*, 1955 [1570]), or from the first published edition of *Historia*, 1632, a copy of which is in the JCBL (where I was also able to consult the 1795 Madrid edition). But as I have been hard pressed to improve on the Maudslay edition and have found the Cohen edition to be almost as reliable, and for the convenience of the reader, I cite one or the other or both of these editions; the references here are Díaz, *The True History*, 1908 [1570]: 39; *Conquest*, 1963 [1570]: 216, with the original passage being in *Historia*, 1632 [1570]: f. 65r.
2. Díaz, *Conquest*, 1963 [1570]: 214.
3. Cortés, letter of 1520; *Letters*, 1986: 102–110. For a scathing discussion of the inadequacy of Díaz's descriptions of Tenochtitlán, see Mund, *Les rapports complexes*, 2001: 57–74.
4. For centuries, historians were able to employ prevailing theories of historical analysis—from Enlightenment progressivism to Marxism—as the tools of their trade. But in recent decades postmodernists and other scholars have argued with growing success that such tools do not work. As philosophy professor Behan McCullagh suggests, it can be a shock to realize that we cannot escape the crushing ubiquity of subjectivity (*Truth*, 1998: 307, 1).
5. This amounts to a straightforward juxtaposition of two historicities, a contrast "between what happened and that which is said to have happened," to borrow a phrase of anthropologist Michel-Rolph Trouillot's, *Silencing the Past*, 1995: 106; his "two historicities" are also discussed on pp. 29 and 118.
6. Again, see Trouillot, *Silencing the Past*, 1995; "conditions of production" and "that which is said to have happened" are phrases borrowed from him (pp. 25 and 106).

7. In the nineteenth century, "myth" commonly implied "fiction" or "invention," as I am using the term here; in the early twentieth century scholars used it to describe stories that were "true" from the viewpoint of the cultures that created and valued such sacred traditions. Forty years ago, Mircea Eliade, the acclaimed French scholar of myth and religion, noted that both meanings of "myth" were then in use, making its usage "somewhat equivocal" (*Myth and Reality*, 1963: 1). The same is true today. Examples of recent uses of the two meanings of the term are Karl Taube's *Aztec and Maya Myths* (1993), which recounts creation mythology, ancient calendrics, and tales of the gods, and Stephen Steinberg's classic, *The Ethnic Myth* (2001 [1981]), which characterizes as a prevailing, popular misconception the idea that individual and group fates in the twentieth-century United States have been determined by ethnic identities and their cultural values. An example of a recent book that argues that a myth in one sense (the semi-fictional or distorted American myth of the "winning of the West") became a myth in the other sense (a treasured tradition of American history and identity) is Prats, *Invisible Natives*, 2002.
8. Doniger, *The Implied Spider*, 1998: 2–3; Eliade, *Myth and Reality*, 1963: 147–57.
9. Veyne, *Greeks*, 1988: 22; Tedlock, *Popol Vuh*, 1985: 64; both quoted in Hill Boone, *Stories in Red and Black*, 2000: 15. Also see Bricker, *The Indian Christ, the Indian King*, 1981: 3–4, and Salomon, "Testimonies," 1999: 51–57.
10. To paraphrase Jenkins, *Re-thinking History*, 1991: 32, whose phrase is "useful fictions."
11. "Something true about the world" and "one fiction among others" are phrases borrowed from McCullagh, *Truth*, 1998: 5 and Trouillot, *Silencing the Past*, 1995: 6, respectively.
12. Valle Inclán's remark is widely quoted; it was brought to my attention by Vargas Llosa, *Essays*, 1996: 325.
13. Prescott, *Conquest of Mexico*, 1909 [1843]: 3.
14. "Void" is the term that French writer J. M. G. Le Clézio uses; *Mexican Dream*, 1993: 176.

Notes to Chapter 1

1. Both quotes in Elliott, *The Old World and the New*, 1970: 10; Gómara assessment also cited in Fernández-Armesto, *Columbus*, 1991: 185, and quoted in Florescano, *Memory*, 1994: 80; Gómara quote at the top of this chapter is in Gómara, *Cortés*, 1964 [1552]: 4. In using Gómara I also consulted a manuscript copy of the first 81 chapters written in the early seventeenth century by the Nahua nobleman, Chimalpahin, but it did not appear to differ significantly from the 1552 publication (as confirmed by David Tavárez, personal communication; the manuscript is in the JCBL as Codex Sp 63).
2. Throughout this book I use the "Discovery" as shorthand for the European discovery of the Americas, the "Contact" for the same process, initial European–Native American contact, and the "Conquest" for the Spanish conquests in the Americas. I hope the reader will accept this device as a convenient way of avoiding both the controversy and baggage attached to "the discovery" and its sibling phrases (see Foner, "Our Monumental Mistakes," 1999, for example) and clumsy alternative formulations.
3. Again, both quoted in Elliott, *The Old World and the New*, 1970: 1.
4. Hanke, *Aristotle*, 1959: 11; Todorov, *Conquest*, 1984: 4.
5. Author's visit to National Air and Space Museum, Washington, D.C., January 2001; "Where Next, Columbus?" web page address is www.nasm.edu/galleries/ gal209. The exhibit is listed as "temporary" but has been up since 1992. The museum's use of Columbus in this way shows how the Genoese's "first voyage is still the world's most powerful metaphor for discovery," as Dor-Ner puts it (*Columbus*, 1991: 1; also quoted in Frederick, "Colonizing Columbus," 2001: 1).
6. Quoted in Trouillot, *Silencing the Past*, 1995: 82.

7. Prescott, *Conquest of Mexico*, 1909 [1843]: 3.

8. Quotes respectively from Keen, *Latin America*, 1996: 71; Diamond, *Guns, Germs, and Steel*, 1997: 91; Elliott, *Imperial Spain*, 1963: 51; Cohen's introduction to Zárate, *Peru*, 1981 [1555]: 15; Markham, *Discovery of Peru*, 1872: xiii; Schwartz, *Victors and Vanquished*, 2000: 1; Clendinnen, "'Fierce and Unnatural Cruelty,'" 1991: 12. There are numerous other examples of both "handful" and "adventurers" being used by scholars of various disciplines, as though it is a reflex association; one example of the former is in Dibble, *Conquest*, 1978: 7; and of latter is in Harris, *Aztecs, Moors, and Christians*, 2000: 117. Examples from older sources, in addition to Markham (just cited), include Henty, *By Right of Conquest*, 1890: ii (also quoted in Cowher, "A Handful of Adventurers?" 2001: 13).

9. The Jerez account is published as Jerez, *Verdadera relación*, 1985 [1534] and in translation in Markham, *Discovery of Peru*, 1872: 1–74; quote on p. 1; also quoted in Seed, "'Failing to Marvel,'" 1991: 15. Vargas Machuca, writing in the 1590s, likewise lauded the success of Spanish conquerors, "outnumbered five hundred to one," as a triumph against the odds that rivaled the ancient Greeks and Romans (*Milicia y Descripción*, 1599: 25v–26v).

10. Quotes, respectively, from Clendinnen, "'Fierce and Unnatural Cruelty,'" 1991: 12; Fernández-Armesto, "'Aztec' auguries," 1992: 287; Wachtel, "The Indian," 1984: 210 also quoted in Guilmartin, "The Cutting Edge," 1991: 42. There are numerous other examples of the same question being posed—a few more are Dibble, *Conquest*, 1978: 7; Todorov, *Conquest*, 1984: 53; Keen, *Latin America*, 1996: 71.

11. Fernández-Armesto, "'Aztec' Auguries," 1992: 287; "the question has not lost its potency through time"—Clendinnen, "'Fierce and Unnatural Cruelty,'" 1991: 12.

12. The painting is variously reproduced elsewhere (see Ades, *Art in Latin America*, 1989: 33, for example) and the original can be seen in the Museo Nacional de Arte, Mexico City.

13. Scott, *1492*, 1992.

14. Berry and Razaf, "Christopher Columbus," 1936. I am grateful to Barry Kernfeld, personal communication, for giving me the date Razaf wrote these lyrics. They are reproduced with permission.

15. Fernández-Armesto, *Columbus*, 1991: 53; Berry and Razaf, "Christopher Columbus," 1936.

16. Scott, *1492*, 1992.

17. Russell, *Inventing the Flat Earth*, 1991; Irving, *Columbus*, 1981 [1828]: 48; Morison, *Columbus*, 1942; Fernández-Armesto, *Columbus*, 1991: 54; Boller, *Not So!* 1995: 3–6.

18. Eco, *Serendipities*, 1998: 4.

19. Eco, *Serendipities*, 1998: 7.

20. Winius, *Portugal*, 1995: 1. The idea that Columbus has been enveloped in myths and misunderstandings about him is standard fare of much of the Columbus literature, from early works such as Goodrich, *Columbus*, 1874 (e.g., p. 177); to the classics of the forties—Morison, *Columbus*, 1942; and Madariaga, *Columbus*, 1949—to publications of the quincentennial boom such as Fernández-Armesto, *Columbus*, 1991 (e.g., pp. vii–x); Wilford, *Columbus*, 1991 (e.g., pp. 247–65); Bushman, *America Discovers Columbus*, 1992 (e.g., pp. 8–14); Davidson, *Columbus*, 1997 (e.g., pp. 467–82). A brief survey of Columbus historiography through to the early 1980s is in Crosby, "The Columbian Voyages," 1993.

21. Fernández-Armesto, *Columbus*, 1991: 21.

22. To paraphrase Fernández-Armesto, *Columbus*, 1991: 21.

23. Fernández-Armesto, *Before Columbus*, 1987: 151–85; "Medieval Atlantic Exploration," 1995: 43–44.

24. Fernández-Armesto, *Before Columbus*, 1987: 185–202; "Medieval Atlantic Exploration," 1995: 44, 65; Keen, *Latin America*, 1996: 56.

25. Fernández-Armesto, *Before Columbus*, 1987: 203–22; "Medieval Atlantic Exploration," 1995: 44–53; Verlinden, "European Participation," 1995: 71–77.

26. Radulet, "Vasco da Gama," 1995: 133–134.
27. Fernández-Armesto, *Columbus*, 1991: 43–65; Radulet, "Vasco da Gama," 1995: 134–35; Pinheiro Marques, "Triumph," 1995: 363–68. On the da Gama quincentennial, see Fox, "No Room for Romantics," 2001.
28. Like so much of Columbus mythology, this point has often been made (from Goodrich, *Columbus*, 1874: 113–42, to Wilson, *Emperor's Giraffe*, 1999: 32) but seems to bounce right off the armor of the mythical Columbus image. Also see Frederick, "Colonizing Columbus," 2001.
29. Fernández-Armesto, *Columbus*, 1991: 186–87; Dutra, "The Discovery of Brazil," 1995: 147–48; Pinheiro Marques, "Triumph," 1995: 371; Keen, *Latin America*, 1996: 62.
30. Pinheiro Marques, "Triumph," 1995: 372, for example.
31. Quoted by Fernández-Armesto, *Columbus*, 1991: 187. The juxtaposition of the two men together in the Blue Room in the White House, in the form of busts sculpted in 1815, is thus significant on more levels than most visitors to the Washington, D.C., tourist attraction surely realize (author's visit of January 2001; see www.whitehouse.gov/history/whtour/blue).
32. Fernández-Armesto, *Columbus*, 1991: 185; Gómara later gives Columbus some credit, however; *Cortés*, 1964 [1552]: 334.
33. Elliott, *The Old World and the New*, 1970: 11–12. For example, in the dedicatory letter to Cortés in Francisco Cervantes de Salazar's *Diálogo de la dignidad del hombre* (1772 [1564?]: 2) Cervantes grants Cortés the title of "Descubridor I Conquistador de la Nueva España [Discoverer and Conqueror of New Spain]." On Lope de Vega's view of Spanish history and the placing of that view in the context of courtly literature, see Wright, *Pilgrimage to Patronage*, 2001.
34. It remains unclear whether Columbus's body is in Santo Domingo, Havana, or Seville, or whether part of it is in one of these cities and part of it in Genoa (Trouillot, *Silencing the Past*, 1995: 179 n21; Giardini, *Columbus*, 1967: 72). As Trouillot observes (*Silencing the Past*, 1995: 122), Columbus was too much of a European figure to work well as a symbol of an independent Latin America.
35. For example, the Knights of Columbus, an Irish-American Catholic fraternity, was founded in 1881 (Trouillot, *Silencing the Past*, 1995: 123). For a detailed study of the invention of the Columbus myth in the nineteenth century, see Bushman, *America Discovers Columbus*, 1992: 81–190.
36. Trouillot, *Silencing the Past*, 1995: 123–140; Bushman, *America Discovers Columbus*, 1992: 152–90. The 1815 bust of Columbus in the White House was put on prominent display in the Blue Room in the early 1990s; www.whitehouse.gov/history/whtour/blue. For a fascinating new book-length study of the quincentennial controversy (effectively a sequel to Bushman, *America Discovers Columbus*, 1992), see Summerhill and Williams, *Sinking Columbus*, 2000. An echo of the controversy is currently resonating through the plans for and discussions of the Vasco da Gama quincentennial (Fox, "No Room for Romantics," 2001).
37. Florescano, *Memory*, 1994: 65.
38. For examples of probanzas and similar letters, see Icaza, *Diccionario*, 1923; Lockhart and Otte, *Letters and People*, 1976. The context for the development of this genre is the centuries of the so-called *reconquista*, the sporadic and protracted war between Christian and Islamic kingdoms in Iberia from 711 to 1492, as well as the Castilian conquest of the Canary islands in the late fourteenth and fifteenth centuries. For the parallel development of a related genre, the *requerimiento*, see Seed, "The Requirement," 1995.
39. Cortés's letters (*Cartas*, 1983, and *Letters*, 1986 [1519–26]) were banned in 1527, Gómara's book (*Cortés*, 1964 [1552]) in 1553; Pagden, *Fall of Natural Man*, 1982: 58; Elliott, "Cortés," 1989: 41; Florescano, *Memory*, 1994: 97.

40. Zamora, *Reading Columbus*, 1993: 5, 9–20.
41. The 1552 and 1558 Díaz letters to the king are published in translation in Lockhart and Otte, *Letters and People*, 1976: 73–82, quotes on pp. 79 and 82.
42. Gómara, *Cortés*, 1964: xxi; Díaz, *Historia*, 1955 [1570]; *Conquest*, 1963: 7–8.
43. Quoted in Florescano, *Memory*, 1994: 92. The Belgian scholar Sabine Mund has recently argued that Díaz was motivated largely by what he heard in the Spanish city of Valladolid in 1550–51, when a now-famous debate on the nature of the "Indian" featured furious denunciations of conquistador practices by the Dominican friar Bartolomé de Las Casas; in response, Díaz sought to defend and promote not just his own record, but the whole Conquest enterprise (*Les rapports complexes*, 2001: 89–99).
44. Florescano, *Memory*, 1994: 67.
45. Florescano, *Memory*, 1994: 77. As mentioned below, Spanish imperial ideology can also be placed in the larger context of western European imperial ideology, which helps explain the nineteenth-century boost given to the glorification of the conquistadors.
46. Elliott, "Cortés," 1989: 39.
47. There are numerous discussions of this literature and Franciscan evangelization in the Americas; see, for example, Klor de Alva, Nicholson, and Quiñones-Keber, *Sahagún*, 1988; Rabasa, *Inventing America*, 1993: 151–64; Chuchiak, "The Indian Inquisition," 2000; and Francis, "la conquista espiritual," 2000.
48. The letter is published in translation in Lockhart and Otte, *Letters and People*, 1976: 220–47, quotes on pp. 246 and 246–47. Another Franciscan, Gerónimo de Mendieta, similarly eulogized Cortés in his *Historia eclesiástica indiana* of 1596; Rabasa, *Inventing America*, 1993: 157–58.
49. Cline, "Revisionist Conquest History," 1988: 93.
50. Cline, "Revisionist Conquest History," 1988.
51. Elliott, "Cortés," 1989: 39–41. The comparison to Caesar would not be the last; see Alcalá, *César y Cortés*, 1950.
52. Gómara, *Cortés*, 1964 [1552]; Todorov, *Conquest*, 1984: 120.
53. Díaz, *Historia*, 1955 [1570]; *Conquest*, 1963 [1570].
54. Lasso de la Vega, *Cortés valeroso*, 1588: 4r et al.
55. For example, the Italian friar, Ilarione da Bergamo, writing in 1770 of his travels in Mexico, explicitly refers his readers to "the letters of Christopher Columbus and other conquistador captains" (Ilarione da Bergamo, *Daily Life*, 2000 [1770]: 69).
56. Florescano, *Memory*, 1994: 96. Mignolo, *Local Histories*, 2000: x, argues that only "hegemonic discourses" were published in the colonial period, suppressing alternative voices such as Huaman Poma's *New Chronicle*, not published until 1936 (Huaman Poma, *Nueva corónica*, 1980 [1615]).
57. Prescott, *Conquest of Mexico*, 1909 [1843]; Gómara, *Cortés*, 1964 [1552]: xvii; Díaz, *Conquest*, 1963: 10.
58. Clendinnen, "'Fierce and Unnatural Cruelty,'" 1991:12–13.
59. Prescott's work also inspired a category of historical romance centered on the Conquest of Mexico, further extending the popular reach of his myth-based vision of the Conquest; good examples are Falkenhorst, *With Cortez in Mexico: A Historical Romance*, 1892, and Marshall, *Cortez and Marina*, 1963.
60. See the Goodrich quote at the top of this chapter (Goodrich, *Columbus*, 1874: 89; also quoted by Frederick, "Colonizing Columbus," 2001: 10). E. H. Carr observed 40 years ago that "the great-man theory of history ... has gone out of fashion in recent years, though it still occasionally rears its ungainly head" (*What Is History?*, 1961: 53); however, two decades later it was still sufficiently alive for a scholar such as Eric Wolf to consider it worth a book-length assault (*Europe*, 1982).

61. Thomas, *Conquest*, 1995; Hill Boone, *Stories*, 2000: 5, makes a similar point. For a critical view of Thomas's coverage of native cultures, see Nicholson, "Hugh Thomas's *Conquest*," 2000. I do not mean to be dismissive of Thomas's book, merely to situate it historiographically; I use it extensively in this book, both to illustrate the seven myths and their counterpoints. There are books on the Conquest of Mexico that embrace Conquest myths in pernicious ways, such as that by Marks, *Cortes*, 1993, but Thomas (*Conquest*, 1995) is not one of them.

62. Even when, in postrevolutionary Mexico, Cortés's reputation was revisited, the principle of "great men" of the Conquest as the tale of a few heroes and villains, was maintained; for example, in a mural by Diego Rivera in the Palacio Nacional in Mexico City, Cortés is portrayed as the villain, and Las Casas the hero (also reproduced in Todorov, *Conquest*, 1984: 178). Similarly, the French writer Le Clézio, whose book on the Conquest embodies modern versions of most of the seven myths, perpetuates the myth of exceptional men by inverting Sepúlveda's trope of bold Cortés and timorous Moctezuma to juxtapose "the wily and threatening words of [Cortés] and the anguished and magical speech of the Mexican king" (*Mexican Dream*, 1993: 22). The modern Mexican attitude toward Cortés is contested and ambiguous; Eulalia Guzmán's attack on the conquistador (*Relaciones*, 1958) produced numerous defenses of him, including a brief one by Manuel Alcalá, who reminded readers of his earlier favorable comparison of the "cortesísimo Cortés" to Julius Caesar (*César y Cortés*, 1950; Cortés, *Cartas*, 1983: ix [Alcalá's essay is dated 1960]).

63. Pagden (in Cortés, *Letters*, 1986: 461) and Elliott, "Cortés," 1989: 41, suggest that Cervantes de Salazar originated the myth; also see Amor y Vásquez ("Apostilla," 1961). The original accounts of the scuttling are in Díaz, *Conquest*, 1963 [1570]: 128–30), and Cortés (*Letters*, 1986 [1522]: 52). The myth has been repeated widely (see, for example, Bricker, *The Indian Christ*, 1981: 16) but recently began to show signs of dying (for examples, Todorov, *Conquest*, 1984: 56; Schwartz, *Victors and Vanquished*, 2000: 43; Burkholder and Johnson, *Colonial Latin America*, 2001: 45). I benefited from conversations on this topic with Jack Crowley.

64. Todorov, *Conquest*, 1984: 56, calls the scuttling of ships one of Cortés's two most "startling" decisions. Although Cortés himself clearly explains (*Letters*, 1986 [1522]: 52) that the scuttling is a temporary measure designed to deter Velázquez loyalists from deserting, Todorov follows the myth generated in the colonial period that Cortés's purpose was to prevent *anyone* from turning back. A succinct colonial-era expression of the myth can be found in Juan de Solórzano's 520-page official condemnation of the admirals who surrendered without resistance the 1628 silver fleet to the Dutch; Solórzano states in the Latin marginalia to the report that Cortés scuttled his ships (not burned; *naves perforarunt*) in order to oblige (all) his men to fight, not flee, a precedent used by Solórzano to make his case for the "cowardice" of the admirals (JCBL, Codex Sp 26: f. 91r; on Solórzano's other work, see Muldoon, *The Americas*, 1994).

65. Chamberlain, *Conquest and Colonization*, 1948: 38–40; Restall, *Maya Conquistador*, 1998: 8. In the same category of action was Antonio de Berrio's slaughter of horses during one of his expeditions into the Orinoco basin (Naipaul, *El Dorado*, 1969: 18).

66. Gibson, *Spain in America*, 1966: 29.

67. Respectively: Clendinnen, "'Fierce and Unnatural Cruelty,'" 1991: 19; Todorov, *Conquest*, 1984: 99; Le Clézio, *Mexican Dream*, 1993: 7, 8. The counterfactual speculation as to whether the Conquest of Mexico would have taken place without Cortés, or if Cortés had perished during the 1519–21 war, as he came close to doing on several occasions, is masterfully articulated by Ross Hassig, "Immolation," 1999. Hassig's task in this article is to imagine a dramatically different history of Mexico without Cortés, but reading between the lines one can see that Hassig is too perceptive a historian not to see the

overwhelming likelihood of the second-order counterfactual (i.e., the reassertion of the original pattern), with a Spanish Conquest led by Alvarado or another of Cortés's fellow captains.

68. I benefited from e-mail exchanges with Grant Jones on this topic.

69. My translation from Cortés, *Cartas*, 1983 [1519]: 18, but also see Cortés, *Letters*, 1986 [1519]: 26, and Schwartz, *Victors and Vanquished*, 2000: 75–76.

70. The only permanent settlement of these was Salamanca de Bacalar, founded in 1544, and soon known simply as Bacalar. Clendinnen, *Ambivalent Conquests*, 1987: 21, 31; Jones, *Maya Resistance*, 1989: 41–45; Restall, *Maya Conquistador*, 1998: 8, 181. My point about unbuilt towns refers only to this early stage of Conquest campaigns; Spaniards placed great emphasis on urban living and began to build provincial capital cities as soon as they could.

71. My translation from Cortés, *Cartas*, 1983 [1519]: 18; but also see Cortés, *Letters*, 1986 [1519]: 25–26, and Schwartz, *Victors and Vanquished*, 2000: 75.

72. Comparisons have been drawn between Cortés and Machiavelli, suggesting, in the vein of the myth of exceptional men, that Cortés was the Machiavellian archetype (see, for example, Todorov, *Conquest*, 1984: 116; Fuentes, *Buried Mirror*, 1992: 129; Pastor, *Armature of Conquest*, 1992: 82–83). However, the lack of evidence of direct influence (as Todorov, Fuentes, and Pastor concede) suggests that both men were products of their time and articulated or acted on ideas that were common currency; if Cortés was Machiavellian, then the latter was "the elder brother of [*all*] the conquistadors" (Fuentes's words, my emphasis). Along the same lines, Elliott has shown how Cortés's use of certain literary references in his letters to the king, often taken as "an impression both of originality and of erudition," were almost always commonplace references, some even clichés, of the day ("Cortés," 1989: 31). Pastor's analysis of Cortés's letters as using "fiction" to represent "rebellion as service" and "the rebel as model conqueror" is insightful, but its focus on Cortés alone misses the larger context of conquistador culture and the essential point that Cortés is not an innovator but a practitioner of standard procedures, not an exception but a part of the pattern (*Armature of Conquest*, 1992: 50–100, quote on p. 63).

73. Restall, *Maya Conquistador*, 1998: 8.

74. Lockhart, *Cajamarca*, 1972: 5–6, 67.

75. Lockhart, *Cajamarca*, 1972: 6, 15–16; letter published in translation in Lockhart and Otte, *Letters and People*, 1976: 54–56, quote on p. 55.

76. Prescott, *Conquest of Peru*, 1847, II: 153–54; Millar, *A Crossbowman's Story*, 1955: xiii; Wallace, *Michael Wood's Conquistadors*, 2000; and Wood, *Conquistadors*, 2000: 187–229.

77. Wood, *Conquistadors*, 2000: 229; when Wood comments that in the end Orellana "was— and remained—a conquistador" he is right, but in a far more mundane way than is usually recognized.

78. The quotations are by Fuentes, *Buried Mirror*, 1992: 83, Bitterli, *Cultures in Conflict*, 1989: 75; and Georg Friederici (quoted by Bitterli from a work of his published in German in 1925). A pithy evocation of the "thirst for gold" submyth is found in Alfred Furman's 1930 play, *Atahualpa: The Last of the Incas*, in which a conquistador exclaims that "Pizarro is insane / His constant thought is gold: his lexicon / Holds that word only" (Smith, "Conquest of Peru," 2001: 15). For an early and partially successful attempt to place the "thirst for gold" theme and myth into a cultural context, see Picón-Salas (*A Cultural History*, 1966: 32–34). Shaffer's 1964 play about the Conquest of Peru has Pizarro interested in fame, not gold (Shaffer, *Royal Hunt*, 1969; Smith, "Conquest of Peru," 2001: 24). But the stereotype lives on; when the two Spaniards in *The Road to El Dorado* are contemplating their demise, one asks the other, "Any regrets?" To which the reply is, "I never had enough gold" (Bergeron and Paul, *El Dorado*, 2000).

79. As Lockhart points out, in Lockhart and Otte, *Letters and People*, 1976: 19.
80. Díaz, *Conquest*, 1963 [1570]: 66); Restall, *Maya Conquistador*, 1998: 7, 180–81.
81. Columbus, *The Four Voyages*, 1969 [1492–96]: 80, 98, 116, 148, 154; Fernández-Armesto, *Columbus*, 1991: 106, 165.
82. Juan Díaz, *Littera mandata*, 1520; Gómara, *Cortés*, 1964 [1552]: 57; Díaz, *Conquest*, 1963 [1570]: 26, 28, 30, 32, 64–65, 231; Thomas, *Conquest*, 1995: 93, 99, 152, 167, 308; Karttunen, "Interpreters," 2000: 217.
83. Restall, "Gaspar Antonio Chi," 2002.
84. Indeed this kind of violence was used by Christians during the Reconquista; one of many examples is the public torture of Moors during the siege of Valencia by the tenth-century Reconquista hero, El Cid (Nelson, "El Cid," 2001: 23). Although some conquistadors no doubt earned their reputations for cruelty and gratuitous violence, the deeds that tend to be cited as evidence of excess are almost always standard procedures. For example, in a brief letter of 1533 describing the early events in the Conquest of Peru, Hernando Pizarro casually refers to three moments when native Andeans were tortured, for which his nineteenth-century English editor, Sir Clements Markham, called him "odious," "ruthless," and a "ruffian" (*Discovery of Peru*, 1872: xiii, xiv, 120; Pizarro's letter on pp. 113–27). Whether Markham's epithets were justified or not, he misses the point that torture was a conventional interrogation technique, and public torture of captives central to the strategy of display violence.
85. During the 1536 siege of Cuzco, Francisco Pizarro ordered severed the right hands of 200 Andean prisoners and later 400 more (Himmerich y Valencia, "Siege of Cuzco," 1998: 414; Herrera in Cieza de León, *Peru*, 1998 [1550]: 458; also see Herrera, *Historia General*, 1601/1615). In 1550, Pedro de Valdivía reported that "two hundred [Araucanians] had their hands and noses cut off for their contumacy" (quoted in Todorov, *Conquest*, 1984: 148). An Araucanian hand-severing incident is also discussed by Vargas Machuca, *Milicia y Descripción*, 1599: 5r. Soto was alleged to have "cut off the hands of fifteen Princes" in Florida, just as Cortés had cut the hands off Nahua "spies" (Ogilby, *America*, 1670: 81, 84).
86. The killing of Inca women, as well as torture by fire and dogs, was used during the siege of Cuzco (Himmerich y Valencia, "Siege of Cuzco," 1998: 414). Cortés casually refers to a similar action of 1519 (*Letters*, 1986 [1519]: 61). A practice commonly associated with the Inquisition but frequently used as a display-violence technique by conquistadors was the public burning alive of native lords; one infamous example is Alvarado's burning of Quiché Maya kings in 1524 (Recinos, *Memorial*, 1950: 125; Kramer, *Encomienda Politics*, 1994: 32).
87. Ogilby, *America*, 1670: 83.
88. Clendinnen, "'Fierce and Unnatural Cruelty,'" 1991: 28. For archaeological evidence that the killings in Cholula were a deliberate and planned massacre—and thus another example of routine display violence by conquistadors—see Peterson and Green, "Massacre at Cholula," 1987; I am grateful to Blanca Maldonado for bringing this article to my attention.
89. Todorov, *Conquest*, 1984: 56. Todorov follows the Jesuit chronicler, José de Acosta, who wrote in 1590 that the seizure of Moctezuma was "a deed that astonished the world" (*Natural and Moral History*, 2002 [1590]: 438).
90. Guilmartin, "The Cutting Edge," 1991: 56; Seed, "'Failing to Marvel,'" 1991; Burkholder and Johnson, *Colonial Latin America*, 2001: 52–53.
91. Lockhart, *Cajamarca*, 1972: 23; Lockhart and Schwartz, *Early Latin America*, 1983: 84.
92. Cieza de León, *Peru*, 1998 [1550]: 166. Kris Lane pointed out this incident to me.
93. Fernández-Armesto, *Columbus*, 1991: 104.

94. Alvarado, *Conquest of Guatemala*, 1924 [1525]: 62; Whitehead, *Lords of the Tiger Spirit*, 1988: 27–29, 73–75; Fernández-Armesto, *Columbus*, 1991: 106; Avellaneda, *Conquerors*, 1995: 120, 133. An example particularly gruesome in its details—but not, in a general sense, unusual—was Nuño de Guzmán's treatment of the Cazonci, the Tarascan king. In an illustration of Conquest procedures six and seven, the Cazonci was subjected to protracted torture, along with members of his family, before being ritually executed in public (Las Casas, *Devastation*, 1992 [1552]: 74–76; Krippner-Martínez, *Rereading the Conquest*, 2001: 21–44).

95. Letter published in translation in Lockhart, *Cajamarca*, 1972: 461–63 and Lockhart and Otte, *Letters and People*, 1976: 4–7.

96. These were the Canary Islands (1478–96), Granada (1482–92), Naples (1497–1503), Mellilla (1497), Oran and Algiers (1509–10), Navarre (1511–14), and, in the Americas, Hispaniola (1495–96), Puerto Rico (1508), Jamaica (1509), Cuba (1511), and Panama and its surroundings (1512–17); Fernández-Armesto, "'Aztec' auguries," 1992: 301.

Notes to Chapter 2

1. Scott, *1492*, 1992.

2. Recent examples of aspects of this interpretation, and the sources of the phrases quoted above, are Elliott, "Cortés," 1989: 31, 35; Clendinnen, "'Fierce and Unnatural Cruelty,'" 1991: 17; Fuentes, *Buried Mirror*, 1992: 128; Keen, *Latin America*, 1996: 65–71; and Foster, *Mexico*, 1997: 45, 46. A few scholars avoid the trap; see, for example, Hassig, "Immolation," 1999. Not surprisingly, the interpretation is easily found in older sources (for example, see Helps, *Cortés*, 1894, I: 227; also cited by Cowher, "A Handful of Adventurers?" 2001: 2). A variant on the theme is the conventional description of Bernal Díaz as a "foot soldier" (Clendinnen, "'Fierce and Unnatural Cruelty,'" 1991: 15; Altman, Cline, and Pescador, *Greater Mexico*, 2002: 94), "a soldier with a soldier's interests" (Schwartz, *Victors and Vanquished*, 2000: 42). To pin such a label on Díaz is very misleading not just for the reasons related to the "myth of the king's army" that I articulate in this chapter, but because he was the social equal of Cortés (albeit related to Velázquez and thus connected to the "wrong" patronage network; see Lockhart and Otte, *Letters and People*, 1976: 72).

3. Jerez, *Verdadera relación*, 1985 [1534]: 60; Markham, *Discovery of Peru*, 1872: 2; also quoted by Seed, "'Failing to Marvel,'" 1991: 15.

4. Clendinnen, "'Fierce and Unnatural Cruelty,'" 1991: 17; Cortés, *Cartas*, 1983 [1519–26]: 32; *Letters* 1986 [1519–26]: 50. Likewise, Pedro de Alvarado, the captain of Cortés who led the Spanish invasion into Guatemala in 1524 and wrote two letters from there to Cortés, refers to men on foot, not soldiers. But Sedley Mackie, in his 1924 edition of the letters, glosses the phrase as "footsoldiers" (Alvarado, *Conquest of Guatemala*, 1924 [1525]).

5. The 1557 manuscript is in the JCBL as Codex Sp 3.

6. ARH, Sig. B. No. 68; Landa, *Relación*, 1982 [1566]: 29; Restall and Chuchiak, *The Friar and the Maya*, n.d.

7. Lockhart and Otte, *Letters and People*, 1976: 3, 15.

8. Díaz, *Historia*, 1955 [1570]: xxviii; *Conquest*, 1963 [1570]: 7. Bernardo de Vargas Machuca, writing in the 1590s, also used *soldado*, though he tended to distinguish between "conquistadors" (leaders and men of social standing, like himself) and "soldiers" (the rest) (*Milicia y Descripción*, 1599).

9. Ilarione da Bergamo, *Daily Life*, 2000 [1770]: 96.

10. See the images, for example, in Milanich and Milbrath, *First Encounters*, 1989: 8, 34; and in Grafton, *New World*, 1992: 64.

11. The irony of this frontispiece is that the "dictionary" was a compilation of summaries of "merit" reports, or *probanzas*, by conquistadors who were clearly not professional soldiers; Icaza, *Diccionario*, 1923; Prescott, *Conquest of Mexico*, 1909 [1843]; 1847.

12. My summary of the military revolution is drawn from Parker, *Military Revolution*, 1996, with additional assistance from Guilmartin, "Logistics of Warfare at Sea," 1993, and Carol Reardon, personal communication.

13. Guilmartin, "Logistics of Warfare at Sea," 1993: 110, for example, though he also points out (pp. 117, 127) that Spanish conquest activities in the Americas produced gold and silver bullion revenues that financed crucial developments in Spain's military capabilities in Europe. The lack of central organization in the sixteenth- and seventeenth-century expeditions is illustrated by late-colonial examples of attempts at planned, organized conquests—such as plans made in 1750 "For the Conquest of the Colorado River," a region that was surveyed in detail as part of the invasion planning (BL, ms Add 17569: fs. 162–68).

14. Vargas Machuca, *Milicia y Descripción*, 1599; Parker, *Military Revolution*, 1996: 120.

15. Klein, "Free Colored Militia," 1966; Sánchez, "African Freedmen," 1994; Lane, *Pillaging the Empire*, 1998: 49–53, 69, 107, 126, 167; Restall, "Black Conquistadors," 2000: 196–99; Vinson, "Race and Badge," 2000.

16. Guilmartin, "The Cutting Edge," 1991: 56.

17. Lockhart, *Cajamarca*, 1972: 23; Guilmartin, "The Cutting Edge," 1991: 67.

18. Guilmartin, "Logistics of Warfare at Sea," 1993: 110, 119.

19. JCBL, Codex Sp 3: fs. 2r–4r. See Chapter 7 for a brief discussion of the role of horses in the Conquest.

20. My translation is made from the transcription in Lockhart, *Cajamarca*, 1972: 462, but is indebted to his translation in *Cajamarca*, 1972: 459–60, and in Lockhart and Otte, *Letters and People*, 1976: 5.

21. Lockhart, *Cajamarca*, 1972: 330; Lockhart and Otte, *Letters and People*, 1976: 4.

22. Lockhart and Otte, *Letters and People*, 1976: 3.

23. The conquistador letters in Lockhart and Otte, *Letters and People*, 1976, illustrate well the different sizes of *encomiendas*; for example, Melchor Verdugo wrote to his mother in 1536 of his grant of "eight or ten thousand vassals" (p. 45), that is, native Andeans in the Trujillo area, while Bartolomé Garcia complained from Paraguay in 1556 of his *encomienda* of just "sixteen Indians" (p. 49).

24. Pedrarias de Avila's letter is published in Lockhart and Otte, *Letters and People*, 1976: 9–14, quote on p. 12. For a detailed account of how Pizarro and his relatives and associates put together the company that invaded Peru, see Varón Gabai, *Pizarro*, 1997: 10–69. Spanish Conquest companies were smaller and less institutionalized precursors to the British and Dutch East India and West India companies that were the vanguard of colonialism in North America and East Asia. The system of private financing, coupled with royal licenses guaranteeing not direct monetary rewards but titles of office, was still the norm in the 1690s, when don Martín de Ursúa y Arizmendi received a royal license to plan, finance, and execute the Conquest of the Petén (northern Guatemala) (Jones, *Conquest*, 1998: 118–24).

25. Avellaneda, *Conquerors*, 1995: 91–95.

26. Lockhart, *Cajamarca*, 1972: 38. For further discussion of the occupations of crier and piper, in the context of the tendency for such posts to be filled by Africans in Spanish America, see Chapter 3 below. This picture (Table 1) could be further complicated by including other sources on horse and slave ownership, and on social rank (probably 10 percent of the 168 were true plebeians and perhaps 20 percent were low nobility, broadly defined).

27. AGI, *México*, 3048: 18–24, 76–81; Cogolludo, *Historia*, 1688 [1654] and *Historia*, 1957 [1654], 2: Chapters I, V); Chamberlain, *Conquest and Colonization*, 1948: 32–33; Kicza, *Patterns*, n.d.: Chapter 7.

28. Lockhart, *Cajamarca*, 1972: 26; Avellaneda, *Conquerors*, 1995: 61–63. As I have implied above, Spanish women were not conquistadors; although there were a few women brought on many expeditions from the 1530s on (to Colombia, for example; op. cit.: 68–70), gender roles in the Conquest era were such that one Basque woman who wished to participate, the famous Catalina de Erauso, had to resort to disguising herself as a man in order to pursue a conquistador's lifestyle in Peru (Erauso, *Lieutenant Nun*, 1996 [1626]).

29. In support of the idea that this impression does not rise to the level of a myth, see Lockhart's comment (*Cajamarca*, 1972: 41) on the undeserved reputation for *illiteracy* among Peru's conquistadors, citing Cohen's introduction to the Zárate account (*Peru*, 1981 [1555]: 9, 15).

30. Avellaneda, *Conquerors*, 1995: 72, 74.

31. Lockhart, *Cajamarca*, 1972: 72, 135. Among the ten leaders of the famous 1532–34 Peru expedition, including the four Pizarro brothers, four were literate, three were semiliterate (they could sign their names), and three were illiterate (op. cit.: 121–207).

32. Avellaneda, *Conquerors*, 1995: 31–36, 62.

33. Gómara, *Cortés*, 1964 [1552]: 19; Thomas, *Conquest*, 1995: 116–17. Bernal Díaz portrays the decision-making process as more of a public and contentious one; *Conquest*, 1963 [1570]: 44–45.

34. Díaz, *Conquest*, 1963 [1570]: 45; Thomas, *Conquest*, 1995: 117, 133–34, 671 n34. Velázquez had conquered Cuba under the patronage of Columbus's son, don Diego Colón, who was the senior Spanish official in the colonies at that time (Gómara, *Cortés*, 1964 [1552]: 11).

35. Gómara, *Cortés*, 1964 [1552]: 11–12; Díaz, *Conquest*, 1963 [1570]: 46–56; Thomas, *Conquest*, 1995: 134, 141.

36. Gómara, *Cortés*, 1964 [1552]: 19, 88–89, 193; Díaz, *Conquest*, 1963 [1570]: 54, 128; Thomas, *Conquest*, 1995: 215–21, 338–54.

37. Thomas, *Conquest*, 1995: 573, 584.

38. ARH, Sig. B. No. 68; Landa, *Relación*, 1982 [1566]: 22); Restall and Chuchiak, *The Friar and the Maya*, n.d.

39. ARH, Sig. B. No. 68; Landa, *Relación*, 1982 [1566]: 24–25); Restall and Chuchiak, *The Friar and the Maya*, n.d.

40. AGI, *México*, 3048: 21–22. Montejo was not the only conquistador funded by his wife; in the 1690s, Ursúa, the above-mentioned Yucatec governor, financed the Conquest of the Itza Mayas of northern Guatemala in part by drawing upon the fortune of his wealthy spouse, doña Juana Bolio (Jones, *Conquest*, 1998: 121).

41. Chamberlain, *Conquest and Colonization*, 1948; Clendinnen, *Ambivalent Conquests*, 1987: 20–29; Restall, *Maya Conquistador*, 1998: 8–11; Thomas, *Conquest*, 1995: 595.

42. Alonso de Ávila, like Montejo but unlike many who had survived the first two invasions of Yucatan, had received an *encomienda* in Mexico and so had something to fall back on. He was still in Mexico City in 1539, when he was one of the sponsors of a great festival celebrating Spanish conquests (Harris, *Aztecs, Moors, and Christians*, 2000: 124). In 1566 both of his sons were beheaded for their roles in the conspiracy to crown don Martín Cortés as king of Mexico (ibid.: 148).

43. Gómara, *Cortés*, 1964 [1552]: 23; Thomas, *Conquest*, 1995: 577.

44. Alvarado's use of such relatives was not at all unusual; Francisco Pizarro brought his three brothers to Peru and all played major roles in the Conquest (Lockhart, *Cajamarca*, 1972; Varón Gabai, *Pizarro*, 1997), while Alonso de Cerrato, Alvarado's successor in Guatemala in the 1550s, extended such familial patronage that Bernal Díaz complained in a

1552 letter to the king that "we are still waiting for him [Cerrato] to make [*encomienda*] grants to two cousins of his, a nephew, and a grandson, and we don't know when another boatload of Cerratos might arrive, to be given Indians" (letter in Lockhart and Otte, *Letters and People*, 1976: 73–80, quote on p. 75).

45. Alvarado, *Conquest of Guatemala*, 1924 [1525]; Recinos, *Memorial*, 1950 [1605]: 124–38; Bricker, *The Indian Christ*, 1981: 29–42; Kramer, *Encomienda Politics*, 1994: 25–46.

46. Kramer, *Encomienda Politics*, 1994: 42–46, 101. In fact, Alvarado was often absent from Guatemala, returning both to Mexico and Spain in the late 1520s.

47. Even his Peruvian expedition was not the end of Alvarado's conquest endeavors; in the late 1530s he sailed again to Spain and acquired a license to "discover and conquer islands in the Pacific," entering into a partnership with Viceroy Mendoza of New Spain for a 1539 expedition that Cortés had hoped to control (Harris, *Aztecs, Moors, and Christians*, 2000: 136).

48. Zárate, *Historia*, 1555; *Peru*, 1981 [1555]: 134–44; Lockhart, *Cajamarca*, 1972: 15; Kramer, *Encomienda Politics*, 1994: 106–7, 120. See Chapter 3 for an example of a black conquistador, Juan Valiente, who accompanied Alvarado from Guatemala and ended up in Chile.

Notes to Chapter 3

1. In the words of Clendinnen, "'Fierce and Unnatural Cruelty,'" 1991: 12. Lanyon observes that "popular history" has for long embraced "the myth of the easy European conquest of Mexico, like the myth of the easy European conquest of Australia" in part because of "our incapacity to comprehend diversity among non-Europeans" (*Malinche's Conquest*, 1999: 103).

2. Spaniards often compared their own heroes who had triumphed against the odds to those of ancient Greece and Rome; in 1631 the great Spanish jurist Juan de Solórzano argued in his 520-page condemnation of the officers who had surrendered the 1628 silver fleet to Dutch pirates without putting up a fight that "Alexander, Cortés, Pizarro, and others, with a few well-disciplined old soldiers, vanquished innumerable opponents" (my translation from a manuscript copy of Solórzano's *Discurso y alegación en derecho* in JCBL, Codex Sp 26: fs. 7r, 76).

3. Another category of "invisible conquistadors" is potentially that of women. A trio of female conquerors tend to be mentioned quite often in the historical literature. The best known is Inés Suárez, who traveled to Venezuela and Peru in search of her husband; when she discovered he was dead, she joined Pedro de Valdivia on his expedition into Chile, where she was his lover and seems also to have fought the Araucanians. The second such figure is doña Isabel de Guevara, who accompanied her husband on the 1550s expedition to the River Plate; the attempt at founding a colony was a disaster, and Guevara ended up having to take on military roles in battle. The third is Catalina de Erauso, the so-called Lieutenant Nun, who wrote a famous account of her experiences as a conquistador of sorts in early seventeenth-century Peru. However, the first two of these women became conquistadors by accident, and the third did so only in disguise as a man, thereby undermining her status as a "conquistadora." All three remained extremely unusual; they do not represent the tip of the iceberg the way that individual black conquerors do. On these three women, see Lockhart and Otte, *Letters and People*, 1976: 14–17; Fuentes, *Buried Mirror*, 1992: 138–39; Erauso, *Lieutenant Nun*, 1996 [1626]; and Velasco, *Lieutenant Nun*, 2000. The topic is also covered by Cesco, "Invisible Conquistador," 2001: 11–12; and Cowher, "A Handful of Adventurers?" 2001: 17–18. Thomas, *Who's Who*, 2000: 400–401 lists 15 "conquistadoras" among the 2,200 Spaniards who

came on the various expeditions to central Mexico in 1519–21, of whom only five or six appear to have done any fighting. Likewise, there were women involved in the Spanish colonization of parts of California in the 1770s, but there is no evidence that any of these female settlers took on military roles (Bouvier, *Women and the Conquest of California*, 2001: 54–79).

4. Ilarione da Bergamo, *Daily Life*, 2000 [1770]: 95–96.

5. Alvarado, *Conquest of Guatemala*, 1924 [1525]: quote on p. 80.

6. Prescott, *Conquest of Mexico*, 1994 [1843]: 580; and as observed by Fernández-Armesto in his introduction to this Folio edition (p. xxvii).

7. Translations mine (aided by Bierhorst's), from the Nahuatl text published in Bierhorst, *Cantares Mexicanos*, 1985: 318–23; also discussed by Harris, *Aztecs, Moors, and Christians*, 2000: 108–9. The cuckolding of Cuauhtémoc by Cortés is based on the fact that the Spaniard later had a child with Tecuichpo, baptized doña Isabel, a former child-bride of Cuauhtémoc's.

8. *In ye huel patiohuay in Tenochtitlan*; Bierhorst, *Cantares Mexicanos*, 1985: 322.

9. Cortés, *Letters*, 1986 [1519]: 57–73; Gómara, *Cortés*, 1964 [1552]: 97–123; Díaz, *Conquest*, 1963 [1570]: 140–88; Schwartz, *Victors and Vanquished*, 2000: 100–15.

10. Prescott, *Conquest of Mexico*, 1994 [1843]: 581; Gómara, *Cortés*, 1964 [1552]: 138; Hassig, *Mexico*, 1994: 101–102; also quoted by Reese, "Myth of Superiority," 2001: 19.

11. Cortés, *Letters*, 1986 [1519]: 69–70. Similarly, Lasso de la Vega, in his epic ode to Cortés, admitted that the Spaniards defeated the Mexica with "one hundred and fifty thousand Indian allies" but gave credit to Cortés for making these allies "disciplined in the Spanish exercise of war, and beneath their feared flags, through his laudable hard work and purpose, drawn to his service and friendship" (*Cortés valeroso*, 1588: prefatory p. 7r).

12. Todorov, *Conquest*, 1984: 57.

13. Letter of 1560, written in Nahuatl, published in various places, but I have used the translation in Lockhart and Otte, *Letters and People*, 1976: 165–72, quotes on p. 168.

14. Alvarado, *Conquest of Guatemala*, 1924 [1525]; Kramer, *Encomienda Politics*, 1994: 25–99.

15. Chamberlain, *Conquest and Colonization*, 1948; Clendinnen, *Ambivalent Conquests*, 1987; Restall, *Maya World*, 1997; *Maya Conquistador*, 1998. Another Mesoamerican example of various native groups viewing the war as a local conflict, not a native-Spanish war, with natives fighting alongside Spaniards as much as against them, is the Conquest of Oaxaca; see Sousa and Terraciano, "Original Conquest," n.d., and on the far more protracted Conquest of Oaxaca's northern sierra, see Chance, *Conquest*, 1989: 16–30.

16. Prescott, *Conquest of Peru*, 1847; Lockhart, *Cajamarca*, 1972. Burkholder and Johnson, *Colonial Latin America*, 2001: 50–58 also offer an excellent brief summary of the Conquest of Peru.

17. Himmerich y Valencia, "Siege of Cuzco," 1998: 414–15.

18. Gómara, *Cortés*, 1964 [1552]: 23.

19. Lockhart and Otte, *Letters and People*, 1976: 168. The context of this quote is one of blatant Huejotzincan self-promotion, but their presence in the war on the Spanish side is undeniable.

20. The Calkiní account is presented in full in translation from Yucatec Maya in Restall, *Maya Conquistador*, 1998: 86–103; on the event discussed above, see pp. 3–4, 85, 87, 89–90.

21. Spanish campaigns to conquer the Petén from highland Guatemala used Mopan and other Mayas as laborers and archers, while the Conquest campaign from Yucatan depended heavily on squads of Yucatec Maya muleteers, road laborers, porters, and warriors—to the extent that Oxkutzcab suffered a severe depletion of its male population (Jones, *Conquest*, 1998: 134–36, 143–44, 219, 258, 263). Precedents for Maya military expeditions into the area went back over a century: the Chontal Mayas under don Pablo

Paxbolon had conducted a long series of such raids (AGI, *México* 97; 138; 2999; Restall, *Maya Conquistador*, 1998: 53–76; Scholes and Roys, *Maya-Chontal Indians*, 1948: 142–290); and the Yucatec Maya governor of Oxkutzcab was commissioned in 1624 to lead 150 archers from his town on a punitive raid into the unconquered zone south of the colony (Jones, *Conquest*, 1998: 48).

22. Letter of 1527 published in translation in Lockhart and Otte, *Letters and People*, 1976: 39–43, quote on p. 42.

23. Both festivals are described by Díaz, *Historia*, 1955 [1570]: 460, 504; and discussed briefly by Harris, *Aztecs, Moors, and Christians*, 2000: 118.

24. The festival is described by Díaz, *Historia*, 1955 [1570]: 545; *True History*, 1908 [1570]: 190; and analyzed by Harris, *Aztecs, Moors, and Christians*, 2000: 123–31. On Mexico City's blacks in the first decades of colonial rule, including the revolt of 1537, see Palmer, *Slaves*, 1976: 44–55, 134–43 and Altman, "Spanish Society," 1991: 436–40.

25. Much of the material presented in the rest of this chapter originally appeared in a different form in Restall, "Black Conquistadors," 2000, which includes Valiente's biography in the form of a table.

26. Boyd-Bowman, "Negro Slaves," 1969: 135, 150–51; Sater, "Black Experience," 1974: 16–17. Valiente and his wife would have at least one child, a son who inherited his father's *encomienda*.

27. As indicated in a letter of 1541 written by Alonso Valiente, quoted at the top of this chapter and published in Boyd-Bowman, "Negro Slaves," 1969: 135, 150.

28. Bowser, *African Slave*, 1974: 4–5; Palmer, *Slaves*, 1976: 7–13; Aguirre Beltrán, *Población Negra*, 1989 [1946]: 17–19, 33–80; Thomas, *Slave Trade*, 1997: 92. Estimates for the number of slaves shipped to sixteenth-century Spanish America range from 75,000 to 120,000. Estimates for the total number of Africans shipped across the Atlantic as slaves also vary. For comprehensive studies of the Atlantic slave trade, see Thomas, *Slave Trade*, 1997; Berlin, *Many Thousands Gone*, 1998; and Klein, *Atlantic Slave Trade*, 1999.

29. AGI, *México* 204, fs.1–2; Icaza, *Diccionario*, 1923, I: 98; Aguirre Beltrán, *Población Negra*, 1989 [1946]: 16–17; Gerhard, "A Black Conquistador," 1978: 451–55; Alegría, *Juan Garrido*, 1990; Thomas, *Slave Trade*, 1997: 91, 95; *Who's Who*, 2000: 60–61.

30. Letter quoted in Alegría, *Juan Garrido*, 1990: 49.

31. On naming patterns, see Boyd-Bowman, "Negro Slaves," 1969: 138–50; Lockhart, *Spanish Peru*, 1994: 193–224; Landers, *Black Society*, 1999: 116–23; Restall, *The Black Middle*, n.d.

32. AGI, *México* 204, f.1; facsimile and transcription also in Alegría, *Juan Garrido*, 1990: 6, 127–38. Cortés later conceded Garrido's role but claimed it was done on his orders.

33. Durán, *History*, 1994 [1581]: 563; Gómara, *Cortés*, 1964 [1552]: 204–5, 238, 397; Cook, *Born to Die*, 1998: 63–65, 68. Spaniards also blamed African slaves for the introduction of smallpox into Colombia; Francis, *Population, Disease*, 2002: 1–2.

34. Díaz, *Conquest*, 1963 [1570]: 55. A judge wrote in 1529 of his dismay at learning how costly African slaves were in Mexico City, but in the same sentence remarked casually that he had sent off "four hundred [black] slaves to mine gold," suggesting not that enslaved Africans were scarce but that demand was even greater than supply (judge's letter in Lockhart and Otte, *Letters and People*, 1976: 194–202, quote on p. 198).

35. Aguirre Beltrán, *Población Negra*, 1989 [1946]: 19; Alegría, *Juan Garrido*, 1990: 117; Díaz, *Conquest*, 1963 [1570]: 55; Icaza, *Diccionario*, 1923, I: 129; Thomas, *Who's Who*, 2000: 155. In addition to Juan Garrido, six other free blacks requested house-plots in the new Mexico City in the 1520s (Altman, "Spanish Society," 1991: 439).

36. Durán, *History*, 1994 [1581]: 510; Lockhart, *We People Here*, 1993: 80–81 (the Nahuatl text reduces the description to invaders with *ocolochtic*, "tightly curled [hair]").

37. The two relevant Durán illustrations are Plates 57 and 58 in Durán, *History*, 1994 [1581]. A similar illustration is in the *Codex Azcatitlán* (MS #59–64 in the Collection Aubin, Paris).

38. Prescott, *Conquest of Mexico*, 1994 [1843]: 637; Gerhard, "A Black Conquistador," 1978: 458. Other examples of Spanish campaigns into the north, for whom there is good evidence of large numbers of African expeditionaries, include those led by Francisco de Ibarra in the 1520s; Lucas Vásquez de Ayllón in 1526 (to the Carolinas; many of the blacks were left there when the surviving Spaniards returned to Santo Domingo); the Florida expeditions of Hernando de Soto in 1537, Tristan de Luna y Arellano in 1559–62, and Menéndez de Avilés in 1565; and the journeys of the famous black, Esteban, in 1528–36 and 1539, the first with Alvar Núñez Cabeza de Vaca. Aguirre Beltrán, *Población Negra*, 1989 [1946]: 20; Cook, *Born to Die*, 1998: 116–19, 159; Landers, *Black Society*, 1999: 12–15; Hoffman, *Florida's Frontiers*, 2002: 39–42; Thomas, *Slave Trade*, 1997: 103; Wright, "Negro Companions," 1902: 221–28; Adorno and Pautz, *Cabeza de Vaca*, 2000, I; II: 414–22.

39. Aguirre Beltrán, *Población Negra*, 1989 [1946]: 20; Lutz, *Santiago*, 1994: 7, 83; Herrera, "People of Santiago," 1997: 254, 261.

40. A number of the black conquistadors who fought with Montejo proved their value not only by acquiring combat experience against the formidable Mayas, but also by learning their language—by 1540 at least one was able to act as an interpreter. AGI, *México* 2999, 2, f. 180; Landa, *Relación*, 1982 [1566]: 23; Restall and Chuchiak, *The Friar and the Maya*, n.d.; Konetzke, *Colección de Documentos*, 1953, I: 511–12; Aguirre Beltrán, *Población Negra*, 1989 [1946]: 19–20, 22; Wright, "Negro Companions," 1902: 220; BL, Rare MS 17,569, f. 181.

41. In addition to the examples in Table 3—Pedro Fulupo in Costa Rica and Juan Bardales in Panama and Honduras—there is also evidence of blacks participating in the Pedrarias conquest of Panama, the expeditions of Vasco Núñez de Balboa, the Gil González company of 1522–23, as well as later campaigns in Costa Rica. Meléndez and Duncan , *El Negro*, 1972: 24–25; Thomas, *Slave Trade*, 1997: 95.

42. Lockhart, *Cajamarca*, 1972: 36, 96–102, 380, 421, 447.

43. Cieza de León, *Peru*, 1998 [1550]: 68, 109, 116, 305, 310, 311, 327, 332, 333, 336, 429, 430, 465 (Peru); 433, 434, 437, 438, 439, 442 (Chile).

44. Bowser, *African Slave*, 1974: 5, 7; Lockhart, *Cajamarca*, 1972: 193; Thomas, *Slave Trade*, 1997: 103; Himmerich y Valencia, "Siege of Cuzco," 1998: 387–418. Himmerich's assertion that there were only "a handful of African slaves" in Cuzco in 1536 is arguably a myth-perpetuating understatement (p. 390).

45. Cook and Cook in Cieza de León, *Peru*, 1998: 8; Thomas, *Slave Trade*, 1997: 96, 102; Avellaneda, *Conquerors*, 1995: 63–66, 160–61; Oviedo y Baños, *Historia*, 1967 [1723]: 347, 390, 394, 438–39.

46. Gerhard, "A Black Conquistador," 1978: 452; Boyd-Bowman, "Negro Slaves," 1969: 151.

47. Bowser, *African Slave*, 1974: 4–5, 11. A merchant writing from Panama to his employers in Seville in 1526 mentioned that a royal permit for 500 Africans to be imported duty free into Peru (as yet vaguely known and unconquered) was slowly being filled (letter in Lockhart and Otte, *Letters and People*, 1976: 17–24.

48. Vásquez de Espinosa, *Compendium*, 1942 [1620]: 743–44; Sater, "Black Experience," 1974: 17.

49. Herrera, "People of Santiago," 1997: 254.

50. AGI, *México* 2999, 2: f. 180.

51. Bowser, *African Slave*, 1974: 7; Thomas, *Slave Trade*, 1997: 103.

52. Rout, *African Experience*, 1969: 13–17; Lovejoy, *Transformations in Slavery*, 1983: 15–18, 23–43; Aguirre Beltrán, *Población Negra*, 1989 [1946]: 180–94.

53. Both quoted in Diouf, *Servants of Allah*, 1998: 146, 148.

54. Vásquez de Espinosa, *Compendium*, 1942 [1620]: 743.

55. Lockhart, *Cajamarca*, 1972: 380, 384; Lane, "Captivity and Redemption," 2000: 231; Cieza de León, *Peru*, 1998 [1550]: 248; Altman, "Spanish Society," 1991: 439. Also see Table 3.

56. A fifth, Cristóbal Varela, may have had some African ancestry; Vásquez de Espinosa, *Compendium*, 1942 [1620]: 743–44; Sater, "Black Experience," 1974: 16–17.
57. Lockhart, *Cajamarca*, 1972: 51.
58. Vásquez de Espinosa, *Compendium*, 1942 [1620]: 744.

Notes to Chapter 4

1. Lockhart and Otte, *Letters and People*, 1976: 56; Simmons, *Last Conquistador*, 1991: 188.
2. I have followed the Dunn and Kelley translation quoted in Zamora, *Reading Columbus*, 1993: 156; checked against the Varela original Spanish text, also quoted by Zamora, with the sole change of glossing *cumplir* as "fulfill" rather than "carry out;" Zamora points out the significance of this term, suggesting that "comply" would be the most accurate translation (Ibid.).
3. Fernández-Armesto, *Columbus*, 1991: 39, 94, 95 (quoted passage); Zamora, *Reading Columbus*, 1993: 155.
4. Millar, *A Crossbowman's Story*, 1955; Prescott, *Conquest of Peru*, 1847, II: 143–59; Simmons, *Last Conquistador*, 1991: 3–6, 84–85, 178–92.
5. As quoted by Clendinnen, *Ambivalent Conquests*, 1987: 28.
6. Cortés, *Letters*, 1986 [1519]: 50–51.
7. Florescano, *Memory*, 1994: 67–81; Muldoon, *The Americas*, 1994; Pagden, *Spanish Imperialism*, 1990: 13–63; *European Encounters*, 1993: 17–87; *Lords of all the World*, 1995: 11–62.
8. Juan López Palacios Rubios, an eminent Castilian legal scholar, wrote in 1512 that "war on the part of the Christians is justified" once natives have been told, but then reject, "the truth"—that God authorized the pope to give the Spanish crown sovereignty over them. This opinion was codified as the *Requerimiento*. See Pagden, *Spanish Imperialism*, 1990: 15–17; *Lords of all the World*, 1995: 91; Seed, "The Requirement," 1995: 72, 92.
9. Seed, "The Requirement," 1995: 81.
10. The seventeenth–century Franciscan chronicler fray Francisco de Cárdenas y Valencia, in his *Relación historial* (manuscript in BL, Egerton 1791: f. 14v).
11. Restall, *Maya Conquistador*, 1998: 13–15.
12. Tozzer, *Landa's Relación*, 1941: 53; Chamberlain, *Conquest and Colonization*, 1948: 168.
13. Quoted in Benjamin, *La Revolución*, 2000: 15.
14. Rabasa, *Inventing America*, 1993: 125–79; Benjamin, *La Revolución*, 2000: 15–17, 120; Gallo, *Cuauhtémoc*, 1978 [1873].
15. Assertions by political figures and historians of terminal dates for the Conquest are too numerous to list; many are mentioned and cited at various points in this and other chapters. For a nineteenth-century example, see Pagden, *Spanish Imperialism*, 1990: 129–30. One common technique is to date specific conquests to the years that regional capitals were founded, and to give the entire Conquest a tidy half century—e.g., from 1492 to the founding of Santiago de Chile in 1541 (Descola, *The Conquistadors*, 1957: 316). Because of the nature of their genre, textbooks (especially older ones) have tended to simplify Conquest chronology and perpetuate the myth of completion with lines such as "By 1535, the conquest of Peru was complete" (Hordern et al., *Conquest of North America*, 1971: 125). Although native historians during the colonial period held the opposite perspective (that the Conquest was *not* a milestone moment marked by any one year; see Restall, *Maya Conquistador*, 1998, for example), there is evidence that native historians in the twentieth century adopted a variant of the colonial Spanish perspective. For example, the indigenous Colombian Manuel Quintín Lame wrote in 1939 that 1492 marked the onset of colonial exploitation, although Spaniards would not begin to conquer his native region until the 1530s (Rappaport, *Cumbe Reborn*, 1994: 161–65).

16. Prescott, *Conquest of Mexico*, 1994 [1843]: 589. The theme appears frequently in more recent studies too; a good example, because his work is otherwise very different from Prescott's, is Pagden's assertion that the Conquest was "technologically . . . a relatively simple matter," that the conquistadors "had little difficulty," and their enterprise "advanced . . . with almost bewildering rapidity" (*Spanish Imperialism*, 1990: 13). A very recent textbook, however, does emphasize the protracted nature of the Conquest: Altman, Cline, and Pescador, *Greater Mexico*, 2002: 73–74.

17. Cortés, *Cartas*, 1983 [1522]: 96; *Letters*, 1986 [1522]: 159 (I have made one small alteration to Pagden's translation).

18. Krippner-Martínez, "The Politics of Conquest," 1990: 182–85; *Rereading the Conquest*, 2001: 9–21; Pollard, *Tariacuri's Legacy*, 1993: 1; Maldonado, "Cultural Diversity," 2001: 25.

19. Schroeder, *Native Resistance*, 1998: xvii.

20. Stern, *Huamanga*, 1993. Nevertheless, in accordance with the myth of completion, a play written in 1930 by Alfred Furman could be titled *Atahualpa: The Last of the Incas* (Smith, "Conquest of Peru," 2001: 14).

21. Another example is highland Guatemala, often alleged to have been conquered by Alvarado with great speed in 1524 (see Alvarado himself, for example; *Conquest of Guatemala*, 1924 [1525]); but, as Kramer (*Encomienda Politics*, 1994) has shown, the wars of the Conquest lasted at least to 1530, with considerable unrest and violence persisting into the 1540s in core areas of the highlands and for decades more in other areas (also see Recinos, *Memorial*, 1950; Lutz, *Santiago*, 1994; Herrera, "People of Santiago," 1997).

22. Villagutierre, *Historia de la Conquista*, 1701: 20–21.

23. Respectively: Landers, *Black Society*, 1999: 11–15; Hoffman, *Florida's Frontiers*, 2002: 1–62; Verdesio, *Forgotten Conquests*, 2001: 39–72; Simmons, *Last Conquistador*, 1991; Knaut, *Pueblo Revolt*, 1995; MacLeod, "Some Thoughts," 1998: 131; Gallup-Díaz, "Tribalize the Darién," 2002; Villagutierre, *Historia de la Conquista*, 1701; and Jones, *Conquest*, 1998.

24. Verdesio, *Forgotten Conquests*, 2001: 151.

25. Fernández-Armesto, "'Aztec' Auguries," 1992: 304; Dumond, *Machete and the Cross*, 1997; Edelman, "A Central American Genocide," 1998; Deeds, "Legacies of Resistance," 2000. The seventeenth-century English chronicler John Ogilby placed the Cortés story in a larger context that emphasized Spanish failures far more than did Spanish-language accounts; "Although several Expeditions of the Spaniards to America prov'd unsuccessful at the first, yet they still undertook them afresh" (*America*, 1670: 81).

26. Susan Schroeder's "Introduction" in Schroeder, *Native Resistance*, 1998: xiii. For details of revolts in colonial Spanish America, see Taylor, *Drinking, Homicide*, 1979; Katz, "Rural Uprisings," 1988; Jones, *Maya Resistance*, 1989; Stern, *Huamanga*, 1993; Knaut, *Pueblo Revolt*, 1995; Deeds, "Legacies," 2000; Verdesio, *Forgotten Conquests*, 2001; and the essays in Schroeder, *Native Resistance*, 1998.

27. In the words of one scholar of the topic, Murdo Macleod, we tend "to look for the lost coin beneath the streetlight" ("Some Thoughts," 1998: 138).

28. Seed, "The Requirement," 1995: 84–87.

29. Lockhart, *The Nahuas*, 1992; Stern, *Huamanga*, 1993; Restall, *Maya World*, 1997; Terraciano, *The Mixtecs Writing and Culture*, 2001; Andrien, *Andean Worlds*, 2001.

30. Ricard, *La Conquête Spirituelle*, 1933.

31. The literature on this topic is extensive, but a good place to begin is two fine collections of essays, Griffiths and Cervantes, *Spiritual Encounters*, 1999, and Schwaller, *The Church*, 2000. One of the most acclaimed and sophisticated recent monographs in this subfield is Burkhart, *Slippery Earth*, 1989. Recent work on the spiritual conquest among the Yucatec Maya and the Muisca of Colombia is, respectively, Chuchiak, "The Indian Inquisition," 2000; and Francis, "la conquista espiritual," 2000. On religious images and the spiritual conquest in Mexico, see Gruzinski, *Images at War*, 2001: 22–214.

32. Francis, "la conquista espiritual," 2000: 99.
33. Restall, "Heirs to the Hieroglyphs," 1997.
34. Burns, *Poverty of Progress*, 1980. Today, the Mexican government recognizes 56 distinct native ethnic groups within the republic (Bonfil Batalla, *México Profundo*, 1996: 20; Maldonado, "Cultural Diversity," 2001: 38.
35. The most recent publication of this analysis is Lockhart, *Of Things*, 1999: 98–119, quote on p. 99.

Notes to Chapter 5

1. Díaz, *Conquest*, 1963 [1570]: 217–18); Gómara, *Cortés*, 1964 [1552]: 139; Cortés, *Letters*, 1986 [1520]: 84–85; Harris, *Navigantum*, 1748: 97. The Jesuit José de Acosta, in his *Natural and Moral History*, 2002 [1590]: 437, simply had the two "greeting one another very courteously," with the addition of a comment by Cortés, surely imagined by Acosta, that Moctezuma was "not to be so sorrowful," as the Spaniard "had not come to take his realm and diminish his authority."
2. Lockhart, *We People Here*, 1993: 116–17. For an interpretation of the meeting, widely read in its day, that took Moctezuma's alleged reverence for Cortés to absurd extremes, see Padden, *Hummingbird*, 1970: 130–32, in which, at the sight of the approaching "supermen," the Mexica emperor's "legs felt weak; he wanted to flee, but the whole empire was watching" (see Chapter 6 below for a discussion of the larger myth-based context behind such an interpretation).
3. A technique not restricted to older movies; it is used in Bergeron and Paul's *The Road to El Dorado*, 2000.
4. Díaz, *Conquest*, 1963 [1570]: 217; Gómara, *Cortés*, 1964 [1552]: 140; Lockhart, *We People Here*, 1993: 118.
5. See the Epilogue for more on the Chontal Mayas, including relevant citations, and for the circumstances under which Malinche returned to their kingdom.
6. An *encomienda* was a grant of native labor and tribute (see Chapter 2). Jaramillo's name is sometimes recorded as Juan Xaramillo de Salvatierra. My paragraphs here on Malinche are drawn from the numerous references to her in Díaz, *Historia*, 1955 [1570]; *Conquest*, 1963 [1570]); and the excellent biography by Karttunen, published in two versions (*Between Worlds*, 1994: 1–23; and "Rethinking Malinche," 1997). Also of some inspiration was Cypess, *La Malinche*, 1991; and Lanyon, *Malinche's Conquest*, 1999. For a fanciful portrait of Malinche that novelizes many Conquest myths and stereotypes, see Marshall, *Cortez and Marina*, 1963.
7. Todorov, *Conquest*, 1984: 33, 98–123.
8. Lanyon, *Malinche's Conquest*, 1999: 17–22.
9. Karttunen, "Rethinking Malinche," 1997: 295. The legend of La Llorona has evolved over the centuries to take many forms, some incorporating Malinche mythology, some not. An example of the latter is a popular song that recounts the tragic tale of a weeping woman; probably colonial or nineteenth century in origin, the song has for long been in the public domain (one recent recording is Downs, "La Llorona," 1998).
10. Salas, *Soldaderas*, 1990: 14; Cypess, *La Malinche*, 1991: 41–152; Karttunen, "Rethinking Malinche," 1997: 296–98; Lanyon, *Malinche's Conquest*, 1999: 187–202. Thus the subtitle to this chapter, "The Myth of (Mis)Communication" is also a rather excrutiating pun that refers to Malinche's legend—"The Myth of Miss (or Ms.?) Communication."
11. Karttunen, "Rethinking Malinche," 1997: 295–96.
12. Díaz, *Conquest*, 1963 [1570]: 153.

13. Quoted by Todorov, *Conquest*, 1984: 98, who does not identify his source and I have not been able to locate the passage in the primary texts.

14. Gómara, *Cortés*, 1964 [1552]: 57.

15. I am indebted to Cesco, "Invisible Conquistador," 2001: 22, for this point.

16. Cortés, *Letters*, 1986 [1520]: 85–87. Columbus sometimes does the same thing; for example, in his account of his third voyage, upon meeting natives on the Venezuelan coast, he states that he "inquired very carefully" of them on various matters, without mentioning an interpreter (*Four Voyages*, 1969 [1498–1500]: 215). This imaginary communication was illustrated literally in the frontispiece to one of the first history texts published for children in the United States; the etching, titled "Columbus's first interview with the natives of America," shows Columbus, dressed as an eighteenth-century gentleman, holding a Native American's hand and seeming to be chatting with him (reproduced in Bushman, *America Discovers Columbus*, 1992: 101).

17. Greenblatt, *Marvelous Possessions*, 1991: 98.

18. There are many versions of the Requirement, as Seed states, but I have used her translated version ("The Requirement," 1995: 69).

19. Las Casas makes the comment in Book III, Chapter 58 of his *Historia de las Indias*, 1971 [1559]: 196; quoted, for example, in Todorov, *Conquest*, 1984: 149; Greenblatt, *Marvelous Possessions*, 1991: 98; and Seed, "The Requirement," 1995: 71.

20. With respect to Columbus's first voyage: Columbus, *Four Voyages*, 1969 [1492–93]: 116; Fernández-Armesto, *Columbus*, 1991: 106. The physician's name was Chanca (Columbus, *Four Voyages*, 1969 [1496]: 151). I am indebted to Vincent, "Use of Signs," 2001, for pointing out a dozen instances where Columbus or Chanca mention interpreters.

21. Greenblatt, *Marvelous Possessions*, 1991: 105.

22. Lockhart, *Cajamarca*, 1972: 6, 448–53; Varón Gabai, *Pizarro*, 1997: 169–70; Karttunen, "Interpreters Snatched from the Shore," 2000: 217.

23. Karttunen, *Between Worlds*, 1994: 84–114, 308; Restall, *Maya Conquistador*, 1998: 144–50; "Gaspar Antonio Chi," 2001.

24. Quoted by Todorov, *Conquest*, 1984: 32.

25. The quoted phrase is Karttunen's (*Between Worlds*, 1994: xi). Also quoted by Vincent, "Use of Signs," 2001: 2. Also see Karttunen, "Interpreters Snatched from the Shore," 2000, which serves as a brief introduction to some of the material and arguments in *Between Worlds*, 1994. For discussion of English attempts to communicate with native peoples in North America, see Axtell, *Natives and Newcomers*, 2000: 46–75. For treatment of this theme in twentieth-century Yucatan and Colombia, respectively, see Sullivan, *Unfinished Conversations*, 1989; and Rappaport, *Cumbe Reborn*, 1994: 97–100, 170–71.

26. "Ignorance" quote in Zamora, *Reading Columbus*, 1993: 84.

27. Todorov, *Conquest*, 1984: 33; Zamora, *Reading Columbus*, 1993: 158; Greenblatt, *Marvelous Possessions*, 1991: 89–90.

28. Todorov, *Conquest*, 1984: 97–123; Clendinnen, "'Fierce and Unnatural Cruelty,'" 1991: 18–36.

29. Elliott, *The Old World and the New*, 1970: quoted passages, 21, 18–19.

30. Le Clézio, *Mexican Dream*, 1993: 12, 16, 17.

31. Schwartz, *Victors and Vanquished*, 2000: 41.

32. Todorov, *Conquest*, 1984: 160; Greenblatt, *Marvelous Possessions*, 1991: 11–12. For a defense of Todorov's position on literacy and an insistence that the distinction he makes "between semiliterate and fully literate communities is not, as it is with his Spanish sources, one of excellence," see Anthony Pagden's "Foreword" to Todorov, *Conquest*, 1999 [1984]: xi. Even accepting Pagden's point, I would argue that because of the prevalence of old myths in modern-day perceptions of the Conquest, Todorov's distinction

by degrees comes too close to colonialist tropes of superiority and thus has the effect of endorsing them—despite Todorov's intention to to the contrary.

33. Diamond, *Guns, Germs, and Steel*, 1997: 78–79.

34. Diamond, *Guns, Germs, and Steel*, 1997: 80, 215–16, 238.

35. Diamond, *Guns, Germs, and Steel*, 1997: 80.

36. The Lévi-Strauss quote, as well as the Aquinas, Las Casas, and Aristotle references, are taken from Seed, "'Failing to Marvel,'" 1991: 8.

37. Seed, "'Failing to Marvel,'" 1991: 16–21.

38. Seed, "'Failing to Marvel,'" 1991: 22–26. Also see the role played by miscommunication in the 1960s play and film, Shaffer, *The Royal Hunt of the Sun*, 1969; and its discussion by Chang-Rodríguez, "Cultural Resistance," 1994, in the context of other accounts, especially a 1957 Bolivian play. Smith, "Conquest of Peru," 2001, compares Shaffer's play to Sheridan's 1800 adaptation of von Kotzebue's *Pizarro: A Tragedy in Five Acts* and other early dramas seeking "to improve upon the facts" (p. 1).

39. Cieza de León, *Peru*, 1998 [1550]: 211–12.

40. For example, the accounts by Pedro Pizarro and Hernando Pizarro—excerpts from which are transcribed in Prescott, *Conquest of Peru*, 1847, II: 475–77, with Hernando's 1533 account included in translation in Markham, *Discovery of Peru*, 1872: 113–27—and the Huaman Poma account summarized by Seed, "'Failing to Marvel,'" 1991: 27–29; Huaman Poma, *Nueva Corónica*, 1980 [1615]: 353–57. The derivative account by the Englishman John Ogilby (*America*, 1670: 96–98) accords most closely with Jerez's.

41. Seed, "'Failing to Marvel,'" 1991: 13; although in a later piece Seed suggests that the Requirement was not read until later, when Pizarro reached Cuzco ("The Requirement," 1995: 98). The latter may in fact be the case, as Juan de Solórzano stated in his great legal treatise on the Conquest, *De Indiarum Jure* (1629–39), that the king sent the Requirement to Pizarro in 1533 (Muldoon, *The Americas*, 1994: 136).

42. Hanke, *Spanish Struggle for Justice*, 1949: 33–34, also quoted by Seed, "'Failing to Marvel,'" 1991: 13.

43. Quoted in Todorov, *Conquest*, 1984: 148.

44. Seed, "The Requirement," 1995: 75–85.

45. An example of the Requirement's absurdity being a part of its function can be found in Alvarado's account of his 1524 invasion of Guatemala, written as a pair of letters to Cortés. Alvarado begins the first letter stating that when he was still three days' journey from highland Guatemala he sent Maya messengers into the highlands with what was clearly a summary of the Requirement. This act had a dual purpose: to demonstrate to Cortés and crown officials that proper procedure had been followed, and to intimidate the Mayas with a warning of impending invasion (Alvarado, *Conquest of Guatemala*, 1924 [1525]: 53).

46. Cortés, *Letters*, 1986 [1520]: 85–86.

47. Gómara, *Cortés*, 1964 [1552]: 140–42.

48. Díaz, *Conquest*, 1963 [1570]: 220). Another account was made by Francisco de Flores, one of the conquistadors of the Spanish-Mexica war, who testified in the proceedings of Cortés's *residencia* (formal investigation into a term of office), which dragged out from the late 1520s to Cortés's death two decades later. Flores, whose view was probably that of most Spaniards at the time, also portrayed Moctezuma's speech as constituting a surrender of sovereignty, adding that the surrender must have been "agreed formally since the said don Hernando always had with him a notary to be present at things which occurred" (testimony excerpted in Thomas, *Conquest*, 1995: 634–35, translation his).

49. Lockhart, *We People Here*, 1993: 116. I have not altered Lockhart's translation save for italicizing *altepetl* and inserting [city-state] after it first appears. The *altepetl* was actually both more and less than a city-state, being the Nahua municipal community and

focus of Nahua identity, ranging in size from a village to the metropolis of Mexico-Tenochtitlan. The five rulers that Moctezuma names in his speech were his five predecessor emperors.

50. For suggestions by other scholars as to how Cortés may have imagined or invented the surrender, see Elliott, "Cortés," 1989: 36–38; and Pagden, *Lords of all the World*, 1995: 32.

51. Sahagún, *Florentine Codex*, 1950–82, Book VI; Karttunen and Lockhart, *Art of Nahuatl Speech*, 1987: including 2–15 for a useful summary of the genre; Maxwell and Hanson, *Manners of Speaking*, 1992; Kicza, "Comparison," 1992: 56–57.

52. Karttunen, "Rethinking Malinche," 1997: 301.

53. Vargas Machuca, *Milicia y Descripción*, 1599: unnumbered prefatory p. 3. For an argument that violence was the primary medium of cultural communication and exchange between Portuguese and natives on the southeastern frontier of eighteenth-century Brazil, see Langfur, "Reversing the Frontier's Advance," 2002.

Notes to Chapter 6

1. Huaman Poma, *Nueva Corónica*, 1980 [1615]; I have also used an unpublished translation of excerpts by James Lockhart.

2. Wachtel, *Vision of the Vanquished*, 1977: 30.

3. www.yale.edu/ynhti/curriculum/units/1992/2/92.02.01.x.html; León-Portilla, *Broken Spears*, 1992: xxxiii; xv in the original 1962 edition. Eminent French anthropologist Claude Lévi-Strauss recently defended this emphasis on native victimhood in a review in *L'Homme* (2001) of the South America volume of the *Cambridge History of the Native Peoples of the Americas* (Salomon and Schwartz, 1999), accusing the editors of perpetrating a form of Holocaust revisionism by emphasizing native agency and protagonism; see Schwartz, "Denounced," 2002, for a summary of and response to Lévi-Strauss's critique.

4. Sale, *Conquest of Paradise*, 1990; Berliner, "Man's Best," 1991.

5. The term "anomie" was coined by the French sociologist Émile Durkheim in his 1897 study of *Le Suicide* (www.britannica.com/eb/article?eu=7804); I first saw it used in the context of Native Americans and the European invasion in Gubler Rotsman, "Acculturative Role," 1985, where it is used extensively, and in Taylor, *Drinking, Homicide*, 1979: 144, where it is mentioned in passing.

6. Le Clézio, *Mexican Dream*, 1993: 176.

7. Whitehead, "Historical Anthropology of Text," 1995: 56; Ralegh, *Discoverie*, 1997 [1596]: 178–79.

8. Whitehead in Ralegh, *Discoverie*, 1997: 91–101; Fernández-Armesto, *Before Columbus*, 1987: 223–45.

9. Letter of 1493 published in Zamora, *Reading Columbus*, 1993: 196–97, who also uses the other quote (p. 170). In the version written by Columbus's son, the Genoese appears to accept that there are Amazons in the Caribbean (Columbus, *Life*, 1992 [1539]: 171). For a brief polemic on Columbus and cannibalism among Caribbean natives as pure myth, see Sale, *Conquest of Paradise*, 1990: 129–35; for a more complex argument on the topic, see Whitehead, *Lords of the Tiger Spirit*, 1988. For a recent, comprehensive, and original monograph on the topic of Amazons, see Weinbaum, *Islands of Women*, 1999.

10. Quoted in Zamora, *Reading Columbus*, 1993: 159.

11. Quoted in Zamora, *Reading Columbus*, 1993: 160, 167; also see Todorov, *Conquest*, 1984: 35.

12. Quoted in Fuentes, *Buried Mirror*, 1992: 125. A century later there were still native groups being described as without any religion at all; for example, this was how Herrera characterized the Chichimecs (*Historia General*, 1601, dec. I: p. 10; dec. III: p. 75).

13. Quoted in Zamora, *Reading Columbus*, 1993: 90; also cited by Arndt, "Mythic After-math," 2001: 16.
14. Quoted in Hanke, "Dawn of Conscience," 1963: 87. Modern heirs of this view include Sale, *Conquest of Paradise*, 1990, and Carl Sauer, who argued that "the tropical idyll of the accounts of Columbus and Peter Martyr was largely true"; natives "suffered no want" and "lived in peace and amity"(quoted in Christensen and Christensen, *Discovery*, 1992: 3–4).
15. Florescano, *Memory*, 1994: 82–90, Mendieta quote on p. 89; Krippner-Martínez, *Rereading the Conquest*, 2001: 71–106. On the sixteenth-century view that Spanish brutality caused demographic decline in the Caribbean, see Las Casas, *Devastation*, 1992 [1552]; on the modern (and now generally accepted) view that the primary cause was disease, see Cook, *Born to Die*, 1998. Arndt, "Mythic Aftermath," 2001: 14, also discusses supposed native malleability.
16. Quoted in Zamora, *Reading Columbus*, 1993: 167.
17. Vargas Machuca, *Milicia y Descripción*, 1599: 140r; also see p. 125v for a passage on native propensities for cruelty and cannibalism. The Dominican and Oviedo are quoted in Todorov, *Conquest*, 1984: 150–51. Mund, *Les rapports complexes*, 2001, argues that Díaz presents the four traits listed above as the principal characteristics of the Mexica as a way of justifying the Spanish destruction of Tenochtitlán (also see Díaz, *Conquest*, 1963 [1570]). The sodomy theme is interestingly contextualized by Trexler, *Sex and Conquest*, 1995. On European perceptions of natives as diabolistic, see Cervantes, *Devil in the New World*, 1994: 5–39. The idea that colonialism was justified by moral superiority was of course a broader European concept; Charles Lemire, a French colonial official in the South Pacific, put it well in 1884 when he wrote, "To colonize is to moralize; to moralize people ignorant of civilization; to moralize men rendered vicious by the abuse of civilization; there is no better way of attaining this goal than through colonizing" (Bullard, *Exile to Paradise*, 2000: 3).
18. Certeau, *Writing of History*, 1988: xxv; Zamora, *Reading Columbus*, 1993: 152–55; Rabasa, *Inventing America*, 1993: 23–48.
19. Quoted in Todorov, *Conquest*, 1984: 156 from Sepúlveda's *Tratados politicos*.
20. Landa, *Relación*, 1982 [1566]: 5–8; Restall and Chuchiak, *The Friar and the Maya*, n.d.: 3–5. For a similar emphasis on the dangers of Yucatan's human and natural environment, in the first European publication about the peninsula (that was still thought to be an island), see Juan Díaz's 16-page book on the Grijalva expedition (Díaz, *Littera mandata*, 1520; facsimile copy in the JCBL). On Guerrero and his legend, see Clendinnen, *Ambivalent Conquests*, 1987: 17–22; Restall, *Maya Conquistador*, 1998: 7; and Vallado Fajardo, "Cristianos españoles e indios yucatecos," 2000.
21. Ellingson, *Noble Savage*, 2001. Contrary to the myth about the myth, Rousseau did not create the Noble Savage concept, as Ellingson demonstrates.
22. The lyrics are by Tim Rice and, on Elton John's soundtrack to the movie, sung by John and Randy Newman (Rice and John, *El Dorado*, 2000; Bergeron and Paul, *El Dorado*, 2000).
23. Obeyesekere, *Apotheosis*, 1992 (who on p. 125 uses the Larson cartoon presented here as Figure 14). For the relevance here of Obeyesekere's work, see my discussion below of the Sahlins-Obeyesekere debate on Captain Cook.
24. Todorov, *Conquest*, 1984: 75; Inclán, "Plucking the Feathered Serpent," 2001: 1.
25. These three translations are all in Zamora, *Reading Columbus*, 1993: 45, 192, 16, respectively (the last one being the letter to Santángel). Cohen also translates *cielo* as "sky" (Columbus, *Four Voyages*, 1969: 118; also quoted by Inclán, "Plucking the Feathered Serpent," 2001: 5.

26. Zamora, *Reading Columbus*, 1993: 201 n8.

27. Bitterli, *Cultures in Conflict*, 1989: 72–73, 25–26; his cited sources are the *Florentine Codex* and Wachtel, *Vision of the Vanquished*, 1977, both of which I discuss below. Another example of the extreme embrace of the apotheosis myth is Le Clézio, who has the Spaniards taken for gods right from the start and their divine status confirmed by military victories and demands for gold (*Mexican Dream*, 1993: 3, 10, 12, 14)—the Nahuatl for gold was *teocuitlatl*, combining the terms for "god" and "extrusion or excrement," but see my point below on meanings of *teotl*, "god." Todorov, *Conquest*, 1984: 81 admits that the Mayas did not take the Spaniards to be gods, but argues that this was because they had writing—a faulty argument, as the Mexica also had writing, and no evidence is presented as to why lack of writing would lead to such credulity.

28. Gómara, *Cortés*, 1964 [1552]: 50, 137, 58, 130, 133, 128. On the Cholula massacre: Pagden in Cortés, *Letters*, 1986: 465–66 n27; Peterson and Green, "Massacre at Cholula," 1987.

29. Lockhart, *Nahuatl As Written*, 2001: 234.

30. Díaz, *Conquest*, 1963 [1570]: 138. Another instance is cited in Todorov, *Conquest*, 1984: 88–89; and another is Díaz, *Discovery*, 1956 [1570]: 266.

31. My translation from Díaz, *Historia*, 1955 [1570]: 65; but also see Díaz, *Discovery*, 1956 [1570]: 73.

32. Elliott, "Cortés," 1989: 37–38.

33. Quoted in Thomas, *Conquest*, 1995: 111.

34. Elliott, "Cortés," 1989: 36. Like the Franciscans who wrote before him, the Jesuit missionary and chronicler José de Acosta presented in his *Natural and Moral History of the Indies* of 1590 the various mythical aspects of the Spanish invasion as evidence of God's role and purpose in the Conquest. Yet, following earlier sources, Acosta merely details Quetzalcoatl's identity as an "ancient and great lord" destined to return, with his status as a god and the consequent apotheosis of Cortés and other Spaniards left muted and ambiguous (*Natural and Moral History*, 2002 [1590]: 433–35).

35. Lockhart, *We People Here*, 1993: 13, 27; Clendinnen, "'Fierce and Unnatural Cruelty,'" 1991: 16; Kicza, "Indian and Spanish Accounts," 1992: 60. The best version of the Book XII, presented in Spanish, Nahuatl, and English, is in Lockhart, *We People Here*, 1993: 48–255. For a skillful appraisal of the *Codex* in the context of other sources on the Conquest of Mexico, see Brooks, "Construction of an Arrest," 1995.

36. Thomas, *Conquest*, 1995: 41–44; Bitterli, *Cultures in Conflict*, 1989: 72–73; Kicza, "Indian and Spanish Accounts," 1992: 59, 62. In his account published in 1590, shortly after his death, Acosta presented the omens as "devised" by God, but he details the appearance of similar omens in the Old Testament and admits that "some of these things may not have happened exactly as described" (*Natural and Moral History*, 2002 [1590]: 427–32). For a succinct analysis and explanation of the omens, see Fernández-Armesto, "'Aztec' Auguries," 1992. For credulous presentations of them, see León-Portilla, *Broken Spears*, 1992: 3–12; Todorov, *Conquest*, 1984: 63–75; and Wolf, *Sons of the Shaking Earth*, 1959: 169. For appropriately skeptical presentations, see Schwartz, *Victors and Vanquished*, 2000: 29–39; Hassig, *Aztec Warfare*, 1988: 219–33; Gillespie, *Aztec Kings*, 1989: chap. 6. Carrasco, *Quetzalcoatl*, 2000: 236–40, deftly walks the line between the two positions.

37. Lockhart, *We People Here*, 1993: 235; Thomas, *Conquest*, 1995: 185; Inclán, "Plucking the Feathered Serpent," 2001: 2–3, 5–15, 22–23, to whom I am grateful for drawing my attention to many of the sources discussed in this section of the chapter. For a discussion of Lockhart's position, and the strongest argument I have seen that the Cortés-as-Quetzalcoatl story was circulating during the Conquest, see Carrasco, *Quetzalcoatl*, 2000: 210–40; also Gruzinski, *Conquest of Mexico*, 1993: 76. The anthropologist H. B. Nicholson is inclined to accept the story as real, but his review of the evidence in "The 'Return of

Quetzalcoatl,'" 2001, concludes that it can only be seen "as a serious working hypothesis" (p. 15); also see his *Topiltzin Quetzalcoatl,* 2001. The myth is presented as historical fact in numerous works of history (especially older publications, textbooks, readers, and works of popular history); see, for example, Wolf, *Sons of the Shaking Earth,* 1959: 169; Padden, *Hummingbird and the Hawk,* 1970: 116–132, Hordern et al., *Conquest of North America,* 1971: 59; Christensen and Christensen, *Discovery,* 1992: 53; Keen, *Latin America,* 1996: 65 (though his position is more ambiguous in *Aztec Image,* 1971: 51, 186, 483); and Baldwin, *Legends of the Plumed Serpent,* 1998: 90–103. A Library of Congress website on "Mexico: The Spanish Conquest," a brief summary containing a number of errors and myths presented as facts, suggests that the main reason for Spanish victory was Moctezuma's belief that Cortés was the "white god," Quetzalcoatl (http://lcweb2.loc.gov/cgi-bin/query/r?frd/cstdy:@field(DOCID+mx0013)). A recent article in the *Chronicle of Higher Education* refers to the myth unquestioningly as a "widespread belief among historians" (Lloyd, "The Scholar," 2002). For an argument that the holes in the Cortés-as-Quetzalcoatl myth mean that Moctezuma thought Cortés was another Nahua god, Tezcatlipoca, see Wasserman, "Montezuma's Passivity," 1983. On Quetzalcoatl as a god and mythical culture hero in pre-Conquest times, see Florescano, *The Myth of Quetzalcoatl,* 1999; and Carrasco, *Quetzalcoatl,* 2000: 11–204.

38. Tuchman, *March of Folly,* 1984: 11–14; Todorov, *Conquest,* 1984: 119. There are many other instances of this view of Moctezuma in published works; e.g., Wolf, *Sons of the Shaking Earth,* 1959: 155–56.

39. Le Clézio, *Mexican Dream,* 1993: 10.

40. Recinos, *Memorial,* 1950: 126 translates the phrase as "Los Señores los tomaron por dioses" (the Maya original is on line 26 of a page reproduced in facsimile facing p. 124). Kramer follows this gloss and states that "the native chroniclers, however, admit that they were in fear of the strangers and that the lords mistook them for gods" (*Encomienda Politics,* 1994: 32).

41. As, indeed, Kramer shows in her treatment of the Conquest (*Encomienda Politics,* 1994: 25–125); her acceptance of the above apotheosis sentence is an exception to her tendency to avoid the traps of Conquest myths. Also see the Maya account in Recinos (*Memorial,* 1950: 124–140) and Alvarado's account in his two letters to Cortés (Alvarado, *Conquest of Guatemala,* 1924 [1525]; also published in Fuentes, *The Conquistadors,* 1963: 184–96).

42. Todorov, *Conquest,* 1984: 93–96; Krippner-Martínez, *Rereading the Conquest,* 2001: 16 (the quotations), 9–69, 109–49 (the critical study of the Conquest, its historiography, and the *Relación*); the Prescott quote atop this chapter.

43. Cieza de León, *Peru,* 1998 [1550]: 217, 313—the only two mentions of the Viracocha nickname in all of Cieza de León's long history of the Conquest. In another volume of his writings, Cieza de León mentions the Spanish-Viracocha association and is openly skeptical of it (Harris, "Coming of the White People," 1995: 13).

44. Sarmiento quoted by Harris, "Coming of the White People," 1995: 13.

45. This is my hybrid translation drawn from Acosta, *Natural and Moral History,* 2002 [1590]: 257; and from the gloss by Harris in "Coming of the White People," 1995: 13.

46. Harris, "Coming of the White People," 1995: 13.

47. Silverblatt, *Moon, Sun, and Witches,* 1987: 177–78.

48. Quoted by Wachtel, *Vision of the Vanquished,* 1977: 22; and Bitterli, *Cultures in Conflict,* 1989: 26. Titu Cusi became Inca upon his brother's death in 1561, ruling an independent Inca kingdom in the Andes until his death in 1571; Titu Cusi's policy toward the Spanish colony of Peru was hostile until 1567, when a treaty was signed whereby the Inca preserved his autonomy by paying lip service to Spanish sovereignty (Andrien, *Andean Worlds,* 2001: 197–98).

49. Interpreting Titu Cusi's words is problematized by the fact that he dictated his account in Quechua to an Augustinian, fray Marcos García, who then wrote it down in Spanish—as Wachtel observes, although his spin on the material is ultimately in support of the apotheosis myth (*Vision of the Vanquished*, 1977: 227 n54).

50. Zárate, *Peru*, 1981 [1555]: 103.

51. The Yucatec governor was Santiago Mendez (Mendez, *Report*, 1921 [1861]: 185). The "terror" quote is Bitterli's (*Cultures in Conflict*, 1989: 26). An interesting variation on the apotheosis myth in the Andes is in Shaffer's *Royal Hunt of the Sun*, in which Pizarro presents himself as a god in order to confuse and amaze Atahuallpa. Shaffer ducks some Conquest myths, but not this one; his Inca is quick to fall for Pizarro's strategy (Shaffer, *Royal Hunt*, 1969; Smith, "Conquest of Peru," 2001: 25). Parallel to the modern perpetuation of the sixteenth-century myth of native desolation is the modern perpetuation of the ethnocentric colonial view that the "Indians" were too uncivilized to have built the ancient ruined cities of the Americas. One advocate of this position, Graham Hancock, is particularly pernicious because of the way he recycles racist colonial perspectives on natives into a supposedly revisionist package; he writes, for example, of the "stolid Aymara Indians who walked slowly in the narrow cobbled streets and sat placidly in the little sunlit plaza. Were these people the descendents of the builders of Tiahuanaco, as the scholars insisted? Or were the legends right? Had the ancient city been the work of foreigners with godlike powers who had settled here, long ages ago?" (*Fingerprints of the Gods*, 1995: 71).

52. Ilarione da Bergamo, *Daily Life*, 2000 [1770]: 96.

53. Lockhart, *The Nahuas*, 1992: 270–72; Restall, *Maya World*, 1997: 181. The horse-rider myth is still alive, of course; Le Clézio, citing Díaz, has "Indians" believing it "for a long time" (*Mexican Dream*, 1993: 6).

54. This was according to both Cortés, *Letters*, 1986 [1526]: 364–65; and Gómara, *Cortés*, 1964 [1552]: 353–54.

55. López Austin, *Places of Mist*, 1997: 23, 209–14. Clendinnen has persuasively argued that the Mexica's elaborate rituals of execution or human sacrifice were designed to achieve control over a phenomenon of which the Mexica were particularly aware, human mortality (*Aztecs*, 1991: 87–152). Also see Clendinnen, "'Fierce and Unnatural Cruelty,'" 1991, and, on various Mesoamerican conceptions of death, López Austin, *Places of Mist*, 1997: 166–69, 186–88, 194.

56. Carrasco, *Quetzalcoatl*, 2000: 28–39.

57. Inclán, "Plucking the Feathered Serpent," 2001: 3, 25, 28.

58. Jemingham, *Fall of Mexico*, 1775; Cowher, "A Handful of Adventurers?" 2001: 20–21. I am grateful to Iris Cowher for drawing my attention to this source and its relevance here. Cowher also discusses a German source of 1800, published in English in 1811, that portrays the conquistadors as motivated by greed and religious fanaticism and the Conquest of Mexico as a suitable morality tale for children; the book's title is *Cortez, or The Conquest of Mexico: As Related by a Father to His Children and Designed for the Instruction of Youth* (Campe, *Cortez*, 1811). A parallel piece is a German play by August von Koztebue, adapted by Sheridan in 1800 as *Pizarro: A Tragedy in Five Acts*, whose finale is the death of Pizarro and the triumph of Atahuallpa (Smith, "Conquest of Peru," 2001: 12). The Spanish Armada of 1588 was a vast fleet intended to spearhead an invasion of England but destroyed mostly by bad weather before a single soldier could land (an older classic account is Mattingly, *Armada*, 1959; a more recent study is Martin and Parker, *Spanish Armada*, 1988).

59. Sahlins, "Individual Experience," 1982: 289–90; *Islands of History*, 1985: 74, 154; "Cosmologies," 1988: 441–42; *How "Natives" Think*, 1995.

60. Obeyesekere, *Apotheosis*, 1992: 123; discussion of Todorov is also on pp. 16–19.
61. Obeyesekere, *Apotheosis*, 1992: 91 et al. A similar point is made by Hassig, *Time, History*, 2001: 156, in a discussion of the Mexica.
62. Motolinía, *Historia*, 1979 [1541]: *trat.* I, chap. 15; Harris, *Aztecs, Moors, and Christians*, 2000: 132–47.
63. As Harris observes; *Aztecs, Moors, and Christians*, 2000: 144.
64. Harris, *Aztecs, Moors, and Christians*, 2000: 137. A further dimension to the slighting of Cortés in the drama is the fact that the governor of Tlaxcala in 1539 was don Luís Xicotencatl, nephew of the Axayacatzin Xicotencatl who had led Tlaxcalan resistance against Cortés in 1519, had reluctantly joined the allied cause in 1521 and then, when he seemed uncooperative, had been hanged by Cortés in Texcoco that year (Gómara, *Cortés*, 1964 [1552]: 100–16; Gibson, *Tlaxcala*, 1952: 98–100; Thomas, *Conquest*, 1995: 490–91; Harris, *Aztecs, Moors, and Christians*, 2000: 139).
65. The exception to the actors being Tlaxcalans was a fictional Caribbean native army, defeated in the middle of the play in their attempt to take Jerusalem. These actors were Otomí natives—reflecting Tlaxcalan insight into colonial Caribbean history and their perception of Caribbean and Otomí natives in a different category from Tlaxcalans (a difference we would define as that between semisedentary and sedentary peoples). Harris, *Aztecs, Moors, and Christians*, 2000: 140–41, 136, 135.
66. Harris, *Aztecs, Moors, and Christians*, 2000: 134.
67. Bricker, *The Indian Christ*, 1981: 129–54; Hill, *Colonial Cakchiquels*, 1992: 1–8; Cohen, "Danza de la Pluma," 1993; Rappaport, *Cumbe Reborn*, 1994: 145–66; Restall, *Maya Conquistador*, 1998: 46, 193–94 n53; Harris, *Aztecs, Moors, and Christians*, 2000.
68. See Restall, "Heirs to the Hieroglyphs," 1997, which includes a fairly comprehensive bibliography of *título* studies. *Títulos* continue to be discovered and published, enriching our understanding of the native views of the Conquest described above; see Colom et al., *Testamento y Título*, 1999.
69. Restall, *Maya Conquistador*, 1998.
70. The only presentation and study of these *títulos* is Sousa and Terraciano, "Original Conquest," 2003; also see Terraciano, *The Mixtecs*, 2001: 336–38.
71. Fernández-Armesto in Prescott, *Conquest of Mexico*, 1994: xxx; Hassig, *Aztec Warfare*, 1988; Hill, *Colonial Cakchiquels*, 1992; Dakin and Lutz, *Nuestro Pesar*, 1996.
72. AGI, *México* 97; 138; 2999; Restall, *Maya Conquistador*, 1998: 53–76; Scholes and Roys, *Maya-Chontal Indians*, 1948: 142–290. The Chontal Maya kingdom and its *título* is further discussed in the Epilogue below, in the context of events of 1525 when don Pablo Paxbolon's grandfather, predecessor, and namesake, Paxbolonacha, was king. The Chontals were not the only Mayas to raid as colonial agents the large unconquered zone that lay between the Spanish provinces in northern Yucatan and southern Guatemala. As mentioned in Chapter 3, in 1624 the Maya governor of Oxkutzcab (a Yucatec Maya town) was commissioned to lead 150 of his warriors on a punitive expedition south, while Spanish campaigns into the Petén region of northern Guatemala, coming from highland Guatemala and Yucatan in the 1690s, made extensive use of squads of Mopan and Yucatec Maya archers (Jones, *Conquest*, 1998: 48, 134–36, 258, 263).
73. Gibson, *Tlaxcala*, 1952: 191; also quoted by Harris, *Aztecs, Moors, and Christians*, 2000: 139.
74. Fernández-Armesto, "'Aztec' Auguries," 1992: 298; Prescott, *Conquest of Mexico*, 1994: xxix; Hassig, *Aztec Warfare*, 1988; Brooks, "Construction of an Arrest," 1995.
75. Cieza de León, *Peru*, 1998 [1550]: 447–66; Sarmiento, *History of the Incas*, 1907 [1572]: 258–61; Prescott, *Conquest of Peru*, 1847, II: chaps. 1–3; Wachtel, *Vision of the Vanquished*, 1977: 169–84; Himmerich y Valencia, "Siege of Cuzco," 1998; Wood, *Conquistadors*, 2000: 155–85.

76. As illustrated in an important and fascinating series of documents of the 1530s to 1620s, most of them petitions to the king from Mexica royalty and other nobles, preserved in the AGI and recently published in Pérez-Rocha and Tena, *La nobleza indígena*, 2000. Complementary sources are the records of legal actions taken over lands and noble privileges by doña Isabel Moctezuma, the emperor's daughter, in the 1540s to 1560s, published in Pérez-Rocha, *Privilegios en Lucha*, 1998. Doña Isabel's descendents received government pensions until 1934, and in 2000 began a legal campaign to have the pensions reinstated (Lloyd, "The Scholar," 2002).

77. They were prominent members of what I have elsewhere termed Yucatan's "dynastic dozen"; Restall, "People of the Patio," 2001: 351–58, 366–68. The collection of documents known as the Xiu Papers, of which Figure 17 is a part, were recently published for the first time, as Quezada and Okoshi, *Papeles de los Xiu*, 2001.

78. For this argument laid out with Maya evidence, see Restall, *Maya World*, 1997: 51–83; for treatments of native *cabildos* in other regions, see Spalding, *Huarochirí*, 1984: 216–26, Haskett, *Indigenous Rulers*, 1991, Stern, *Peru's Indian Peoples*, 1993: 92–96, and Terraciano, *The Mixtecs*, 2001: 182–97.

79. Lockhart, *Of Things*, 1999: 98. Also see Restall, "Interculturation," 1998: 141–62.

80. Cook, *Born to Die*, 1998. Note that there is much disagreement on the size of native populations in the ancient Americas, with estimates on sixteenth-century losses varying above and below the middle-ground figure of 40 million. But even at, say, 25 million, the death toll was still greater than Europe's Black Death, for example.

81. See Powers, "Battle of Wills," 1998: 183–213.

82. For readings on this issue with respect to central Mexico and Yucatan, for example, see Harvey, *Land and Politics*, 1991; Lockhart, *The Nahuas*, 1992: 141–202; Horn, *Postconquest Coyoacan*, 1997: 111–165; and Restall, *Maya World*, 1997: 169–225.

83. "Nothingness" is Le Clézio's term (*Mexican Dream*, 1993: 5).

84. Clendinnen, "'Fierce and Unnatural Cruelty,'" 1991: 19.

Notes to Chapter 7

1. Wilson, *Emperor's Giraffe*, 1999: 5, 7.

2. Quoted in Fuentes, *Buried Mirror*, 1992: 126. Sepúlveda was not the only sixteenth-century European to compare natives to animals; Villegagnon wrote to Calvin that the Tupinamba of Brazil struck him as "a wild and savage people, remote from all courtesy and humanity," like "beasts bearing a human countenance" (quoted in Greenblatt, *Marvelous Possessions*, 1991: 154 n13).

3. Trouillot, *Silencing the Past*, 1995: 82. Both Trouillot and I quote Diderot somewhat out of context; for a detailed discussion of Diderot's ideas on colonization, the nature of Native Americans, and native-European contact, see Pagden, *European Encounters*, 1993: 141–88.

4. The Quincentennial produced extreme expressions of old views from both sides of the debate; the vice mayor of Pasadena, commenting on the controversy over a planned Columbus Day parade in that Californian city, called the direct descendent of Columbus who had originally been picked to lead the parade "a symbol of greed, slavery, rape, and genocide." George Black, then foreign editor of the *Nation*, decried "the smug assumption of white cultural supremacy" that ran "across the mainstream political spectrum" and lay behind "official celebrations of Columbus" (Black, "1492," 1991; Berliner, "Man's Best," 1991). Two fine treatments of the Quincentennial, one brief, the other book length, are Trouillot, *Silencing the Past*, 1995: 108–40; and Summerhill and Williams, *Sinking Columbus*, 2000.

5. It has only been a few decades since the eminent British historian Hugh Trevor-Roper summarized non-European history as "the unrewarding gyrations of barbarous tribes in picturesque but irrelevant corners of the globe"—in his *The Rise of Christian Europe*, published in the United States in 1974; quoted by Parenti, *History as Mystery*, 1999: xiv.

6. Marquina's letter, also quoted in Chapters 1 and 2, is in Lockhart and Otte, *Letters and People*, 1976: 4–7; this quote on p. 5; also in Lockhart, *Cajamarca*, 1972: 462.

7. Avila's letter is in Lockhart and Otte, *Letters and People*, 1976: 9–14; this quote on p. 11.

8. As Himmerich y Valencia observes in "Siege of Cuzco," 1998: 398–99, 416–17; also see Herrera, *Historia General*, 1615, decada VI, pp. 52–59. Santiago allegedly appeared to Spaniards during the war against the Mexica too (according to Bernal Díaz, cited in Fernández-Armesto, "'Aztec' Auguries," 1992: 302). Lasso de la Vega described Cortés's life as one of "miraculous histories" (or "miraculous stories"; *Cortés valeroso*, 1588: prefatory p. 6v).

9. Cline, "Revisionist Conquest History," 1988: Sahagún quote on p. 97; manuscript copy of Bartolomé de las Casas, *Historia general de las Indias*, archived in JCBL as Codex Sp 4, relevant passages on fs. 31–35; Fernández-Armesto, "'Aztec' Auguries," 1992: 296; Villagutierre, *Historia*, 1701: 21.

10. Cortés, *Letters*, 1986 [1522]: 166.

11. The phrase is from Gómara's version of the speech (*Cortés*, 1964 [1552]: 240–41), quoted atop this chapter and also by Reese, "Myth of Superiority," 2001: 1.

12. Quoted by Florescano, *Memory*, 1994: 78.

13. Quoted by Florescano, *Memory*, 1994: 80. The "miracle" explanation occasionally pops up in modern histories too; Elliott, *Imperial Spain*, 1963: 63, for example, has the Spanish American empire "triumphantly and almost miraculously established." Another variant on the theme is illustrated by Cunninghame Graham's phrase "the *conquistadores* (after God) owed their conquest to their horses" (*Horses of the Conquest*, 1949: 12).

14. Elliott, *Imperial Spain*, 1963: 66; Reese, "Myth of Superiority," 2001: 6, drew my attention to this passage. Elliott's juxtaposition of "confidence" and "fatalism" is reminiscent of Vargas Machuca's explanation for Spanish success as a contrast between the Spanish "spirit of internal fortitude, which excluded all cowardice," and native weakness of spirit and lack of resolve (*Milicia y Descripción*, 1599: 18v–20r).

15. Mendez, *Report on the Indians*, 1921 [1861]: 185.

16. Hergé, *Prisoners of the Sun*, 1962 [1946–47].

17. Peeters, *Tintin*, 1992. *Prisoners* originally appeared in 1946–47 in serial format in the Belgian *Tintin* magazine as *Le Temple du Soleil*, then somewhat abbreviated as a book in 1949; it is a continuation of the story begun in *The Seven Crystal Balls*, first serialized in *Le Soir* beginning in 1943. Hergé's source on Andean civilization was Charles Wiener's *Perou et Bolivie*, published in 1880 (Peeters, *Tintin*, 1992: 79–83).

18. For one English writer's account of his realization of this fact, see Wright, *Stolen Continents*, 1992: 5–10.

19. Wood, *Conquistadors*, 2000: 100; Le Clézio, *Mexican Dream*, 1993: 9–10. Note that additionally the peoples listed were not "tribes," nor were they ruled by "priest-kings." As befits an animated movie, *The Road to El Dorado* evokes with little subtlety the theme of native credulity and superstition; one of the cartoon Spaniards describes El Dorado as "an entire city of suckers" (Bergeron and Paul, *El Dorado*, 2000).

20. Dibble, *The Conquest*, 1978: 10–23.

21. Keen, *Latin America*, 1996: 72; Soustelle, *Daily Life*, 1964: 218.

22. Columbus quote in Zamora, *Reading Columbus*, 1993: 159; Le Clézio, *Mexican Dream*, 1993: 34; Todorov, *Conquest*, 1984: 61, 62. Clendinnen, "'Fierce and Unnatural Cruelty,'" 1991, debunks Todorov's treatment of Cortés and "signs" in some detail. Also see Fernández-Armesto, "'Aztec' Auguries," 1992: 303.

23. Included among a myriad such uses are Todorov, *Conquest*, 1984: 123; Greenblatt, *Marvelous Possessions*, 199: 145; and Seed, "'Failing to Marvel,'" 1991: 11.
24. Purchas is quoted and discussed in Greenblatt, *Marvelous Possessions*, 199: 9–11 (and also quoted by Reese, "Myth of Superiority," 2001: 10). Also see Todorov, *Conquest*, 1984: 80; Diamond, *Guns, Germs and Steel*, 1997: 78–80. Sowell, *Conquests and Cultures*, 1998: 251 also suggests that writing was a factor helping to explain the Conquest.
25. To remove from context (as she does not mention the Díaz frontispiece) a phrase from Seed, "'Failing to Marvel,'" 1991: 12. The frontispiece is reproduced in Schwartz, *Victors and Vanquished*, 2000: 19, but not discussed in his text.
26. Quoted in Seed, "'Failing to Marvel,'" 1991: 17–18.
27. Ilarione da Bergamo, *Daily Life*, 2000 [1770]: 96.
28. Fuentes, *Buried Mirror*, 1992: 119.
29. Typical such phrases are "the Spanish superiority with regard to weapons," "Spanish military superiority," the Andean "heavy reliance on crushing weapons . . . does much to explain Spanish superiority," "the Spaniards's far superior armament," and so on (Todorov, *Conquest*, 1984: 61; Guilmartin, "The Cutting Edge," 1991: 42, 52; Diamond, *Guns, Germs, and Steel*, 1997: 76; also see Himmerich y Valencia, "Siege of Cuzco," 1998: 411).
30. The quote is from one of many examples of these perspectives on web sites; for example, www.bergen.org/AAST/projects/Cortes/cortes.html.
31. The original study of this phenomenon is Crosby, *Columbian Exchange*, 1972. An accessible brief explanation is in Diamond, *Guns, Germs and Steel*, 1997: 195–214. The best recent study of the impact of disease during the Conquest is Cook, *Born to Die*, 1998.
32. Observation on Prescott made by Fernández-Armesto in Prescott, *Conquest of Mexico*, 1994: xxviii; Cook, *Born to Die*, 1998: 63–70; quote on p. 67, citing Sahagún's *Historia General*.
33. Cook, *Born to Die*, 1998: 72–82.
34. Whitehead, "Ancient Amerindian Polities," 1994; Cook, *Born to Die*, 1998: 82–94, 131–32, 148–49, 154–55, 189–90, 209; Diamond, *Guns, Germs, and Steel*, 1997: 211–12; Wood, *Conquistadors*, 2000: 199, 217–27; Mann, "1491," 2002.
35. As quoted above; Cortés, *Letters*, 1986 [1522]: 166.
36. Guilmartin, "The Cutting Edge," 1991: 61. Even during the 1521 siege of Tenochtitlán, Mexica warriors used captured crossbows after forcing Spanish prisoners to demonstrate their use (Clendinnen, "'Fierce and Unnatural Cruelty,'" 1991: 26, citing Díaz and Durán).
37. As Himmerich y Valencia argued in his study of the "Siege of Cuzco," 1998.
38. Vargas Machuca, *Milicia y Descripción*, 1599: 50v–51r; Herrera, *Historia General*, 1601, dec. I: 162.
39. Guilmartin, "The Cutting Edge," 1991: 53; note that Guilmartin (pp. 53–55) places more emphasis on horses as an advantage than I have. For an example of Spaniards seizing a rare opportunity to use horses on an open battlefield, see Alvarado, *Conquest of Guatemala*, 1924 [1525]: 59. Clendinnen, "'Fierce and Unnatural Cruelty,'" 1991: 29–30, argues that the Mexica accorded the respect of warriors to horses, but she does not present them as offering a great advantage to Spaniards. For a fanciful ode to the role of horses in the Conquest, which glosses over the vulnerability of Spanish horses in the tropical Americas to colic, worms, and various diseases, see Graham, *Horses of the Conquest*, 1949.
40. Vargas Machuca, *Milicia y Descripción*, 1599: 60v–62r.
41. For an argument that this was true of the Conquest of Peru, but not Mexico, see Guilmartin, "The Cutting Edge," 1991: 57, 68 n62.
42. Cieza de León, *Peru*, 1998 [1550]; Cortés, *Letters*, 1986 [1519–26]; Díaz, *The True History*, 1908 [1570]; Gómara, *Cortés*, 1964 [1552]; Jerez, *Verdadera relación*, 1985 [1534]; Oviedo y Baños, *Historia*, 1967 [1723]; Zárate, *Historia*, 1555 and *Peru*, 1981 [1555]; Guilmartin, "The Cutting Edge," 1991: 53.

43. Clendinnen, "'Fierce and Unnatural Cruelty,'" 1991: 24. In Felipe Fernández-Armesto's words, "The conquest of Mexico was, it seems to me, a clash of equally aggressive, equally dynamic, equally self-confident warrior-societies, the outcome of which was nicely balanced" ("'Aztec' Auguries," 1992: 288).

44. Restall, *Maya Conquistador*, 1998: 5–18; Chance, *Conquest of the Sierra*, 1989: 16–30. Other examples of failed expeditions include Gonzalo Jiménez de Quesada's quest for the mythical city of El Dorado and the three follow-up expeditions by his nephew-in-law, Antonio de Berrio (Picón-Salas, *Cultural History*, 1966: 35–36; Naipaul, *Loss of El Dorado*, 1969: 18–90).

45. As observed by Keen, *Latin America*, 1996: 72. Also see Hassig, *Aztec Warfare*, 1988.

46. Clendinnen, "'Fierce and Unnatural Cruelty,'" 1991; *Aztecs*, 1991: 87–152, 259–73.

47. Although note that Himmerich argues that the 1536–1537 Inca siege of Cuzco failed in part because "the Incas seem to have clung almost entirely to their traditional mode of warfare" ("Siege of Cuzco," 1998: 403).

48. As quoted above; Cortés, *Letters*, 1986 [1522]: 166.

49. Dibble, *The Conquest*, 1978: 24.

50. Fernández-Armesto, "'Aztec' Auguries," 1992: 305; Adas, *Islamic and European Expansion*, 1993; Hassig, *Aztec Warfare*, 1988.

51. This summary is loosely drawn from an argument whose classic expression is Crosby, *The Columbian Exchange*, 1972, and whose most recent and accessible expressions are Diamond, *Guns, Germs, and Steel*, 1997; and Fernández-Armesto, *Civilizations*, 2000. For yet another variant on the argument, couched in terms of "human capital" and "cultural capital" but still privileging environment over "race," see Sowell, *Conquests and Cultures*, 1998: 329–79. A classic anthropology trade book that is relevant here for its emphasis on ecological conditions, rather than race or cultural superiority, as determinants of human behavior is Harris, *Cannibals and Kings*, 1977. A more recent study of civilizational differences that also avoids old "superiority" models but seeks to explain differences in terms of game theory is Wright, *Nonzero*, 2000.

Notes to Epilogue

1. Or Canoetown. Bernal Díaz calls it *Acala* and *Gueyacala*, which is *Huey Acalan*, meaning "Great Acalan"; *Historia*, 1955 [1570]: 466–71.

2. For Cortés and Gómara I have followed Pagden's and Simpson's translations in Cortés, *Letters*, 1986 [1526]: 362–68; and Gómara, *Cortés*, 1964 [1552]: 352–57, respectively, although I was also able to consult a 1540 manuscript copy of Cortés's letter archived in the JCBL as Codex Sp 2. For Díaz I have made my own translation from Díaz, *Historia*, 1632 [1570]: 200r–201r; also see *Historia*, 1955 [1570]: 469–70; the English-language editions most frequently cited in previous chapters (*Discovery*, 1956; *Conquest*, 1963) do not go beyond the events of 1521. For Ixtlilxóchitl I have made my own translations from the Spanish in Ixtlilxóchitl, *Obras*, 1891–92. For the Mactun Mayas' version I have used my own translation from Chontal Maya, previously published in Restall, *Maya Conquistador*, 1998: 62–64. There is also a summary of the incident, drawing upon these same sources, in Scholes and Roys, *Maya-Chontal Indians*, 1948: 112–22. I also consulted an additional colonial Spanish source, Antonio de Herrera's *Historia General* of 1601/1615, but its account follows Cortés and Gómara too closely to constitute a separate version (1601, dec. III: 287).

3. Cortés, *Letters*, 1986 [1526]: 367.

4. My translations from Díaz, *Historia*, 1955 [1570]: 470. Herrera stops short of criticizing Cortés, but he does praise Cuauhtémoc as "a valiant man" and defend his alleged plot-

ting (*Historia General*, 1601, *dec.* III: 287). The Franciscan López de Cogolludo uses Díaz and Herrera as the basis of his account, pointing out the differences between the two (1688: 48–52). In later colonial-period versions of the incident, especially those compiled from various sources for non-Spanish readers, such as the vast *Voyages and Travels* compendium by John Harris, the Maya context is removed completely: "All his [Cortés's] great Conquests, however, could not procure him Rest, and a peaceable Establishment; for sometimes he was in Danger from the Intrigues of the *Indians*, who were very desirous of recovering their Country, and driving out or destroying the *Spaniards*: And to put an End to these Contrivances, he, in 1527, found himself obliged to hang *Guatimozin*, and two other *Indian* Princes, whom he had detected in a Conspiracy against him" (Harris, *Navigantum*, 1748, vol. 2: 134).

5. Ixtlilxóchitl's perspective is the one that was adopted by Eduardo Gallo in his biography of Cuauhtémoc published in 1873 as part of his influential *Hombres ilustres mexicanos* series (Gallo, *Cuauhtémoc*, 1978 [1873]; I am grateful to William Pencak for giving me a copy). It was also adopted as part of the Porfirian Mexican attempt to appropriate the "Aztec" past for the purposes of national identity formation; the three kings, Cuauhtémoc, Coanacoch, and Tetlepanquetzal, are all immortalized on the 1887 Monument to Cuauhtémoc in Mexico City (author's personal observation; Gallo, *Cuauhtémoc*, 1978 [1873]: 84–85; Benjamin, *La Revolución*, 2000: 1, 120).

6. Restall, *Maya Conquistador*, 1998: 63–64. The Maya phrase, *tzepci u lukub*, literally means "his neck was cut," but the passage makes it clear that full decapitation is being described. This differs, of course, from the hanging described in the Spanish-language sources and depicted on the title page to Herrera's sixth volume (see Figure 20). It is possible that the emperor was hanged and then his head cut off and diplayed. Or (as I implied above) he was decapitated and then hanged by his feet, as shown in the drawing of the execution in a sixteenth-century pictorial manuscript, the *Mapa de Tepechpan* (Morley 1937–38, I: 15; Scholes and Roys, *Maya-Chontal Indians*, 1948: 116; Gallo, *Cuauhtémoc*, 1978 [1873]: 68). Despite the Maya claim that Cuauhtémoc was baptized the morning of his death, other sources confirm that he was baptized years before in Tenochtitlán, with Cortés's name Hernando (see the *Songs* quote atop this Epilogue); indeed, it would be odd if Cuauhtémoc had *not* been baptized shortly after the city's fall in 1521 and, as the top ranking Mexica, had *not* been given the name of the top ranking Spaniard.

7. The historians Scholes and Roys, writing over a half century ago when historians were expected to judge the protagonists of the past, were harsh in their "condemnation" of Paxbolonacha's "equivocal conduct," although they later admit that while his actions were "not courageous," they were "realistic and sensible" (*Maya-Chontal Indians*, 1948: 119, 121).

8. As Sahlins has written of "the incidents of Cook's life and death in Hawaii" (*Historical Metaphors*, 1981: 11).

9. To echo Fernández-Armesto, in sensing an "intimation of truth," I have sought to "express it for others" (*Truth*, 1999: 229).

10. "Constellation" phrase by Richard Slotkin, quoted by Amado, "Mythic Origins," 2000: 784; Díaz, *Conquest*, 1963 [1570]: 216, 14, and *Historia*, 1955 [1570]: 160, xxxv.

References

Primary Archival Sources and Their Abbreviations

AGI   Archivo General de las Indias, Seville, Spain
ARH   Biblioteca de la Academia Real de la Historia de Madrid, Madrid, Spain
BL   British Library, London, UK
JCBL   John Carter Brown Library, Providence, Rhode Island

Primary and Secondary Published Sources

Acosta, José de. *Natural and Moral History of the Indies* [1590]. Jane E. Mangan, ed. Frances López-Morillas, trans. Durham: Duke University Press, 2002.

Adas, Michael, ed. *Islamic and European Expansion: The Forging of a Global Order.* Philadelphia: Temple University Press, 1993.

Ades, Dawn. *Art in Latin America: The Modern Era, 1820–1980.* London: The South Bank Centre, 1989.

Adorno, Rolena, and Patrick Charles Pautz. *Alvar Núñez Cabeza de Vaca: His Account, His Life, and the Expedition of Panfilo de Narváez.* 3 vols. Lincoln: University of Nebraska Press, 2000.

Aguirre Beltrán, Gonzalo. *La Población Negra de México: Estudio etnohistórico* [1946]. Mexico City: Fondo de Cultura Económica, 1989.

Alcalá, Manuel. *César y Cortés.* Mexico City: Editorial Jus, 1950.

Alegría, Ricardo E. *Juan Garrido, el Conquistador Negro en las Antillas, Florida, México y California, c.1503–1540.* San Juan: Centro de Estudios Avanzados de Puerto Rico y El Caribe, 1990.

Altman, Ida. "Spanish Society in Mexico City After the Conquest," in *Hispanic American Historical Review* 71:3 (1991): 413–45.

Altman, Ida, Sarah Cline, and Juan Javier Pescador. *The Early History of Greater Mexico.* Upper Saddle River, N.J.: Prentice Hall, 2002.

Alvarado, Pedro de. *An Account of the Conquest of Guatemala in 1524* [1525]. Sedley J. Mackie, ed. New York: The Cortés Society, 1924.

Amado, Janaína. "Mythic Origins: Caramuru and the Founding of Brazil," in *Hispanic American Historical Review* 80:4 (November 2000): 783–811.

Amor y Vázquez, José. "Apostilla a la 'quema de las naves' por Cortés," in *Hispanic Review* 39 (1961): 45–52.

Andrien, Kenneth J. *Andean Worlds: Indigenous History, Culture, and Consciousness Under Spanish Rule, 1532–1825.* Albuquerque: University of New Mexico Press, 2001.

Avellaneda, José Ignacio. *The Conquerors of the New Kingdom of Granada.* Albuquerque: University of New Mexico Press, 1995.

Axtell, James. *Natives and Newcomers: The Cultural Origins of North America.* New York: Oxford University Press, 2000.

Baldwin, Neil. *Legends of the Plumed Serpent: Biography of a Mexican God.* New York, Public Affairs, 1998.

Benjamin, Thomas. *La Revolución: Mexico's Great Revolution as Memory, Myth, and History.* Austin: University of Texas Press, 2000.

Berlin, Ira. *Many Thousands Gone: The First Two Centuries of Slavery in North America.* Cambridge: Belknap Press of Harvard University, 1998.

Berliner, Michael S. "Man's Best Came with Columbus," in *Los Angeles Times,* 30 December 1991.

Bierhorst, John, ed. *Cantares Mexicanos: Songs of the Aztecs.* Stanford: Stanford University Press, 1985.

Bitterli, Urs. *Cultures in Conflict: Encounters Between European and Non-European Cultures, 1492–1800.* Stanford: Stanford University Press, 1989.

Black, George. "1492 and the Burden of the White Man," in *Los Angeles Times,* 9 July 1991.

Boller, Paul F., Jr. *Not So! Popular Myths About America from Columbus to Clinton.* New York: Oxford University Press, 1995.

Bonfil Batalla, Gustavo. *México Profundo: Reclaiming a Civilization.* Austin: University of Texas Press, 1996.

Bouvier, Virginia M. *Women and the Conquest of California, 1542–1840: Codes of Silence.* Tucson: University of Arizona Press, 2001.

Boyd-Bowman, Peter. "Negro Slaves in Early Colonial Mexico," in *The Americas* 26:2 (1969): 134–51.

Bowser, Frederick P. *The African Slave in Colonial Peru, 1524–1650.* Stanford: Stanford University Press, 1974.

Bricker, Victoria R. *The Indian Christ, the Indian King: The Historical Substrate of Maya Myth and Ritual.* Austin: University of Texas Press, 1981.

Brooks, Francis J. "Motecuzoma Xocoyotl, Hernán Cortés, and Bernal Díaz del Castillo: The Construction of an Arrest," in *Hispanic American Historical Review* 75:2 (1995): 149–83.

Bullard, Alice. *Exile to Paradise: Savagery and Civilization in Paris and the South Pacific, 1790–1900.* Stanford: Stanford University Press, 2000.

Burkhart, Louise M. *The Slippery Earth: Nahua-Christian Moral Dialogue in Sixteenth-Century Mexico.* Tucson: University of Arizona Press, 1989.

Burkholder, Mark, and Lyman Johnson. *Colonial Latin America.* 4th ed. New York: Oxford University Press, 2001.

Burns, E. Bradford. *The Poverty of Progress: Latin America in the Nineteenth Century.* Berkeley and Los Angeles: University of California Press, 1980.

Bushman, Claudia L. *America Discovers Columbus: How an Italian Explorer Became An American Hero.* Hanover, N.H.: University Press of New England, 1992.

Campe, Joachim Heinrich. *Cortez, or The Conquest of Mexico: As Related by a Father to His Children and Designed for the Instruction of Youth* [1800], Elizabeth Helme, trans. London: Cradock and Joy, 1811.

Carr, E. H. *What Is History?* London: Macmillan, 1961.

Carrasco, David. *Quetzalcoatl and the Irony of Empire: Myths and Prophesies in the Aztec Tradition.* Revised Edition. Boulder: University Press of Colorado, 2000.

Carrillo y Ancona, Crescencio. *Catecismo de Historia y de Geografía de Yucatán.* Mèrida, Yuc.: Libreria Catolica, 1880.

Castellano, Juan de. *Las Elegias de Varones Illustres de Indias.* Madrid, 1589 (copy in JCBL).

Certeau, Michel de. *The Writing of History.* Tom Conley, trans. New York: Columbia University Press, 1988.

Cervantes, Fernando. *The Devil in the New World: The Impact of Diabolism in New Spain.* New Haven: Yale University Press, 1994.

Cervantes de Salazar, Francisco. *Dialogo de la dignidad del hombre* [1564?], in *Obras.* Madrid: Antonio de Sancha, 1772 (copy in JCBL).

Chamberlain, Robert S. *The Conquest and Colonization of Yucatán.* Washington, D.C.: Carnegie Institution, 1948.

Chance, John K. *Conquest of the Sierra: Spaniards and Indians in Colonial Oaxaca.* Norman: University of Oklahoma Press, 1989.

Chang-Rodríguez, Raquel. "Cultural Resistance in the Andes and Its Depiction in *Atau Wallpaj P'uchukakuyninpa Wankan* or *Tragedy of Atahualpa's Death,*" in *Coded Encounters: Writing, Gender, and Ethnicity in Colonial Latin America.* Francisco Javier Cevallos-Candau et al., eds., 115–34. Amherst: University of Massachusetts Press, 1994.

Christensen, Thomas, and Carol Christensen. *The Discovery of America and Other Myths: A New World Reader.* San Francisco: Chronicle Books, 1992.

Chuchiak, John F. "The Indian Inquisition and the Extirpation of Idolatry: The Process of Punishment in the Provisorato de Indios of the Diocese of Yucatan, 1563–1812." PhD dissertation, Tulane University, 2000.

Churchill, John. *A Collection of Travels and Voyages,* 4 vols. London: Awnsham & John Churchill, 1704 (copy in JCBL).

Cieza de León, Pedro de. *The Discovery and Conquest of Peru* [ca. 1550]. Alexandra Parma Cook and Noble David Cook, eds. Durham: Duke University Press, 1998.

Clendinnen, Inga. *Ambivalent Conquests: Maya and Spaniard in Yucatan, 1517–1570.* Cambridge: Cambridge University Press, 1987.

——. "'Fierce and Unnatural Cruelty': Cortés and the Conquest of Mexico," in *Representations* 33 (Winter 1991) (reprinted in *New World Encounters.* Stephen Greenblatt, ed., 12–47. Berkeley: University of California Press, 1993).

——. *Aztecs: an interpretation.* Cambridge: Cambridge University Press, 1991.

Cline, S. L. "Revisionist Conquest History: Sahagún's Revised Book XII," in *The Work of Bernardino de Sahagún: Pioneer Ethnographer of Sixteenth-Century Aztec Mexico.* Jorge Klor de Alva, H. B. Nicholson, and Eloise Quiñones-Keber, eds., 93–106. Austin and Albany: SUNY-Albany Institute of Mesoamerican Studies and University of Texas Press, 1988.

Cogolludo, fray Diego López de. *Historia de Yucathan* [1654]. Madrid: Juan García Infanzón, 1688 (copy in JCBL).

——. *Historia de Yucatán* [1654]. Mexico City: Editorial Academia Literaria, 1957.

Cohen, Jeffrey H. "Danza de la Pluma: Symbols of Submission andSeparation in a Mexican Fiesta," in *Anthropological Quarterly* 66 (1993): 149–58.

Colom, Alejandra, et al., eds. *Testamento y Título de los Antecesores de los Señores de Cagcoh (San Cristóbal Verapaz).* Guatemala City: Universidad del Valle de Guatemala, 1999.

Columbus, Christopher. *The Four Voyages* [1492–1571]. J. M. Cohen, ed. London: Penguin, 1969.

Columbus, Ferdinand. *The Life of the Admiral Christopher Columbus, By His Son Ferdinand* [1539], Benjamin Keen, ed. 2nd ed. New Brunswick: Rutgers University Press, 1992.

Cook, Noble David. *Born to Die: Disease and the New World Conquest, 1492–1650.* Cambridge: Cambridge University Press, 1998.

Cortés, Hernán. *Cartas de Relación* [1519–26]. Mexico City: Editorial Porrúa, 1983.

——. *Letters from Mexico* [1519–26]. Anthony Pagden, ed. New Haven: Yale University Press, 1986.

Crosby, Alfred. *The Columbian Exchange: Biological Consequences of 1492.* Westport, Conn.: Greenwood, 1972.

——. "The Columbian Voyages and Their Historians," in *Islamic and European Expansion: The Forging of a Global Order.* Michael Adas, ed., 141–64. Philadelphia: Temple University Press, 1993.

Cypess, Sandra Messinger. *La Malinche in Mexican Literature: From History to Myth*. Austin: University of Texas Press, 1991.

Dakin, Karen, and Christopher H. Lutz. *Nuestro Pesar, Nuestra Aflicción: Memorias en lengua náhuatl enviadas a Felipe II por indígenas del valle de Guatemala hacia 1572*. Mexico City: Universidad Nacional Autónoma de México and CIRMA, 1996.

Davidson, Miles H. *Columbus Then and Now: A Life Reexamined*. Norman: University of Oklahoma Press, 1997.

Deeds, Susan M. "Legacies of Resistance, Adaptation, and Tenacity: History of the Native Peoples of Northwest Mexico," in *The Cambridge History of the Native Peoples of the Americas*, vol. II, *Mesoamerica*, part 2. Richard E. W. Adams and Murdo J. MacLeod, eds., 44–88. Cambridge: Cambridge University Press, 2000.

Descola, Jean. *The Conquistadors*. New York: Viking, 1957.

Diamond, Jared. *Guns, Germs, and Steel: The Fates of Human Societies*. New York: Norton, 1997.

Díaz, Bernal. *Historia verdadera de la conquista de la Nueva España*. Madrid, 1632 (copy in JCBL).

———. *The True History of the Conquest of New Spain* [ca. 1570]. Alfred P. Maudslay, ed. London: Hakluyt Society, 1908.

———. *Historia de la Conquista de Nueva España* [ca. 1570]. Joaquín Ramírez Cabañas, ed. Mexico City: Porrúa, 1955.

———. *The Discovery and Conquest of Mexico* [ca. 1570]. Alfred P. Maudslay, ed. New York: Farrar, Straus and Cudahy, 1956.

———. *The Conquest of Mexico* [ca. 1570]. J. M. Cohen, ed. London: Penguin, 1963.

Díaz, Juan. *Littera mandata della Insula de Cuba*. Venice, 1520 (facsimile copy in JCBL).

Dibble, Charles E. *The Conquest Through Aztec Eyes*. Salt Lake City: University of Utah Press, Reynolds Lectures, 1978.

Diouf, Sylviane A. *Servants of Allah: African Muslims Enslaved in the Americas*. New York: New York University Press, 1998.

Doniger, Wendy. *The Implied Spider: Politics and Theology in Myth*. New York: Columbia University Press, 1998.

Dor-Ner, Zvi. *Columbus and the Age of Discovery*. New York: William Morrow & Co., 1991.

Dumond, Don E. *The Machete and the Cross: Campesino Rebellion in Yucatan*. Lincoln: University of Nebraska Press, 1997.

Durán, fray Diego de. *The History of the Indies of New Spain* [1581]. Doris Heyden, ed. Norman: University of Oklahoma Press, 1994.

Dutra, Francis A. "The Discovery of Brazil and its Immediate Aftermath," in *Portugal, The Pathfinder: Journeys from the Medieval toward the Modern World, 1300–ca. 1600*. George D. Winius, ed., 145–168. Madison: Hispanic Seminary of Medieval Studies, 1995.

Eco, Umberto. *Serendipities: Language and Lunacy*. San Diego and New York: Harcourt Brace, 1998.

Edelman, Marc. "A Central American Genocide: Rubber, Slavery, Nationalism, and the Destruction of the Guatusos-Malekus," in *Comparative Studies in Society and History* 40:2 (April 1998): 356–89.

Eliade, Mircea. *Myth and Reality*. New York: Harper & Row, 1963.

Ellingson, Ter. *The Myth of the Noble Savage*. Berkeley: University of California Press, 2001.

Elliott, John H. *Imperial Spain, 1469–1716*. London: Arnold, 1963.

———. *The Old World and the New, 1492–1650*. Cambridge: Cambridge University Press, 1970.

———. "The Mental World of Hernán Cortés," in *Spain and Its World, 1500–1700*, 27–41. New Haven: Yale University Press, 1989.

Erauso, Catalina de. *Lieutenant Nun: Memoir of a Basque Transvestite in the New World* [1626]. Michele and Gabriel Stepto, eds. Boston, Beacon Press, 1996.

Falkenhorst, C. *With Cortez in Mexico: A Historical Romance.* New York: Worthington, 1892.

Fernández-Armesto, Felipe. *Before Columbus: Exploration and Colonization from the Mediterranean to the Atlantic, 1229–1492.* Philadelphia: University of Pennsylvania Press, 1987.

———. *Columbus.* Oxford: Oxford University Press, 1991.

———. "'Aztec' Auguries and Memories of the Conquest of Mexico," in *Renaissance Studies* 6:3–4 (1992): 287–305.

———. "Medieval Atlantic Exploration: The Evidence of Maps," in *Portugal, The Pathfinder: Journeys from the Medieval toward the Modern World, 1300–ca. 1600.* George D. Winius, ed., 41–70. Madison: Hispanic Seminary of Medieval Studies, 1995.

———. *Truth: A History and a Guide for the Perplexed.* New York: St. Martin's Press, 1999.

———. *Civilizations.* London: Macmillan, 2000.

Florescano, Enrique. *Memory, Myth, and Time in Mexico: From the Aztecs to Independence.* Austin: University of Texas Press, 1994.

———. *The Myth of Quetzalcoatl.* Baltimore: Johns Hopkins University Press, 1999.

Foner, Eric. "Our Monumental Mistakes," in *The Nation* (1999) (accessed online, 11/8/99).

Foster, Lynn V. *A Brief History of Mexico.* New York: Facts on File, Inc., 1997.

Fox, Justin. "No Room for Romantics," in *Leadership* 17:2 (2001)(accessed online, 4/24/01).

Francis, J. Michael. "'La tierra clama por remedio:' la conquista espiritual del territorio muisca," in *Fronteras de la historia* 5 (2000): 93–118.

———. *Population, Disease and Demographic Change, 1537–1636: The Historical Demography of Tunja.* Unpublished manuscript, 2002.

Fuentes, Carlos. *The Buried Mirror: Reflections on Spain and the New World.* Boston: Houghton Mifflin, 1992.

Fuentes, Patricia de, ed. *The Conquistadors: First-Person Accounts of the Conquest of Mexico.* New York: Orion, 1963.

Gallo, Eduardo L. *Cuauhtémoc, último emperador de México* [1873]. César Macazaga Ordoño, ed. Mexico City: Editorial Innovación, 1978.

Gallup-Díaz, Ignacio. "The Spanish Attempt to Tribalize the Darién, 1735–50," in *Ethnohistory* 49:2 (Spring 2002): 281–317.

Gerhard, Peter. "A Black Conquistador in Mexico," in *Hispanic American Historical Review* 58:3 (August 1978): 451–59.

Giardini, Cesare. *The Life and Times of Columbus.* New York: Mondadori Editore and Curtis Books, 1967.

Gibson, Charles. *Tlaxcala in the Sixteenth Century.* New Haven: Yale University Press, 1952.

———. *Spain in America.* New York: Harper Colophon, 1966.

Gillespie, Susan D. *The Aztec Kings: The Construction of Rulership in Mexica History.* Tucson: University of Arizona Press, 1989.

Goodrich, Aaron. *A History of the Character and Achievements of the So-Called Christopher Columbus.* New York: Appleton & Co., 1874.

Gómara, Francisco López de. *Cortés: The Life of the Conqueror by His Secretary.* Lesley Byrd Simpson, ed. (trans. of *Istoria de la conquista de México* [1552]). Berkeley: University of California Press, 1964.

Grafton, Anthony. *New World, Ancient Texts: The Power of Tradition and the Shock of Discovery.* Cambridge: Harvard University Press, 1992.

Graham, R. B. Cunninghame. *The Horses of the Conquest* [1930]. Norman: University of Oklahoma Press, 1949.

Greenblatt, Stephen. *Marvelous Possessions: The Wonder of the New World.* Chicago: University of Chicago Press, 1991.

Griffiths, Nicholas, and Fernando Cervantes, ed. *Spiritual Encounters: Interactions between Christianity and Native Religions in Colonial America.* Birmingham, UK: University of Birmingham Press, 1999.

Gruzinski, Serge. *The Conquest of Mexico: The Incorporation of Indian Societies into the Western World, 16th–18th Centuries.* Cambridge, Mass.: Polity Press, 1993.

———. *Images at War: Mexico from Columbus to Blade Runner (1492–2019).* Durham: Duke University Press, 2001.

Gubler Rotsman, Ruth. "The Acculturative Role of the Church in 16th Century Yucatan (Culture Contact, Shock, Positive Ethnocentrism, Domination, Directed Change, Dysnomia, Anomie)." PhD dissertation, University of California, Los Angeles, 1985.

Guilmartin, John F., Jr. "The Cutting Edge: An Analysis of the Spanish Invasion and Overthrow of the Inca Empire, 1532–1539," in *Transatlantic Encounters: Europeans and Andeans in the Sixteenth Century.* Kenneth Andrien and Rolena Adorno, eds., 40–69. Berkeley: University of California Press, 1991.

———. "The Logistics of Warfare at Sea in the Sixteenth Century: The Spanish Perspective," in *Feeding Mars: Logistics in Western Warfare from the Middle Ages to the Present.* John A. Lynn, ed., 109–36. Boulder: Westview, 1993.

Guzmán, Eulalia. *Relaciones de Hernán Cortés a Carlos V sobre la invasión de Anáhuac: aclaraciones y rectificaciones.* Mexico City: Libros Anáhuac, 1958.

Hancock, Graham. *Fingerprints of the Gods: The Evidence of the Earth's Lost Civilization.* New York: Doubleday, 1995.

Hanke, Lewis. *The Spanish Struggle for Justice.* Philadelphia: University of Pennsylvania Press, 1949.

———. *Aristotle and the American Indians.* Chicago: Henry Regnery Co., 1959.

———. "The Dawn of Conscience in America: Spanish Experiments and Experiences with Indians in the New World," in *Proceedings of the American Philosophical Society* 107: 2 (April 1963): 83–92.

Harris, John. *Navigantum atque Itinerantium Bibliotheca, or, A Complete Collection of Voyages and Travels.* 2 vols. London: Woodward et al., 1744–48 (copy of this and other rare editions in JCBL).

Harris, Marvin. *Cannibals and Kings.* New York: Random House, 1977.

Harris, Max. *Aztecs, Moors, and Christians: Festivals of Reconquest in Mexico and Spain.* Austin: University of Texas Press, 2000.

Harris, Olivia. "The Coming of the White People: Reflections on the Mythologization of History in Latin America," in *Bulletin of Latin American Research* 14: 1 (1995): 9–24.

Harvey, H. R., ed. *Land and Politics in the Valley of Mexico: A Two Thousand Year Perspective.* Albuquerque: University of New Mexico Press, 1991.

Haskett, Robert. *Indigenous Rulers: An Ethnohistory of Town Government in Colonial Cuernavaca.* Albuquerque: University of New Mexico Press, 1991.

Hassig, Ross. *Aztec Warfare: Imperial Expansion and Political Control.* Norman: University of Oklahoma Press, 1988.

———. *Mexico and the Spanish Conquest.* New York: Longman, 1994.

———. "The Immolation of Hernán Cortés," in *What If? The World's Foremost Military Historians Imagine What Might Have Been.* Robert Cowley, ed., 121–38. New York: Putnam, 1999.

———. *Time, History, and Belief in Aztec and Colonial Mexico.* Austin: University of Texas Press, 2001.

Helps, Arthur. *The Life of Hernando Cortés.* 2 vols. London: George Bell & Sons, 1894.

Henty, G. A. *By Right of Conquest, or, With Cortez in Mexico.* New York: A. L. Burt, 1890.

Herrera, Antonio. *Historia General de los Hechos de los Castellanos en las Islas i Tierra Firme del Mar Oceano.* 8 vols. (*decadas*). Madrid: Juan de la Cuesta, 1610–1615 (copy in JCBL).

Herrera, Robinson. "The People of Santiago: Early Colonial Guatemala, 1538–1587." PhD dissertation, University of California, Los Angeles, 1997.

Hill, Robert M., II. *Colonial Cakchiquels: Highland Maya Adaptation to Spanish Rule, 1600–1700*. Fort Worth: Harcourt Brace, 1992.

Hill Boone, Elizabeth. *Stories in Red and Black: Pictorial Histories of the Aztecs and Mixtecs*. Austin: University of Texas Press, 2000.

Himmerich y Valencia, Robert. "The 1536 Siege of Cuzco: An Analysis of Inca and Spanish Warfare," in *Colonial Latin American Historical Review* 7:4 (Fall 1998): 387–418.

Hoffman, Paul E. *Florida's Frontiers*. Bloomington: Indiana University Press, 2002.

Hordern, Nicholas, et al. *The Conquest of North America*. London: Aldus, 1971.

Horn, Rebecca. *Postconquest Coyoacan: Nahua-Spanish Relations in Central Mexico, 1519–1650*. Stanford: Stanford University Press, 1997.

Huaman Poma de Ayala, don Felipe. *Nueva corónica y buen gobierno* [1615]. Rolena Adorno and John Murra, eds. Mexico City: Siglo Veintiuno, 1980.

Icaza, Francisco A. de. *Diccionario autobiográfico de conquistadores y pobladores de Nueva España*. 2 vols. Madrid: Biblioteca de Facsimiles Mexicanos, 1923.

Ilarione da Bergamo, Friar. *Daily Life in Colonial Mexico: The Journey of Friar Ilarione da Bergamo, 1761–1768* [trans. of *Viaggio al Messico*, 1770]. Robert Ryal Miller and William J. Orr, eds. Norman: University of Oklahoma Press, 2000.

Irving, Washington. *Life and Voyages of Christopher Columbus* [1828]. John Harmon McElroy, ed. Boston: Twayne, 1981.

Ixtlilxochitl, Fernando de Alva. *Obras Históricas*. 2 vols. Mexico City: Secretaria de Fomento, 1891–92. (Also published by Universidad Nacional Autónoma de México, 1977.)

Jemingham, Mrs. Edward. *The Fall of Mexico: A Poem*. London: J. Robson, 1775.

Jenkins, Keith. *Re-thinking History*. London and New York: Routledge, 1991.

Jerez, Francisco de. *Verdadera relación de la conquista del Perú* [1534]. Madrid: Historia 16, 1985.

Jones, Grant D. *Maya Resistance to Spanish Rule: Time and History on a Colonial Frontier*. Albuquerque: University of New Mexico Press, 1989.

———. *The Conquest of the Last Maya Kingdom*. Stanford: Stanford University Press, 1998.

Karttunen, Frances. *Between Worlds: Interpreters, Guides, and Survivors*. New Brunswick: Rutgers University Press, 1994.

———. "Rethinking Malinche," in *Indian Women of Early Mexico*. Susan Schroeder et al., eds., 291–312. Norman: University of Oklahoma Press, 1997.

———. "Interpreters Snatched from the Shore: The Successful and the Others," in *The Language Encounter in the Americas, 1492–1800*. Edward G. Gray and Norman Fiering, eds., 215–29. New York: Berghahn Books, 2000.

Karttunen, Frances, and James Lockhart. *The Art of Nahuatl Speech: The Bancroft Dialogues*. Los Angeles: UCLA Latin American Center, 1987.

Katz, Friedrich. "Rural Uprisings in Preconquest and Colonial Mexico," in *Riot, Rebellion, and Revolution: Rural Social Conflict in Mexico*. Friedrich Katz, ed., 65–94. Princeton: Princeton University Press, 1988.

Keen, Benjamin. *The Aztec Image in Western Thought*. New Brunswick: Rutgers University Press, 1971.

———. *A History of Latin America, Vol. I: Ancient America to 1910*. Fifth ed. Boston: Houghton Mifflin, 1996.

Kellogg, Susan, and Matthew Restall, eds. *Dead Giveaways: Indigenous Testaments of Colonial Mesoamerica and the Andes*. Salt Lake City: University of Utah Press, 1998.

Kicza, John E. "A Comparison of Indian and Spanish Accounts of the Conquest of Mexico," in *Five Centuries of Mexican History*. Virginia Guedea and Jaime E. Rodriguez O., eds., 49–63. Irvine: University of California at Irvine Press and Instituto Mora, 1992.

———. *Patterns in Spanish Overseas Encounters to 1600: The Factors Underlying Success and Failure in Warfare Against Non-Western People*. Unpublished manuscript. Albuquerque: University of New Mexico Press, n.d.

Klein, Herbert S. "The Free Colored Militia of Cuba, 1568–1868," in *Caribbean Studies* 6:2 (1966): 17–27.

——. *The Atlantic Slave Trade*. Cambridge: Cambridge University Press, 1999.

Klor de Alva, Jorge, H. B. Nicholson, and Eloise Quiñones-Keber, eds. *The Work of Bernardino de Sahagún: Pioneer Ethnographer of Sixteenth-Century Aztec Mexico*. Austin and Albany: SUNY-Albany Institute of Mesoamerican Studies and University of Texas Press, 1988.

Knaut, Andrew L. *The Pueblo Revolt of 1680: Conquest and Resistance in Seventeenth-Century New Mexico*. Norman: University of Oklahoma Press, 1995.

Konetzke, Richard, ed. *Colección de Documentos para la Historia de la Formación Social de Hispanoamérica, 1493–1810*. 2 vols. Madrid: Consejo Superior de Investigaciones Superiores, 1953.

Kramer, Wendy. *Encomienda Politics in Early Colonial Guatemala, 1524–1544: Dividing the Spoils*. Boulder: Westview Press, 1994.

Krippner-Martínez, James. "The Politics of Conquest: An Interpretation of the *Relación de Michoacán*," in *The Americas* 48:2 (October 1990): 177–98.

——. *Rereading the Conquest: Power, Politics, and the History of Early Colonial Michoacán, Mexico, 1521–1565*. University Park: Pennsylvania State University Press, 2001.

Landa, fray Diego de. *Relación de las Cosas de Yucatán* [1566]. Mexico City: Editorial Porrúa, 1982.

Landers, Jane. *Black Society in Spanish Florida*. Urbana: University of Illinois Press, 1999.

Lane, Kris E. *Pillaging the Empire: Piracy in the Americas, 1500–1750*. Armonk, N.Y.: M. E. Sharpe, 1998.

——. "Captivity and Redemption: Aspects of Slave Life in Early Colonial Quito and Popayán," in *The Americas* 57:2 (October 2000): 225–46.

Langfur, Hal. "Reversing the Frontier's Advance: Native Opposition to Colonial Settlement in the Eastern Sertão of Minas Gerais, Brazil." Paper presented to the American Historical Association, San Francisco, 2002.

Lanyon, Anna. *Malinche's Conquest*. St. Leonards, Australia: Allen & Unwin, 1999.

Las Casas, fray Bartolomé de. *History of the Indies* [1559]. New York: Harper & Row, 1971.

——. *The Devastation of the Indies: A Brief Account* [1552]. Herman Briffault, trans. Baltimore: Johns Hopkins University Press, 1992.

Lasso de la Vega, Gabriel. *Cortés valeroso, y Mexicana*. Madrid: Pedro Madrigal, 1588 (copy in JCBL).

Le Clézio, J.M.G. *Le rêve mexicain, ou la pensée interrompue*. Paris: Gallimard, 1988.

——. 1993. *The Mexican Dream. Or, The Interrupted Thought of Amerindian Civilizations* [translation of *Le rêve mexicain*]. Chicago: University of Chicago Press, 1993.

León-Portilla, Miguel. *The Broken Spears: The Aztec Account of the Conquest of Mexico* [1962]. Revised ed. Boston: Beacon Press, 1992.

Lloyd, Marion. "The Scholar as P.I.: A Historian Takes on the Case of Moctezuma's Heir," in *The Chronicle of Higher Education* (12 April 2002), p. A14 (accessed online).

Lockhart, James. *The Men of Cajamarca*. Austin: University of Texas Press, 1972.

——. *The Nahuas After the Conquest*. Stanford: Stanford University Press, 1992.

——. *We People Here: Nahuatl Accounts of the Conquest of Mexico*. Berkeley: University of California Press, 1993.

——. *Spanish Peru, 1532–1560: A Social History* [1968]. 2nd ed. Madison: University of Wisconsin Press, 1994.

——. *Of Things of the Indies: Essays Old and New in Early Latin American History*. Stanford: Stanford University Press, 1999.

——. *Nahuatl as Written: Lessons in Older Written Nahuatl*. Stanford: Stanford University Press, 2001.

Lockhart, James, and Enrique Otte. *Letters and People of the Spanish Indies: The Sixteenth Century*. Cambridge: Cambridge University Press, 1976.

Lockhart, James, and Stuart B. Schwartz. *Early Latin America: A History of Colonial Spanish America and Brazil*. Cambridge: Cambridge University Press, 1983.

López Austin, Alfredo. *Tamoanchan, Tlalocan: Places of Mist*. Niwot: University Press of Colorado, 1997.

Lovejoy, Paul E. *Transformations in Slavery: A History of Slavery in Africa*. Cambridge: Cambridge University Press, 1983.

Lutz, Christopher. *Santiago de Guatemala, 1541–1773: City, Caste, and the Colonial Experience*. Norman: University of Oklahoma Press, 1994.

Macleod, Murdo J. "Some Thoughts on the Pax Colonial, Colonial Violence, and Perceptions of Both," in *Native Resistance and the Pax Colonial in New Spain*. Susan Schroeder, ed., 129–42. Lincoln: University of Nebraska Press, 1998.

Madariaga, Salvador de. *Christopher Columbus* [1939]. London: Hollis & Carter, 1949.

Mann, Charles C. "1491," in *The Atlantic Monthly* (March 2002): 41–53.

Markham, Sir Clements R., ed. *Reports on the Discovery of Peru*. London: Hakluyt Society, 1872.

Marks, Richard Lee. *Cortes: The Great Adventurer and the Fate of Aztec Mexico*. New York: Knopf, 1993.

Marshall, Edison. *Cortez and Marina: A Novel about the Conquest of Mexico*. Garden City, N.J.: Doubleday, 1963.

Martin, Colin J. M., and Geoffrey Parker. *The Spanish Armada*. New York: Norton, 1988.

Mattingly, Garrett. *The Armada*. Boston: Houghton Mifflin, 1959.

Maxwell, Judith M., and Craig A. Hanson. *Of the Manners of Speaking That the Old Ones Had: The Metaphors of Andrés de Olmos In the TULAL Manuscript*. Salt Lake City: University of Utah Press, 1992.

Mendez, Santiago. *Report on the Indians of Yucatan* [1861]. Marshall H. Saville, ed. New York: Museum of the American Indian, Heye Foundation, 1921.

McCullagh, C. Behan. *The Truth of History*. London and New York: Routledge, 1998.

Meléndez, Carlos and Quince Duncan. *El Negro en Costa Rica*. San José: Editorial Costa Rica, 1972.

Mignolo, Walter D. *Local Histories/Global Designs: Coloniality, Subaltern Knowledges, and Border Thinking*. Princeton: Princeton University Press, 2000.

Milanich, Jerald T., and Susan Milbrath. *First Encounters: Spanish Explorations in the Caribbean and the United States, 1492–1570*. Gainesville: University Press of Florida, 1989.

Millar, George. *A Crossbowman's Story of the First Exploration of the Amazon*. New York: Knopf, 1955 (U.S. edition of *Orellana*. London: Heinemann, 1954).

Morison, Samuel Eliot. *Admiral of the Ocean Sea: A Life of Christopher Columbus*. Boston: Little, Brown, & Co., 1942.

Morley, Sylvanus G. *The Inscriptions of Peten*. 5 vols. Washington, D.C.: Carnegie Institution, 1937–38.

Motolinía, fray Toribio de. *Historia de los indios de la Nueva España* [1541]. Edmundo O'Gorman, ed. Mexico City: Porrúa, 1979.

Muldoon, James. *The Americas in the Spanish World Order: The Justification for Conquest in the Seventeenth Century*. Philadelphia: University of Pennsylvania Press, 1994.

Mund, Sabine. *Les rapports complexes de l'Historia verdadera de Bernal Díaz avec la vérité*. Brussels: Academie Royale des Sciences D'Outre-Mer, 2001.

Naipaul, V. S. *The Loss of El Dorado*. London: Andre Deutsch, 1969.

Nicholson, H. B. "Hugh Thomas' *Conquest*: Observations on the Coverage of the Indigenous Cultures," in *In Chalchihuitl in Quetzalli, Precious Greenstone Precious Quetzal Feather: Mesoamerican Studies in Honor of Doris Heyden*, Eloise Quiñones Keber, ed., 129–36. Lancaster, Calif.: Labyrinthos, 2000.

———. *Topiltzin Quetzalcoatl: The Once and Future Lord of the Toltecs*. Boulder: University Press of Colorado, 2001.

———. "The 'Return of Quetzalcoatl': Did It Play a Role in the Conquest of Mexico?" Pamphlet. Lancaster, Calif.: Labyrinthos, 2001.

Obeyesekere, Gananath. *The Apotheosis of Captain Cook: European Mythmaking in the Pacific*. Princeton: Princeton University Press, 1992.

Ogilby, John. *America*. London, 1670 (copy in JCBL).

Oviedo y Baños, José de. *Historia de la conquista y población de la provincia de Venezuela* [1723]. Caracas: Publications of the quadricentennial, 1967.

Padden, R. C. *The Hummingbird and the Hawk: Conquest and Sovereignty in the Valley of Mexico, 1503–1541* [1967]. New York: Harper & Row, 1970.

Pagden, Anthony. *The Fall of Natural Man*. Cambridge: Cambridge University Press, 1982.

———. *Spanish Imperialism and the Political Imagination: Studies in European and Spanish-American Social and Political Theory 1513–1830*. New Haven: Yale University Press, 1990.

———. *European Encounters with the New World: From Renaissance to Romanticism*. New Haven: Yale University Press, 1993.

———. *Lords of All the World: Ideologies of Empire in Spain, Britain and France, c. 1500–c. 1800*. New Haven: Yale University Press, 1995.

Palmer, Colin A. *Slaves of the White God: Blacks in Mexico, 1570–1650*. Cambridge: Harvard University Press, 1976.

Pané, fray Ramón. *An Account of the Antiquities of the Indians* [1498]. Juan José Arrom, ed. Durham: Duke University Press, 1999. (A Spanish version is also in *A Collection of Voyages and Travels* [London: Awnsham and John Churchill, 1704], vol. II, 622–33; copy in JCBL.)

Parenti, Michael. *History as Mystery*. San Francisco: City Lights Books, 1999.

Parker, Geoffrey. *The Military Revolution: Military Innovation and the Rise of the West, 1500–1800*. Second ed. Cambridge: Cambridge University Press, 1996.

Pastor Bodmer, Beatriz. *The Armature of Conquest: Spanish Accounts of the Discovery of America, 1492–1589*. Stanford: Stanford University Press, 1992.

Peeters, Benoît. *Tintin and the World of Hergé* [1988]. Boston: Bulfinch, 1992.

Pérez-Rocha, Emma. *Privilegios en lucha: La información de doña Isabel Moctezuma*. Mexico City: Instituto Nacional de Antropología e Historia (Colección científica), 1998.

Pérez-Rocha, Emma, and Rafael Tena. *La nobleza indígena del centro de México después de la conquista*. Mexico City: Instituto Nacional de Antropología e Historia (Colección obra diversa), 2000.

Peterson, David A., and Z. D. Green. "The Spanish Arrival and the Massacre at Cholula," in *Notas Mesoamericanas* 10 (1987): 203–23.

Picón-Salas, Mariano. *A Cultural History of Spanish America: From Conquest to Independence* [1944]. Irving Leonard, trans. Berkeley: University of California Press, 1966.

Pinheiro Marques, Alfredo. "Triumph (for da Gama) and Disgrace (for Columbus)," in *Portugal, The Pathfinder: Journeys from the Medieval toward the Modern World, 1300–ca. 1600*, George D. Winius, ed., 363–72. Madison: Hispanic Seminary of Medieval Studies, 1995.

Pollard, Helen Perlstein. *Tariacuri's Legacy: The Prehispanic Tarascan State*. Norman: University of Oklahoma Press, 1993.

Powers, Karen Vieira. "A Battle of Wills: Inventing Chiefly Legitimacy in the Colonial North Andes," in *Dead Giveaways: Indigenous Testaments of Colonial Mesoamerica and the Andes*. Susan Kellogg and Matthew Restall, eds., 183–214. Salt Lake City: University of Utah Press, 1998.

Prats, Armando José. *Invisible Natives: Myth and Identity in the American Western*. Ithaca: Cornell University Press, 2002.

Prescott, William H. *History of the Conquest of Peru*. 2 vols. Philadelphia: Lippincott & Co., 1847.

———. *The Conquest of Mexico* [1843]. London: Dent, 1909.

———. *History of the Conquest of Mexico* [1843]. Introduction by Felipe Fernández-Armesto. London: The Folio Society, 1994.

Quezada, Sergio, and Tsubasa Okoshi Harada. *Papeles de los Xiu de Yaxá, Yucatán*. Mexico City: Universidad Nacional Autónoma de México, 2001.

Rabasa, José. *Inventing America: Spanish Historiography and the Formation of Eurocentrism*. Norman: University of Oklahoma Press, 1993.

Radulet, Carmen M. "Vasco da Gama and His Successors," in *Portugal, The Pathfinder: Journeys from the Medieval toward the Modern World, 1300–ca. 1600*, George D. Winius, ed., 133–44. Madison: Hispanic Seminary of Medieval Studies, 1995.

Ralegh, Sir Walter. *The Discoverie of the Large, Rich, and Bewtiful Empyre of Guiana* [1596]. Neil L. Whitehead, ed. Norman: University of Oklahoma Press, 1997.

Rappaport, Joanne. *Cumbe Reborn: An Andean Ethnography of History*. Chicago: Chicago University Press, 1994.

Recinos, Adrián ed. *Memorial de Sololá: Anales de los Cakchiqueles* [1605]. Mexico City: Fondo de Cultura Económica, 1950.

Restall, Matthew. *The Maya World: Yucatec Culture and Society, 1550–1850*. Stanford: Stanford University Press, 1997.

———. "Heirs to the Hieroglyphs: Indigenous Writing in Colonial Mesoamerica," in *The Americas* 54:2 (October 1997): 239–267.

———. *Maya Conquistador*. Boston: Beacon Press, 1998.

———. "Interculturation and the Indigenous Testament in Colonial Yucatan," in *Dead Giveaways: Indigenous Testaments of Colonial Mesoamerica and the Andes*. Susan Kellogg and Matthew Restall, eds., 141–62. Salt Lake City: University of Utah Press, 1998.

———. "Black Conquistadors: Armed Africans in Early Spanish America," in *The Americas* 57:2 (October 2000): 171–205.

———. "The People of the Patio: Ethnohistorical Evidence of Yucatec Maya Royal Courts," in *Royal Courts of the Ancient Maya, Volume 2: Data and Case Studies*. Takeshi Inomata and Stephen D. Houston, eds., 335–90. Boulder: Westview, 2001.

———. "Gaspar Antonio Chi: Bridging the Conquest of Yucatán," in *The Human Tradition in Colonial Latin America*. Kenneth J. Andrien, ed., 6–21. Wilmington: Scholarly Resources, 2002.

———. *The Black Middle: Slavery, Society, and African-Maya Relations in Colonial Yucatan*. Unpublished manuscript, n.d.

Restall, Matthew, and John F. Chuchiak. *The Friar and the Maya: Fray Diego de Landa's Relación de las Cosas de Yucatán*. Unpublished manuscript, n.d.

Ricard, Robert. *La "conquête spirituelle" du Mexique: Essai sur l'apostolat et les méthodes missionaires des ordres mendicants en Nouvelle Espagne de 1523–24 à 1572*. Paris: Université de Paris, 1933. Published in English as *The Spiritual Conquest of Mexico*. Lesley Bird Simpson, trans. Berkeley and Los Angeles: University of California Press, 1966.

Rout, Leslie B., Jr. *The African Experience in Spanish America*. London: Longman, 1969.

Russell, Jeffrey Burton. *Inventing the Flat Earth: Columbus and Modern Historians*. New York: Praeger, 1991.

Sahagún, fray Bernardino de. *Florentine Codex: General History of the Things of New Spain* [1547–79]. Arthur J. O. Anderson and Charles E. Dibble, trans. 13 parts. Salt Lake City and Santa Fe: University of Utah Press and School of American Research, 1950–82.

Sahlins, Marshall. *Historical Metaphors and Mythical Realities: Structure in the Early History of the Sandwich Islands Kingdom*. Ann Arbor: University of Michigan Press, 1981.

———. "Individual Experience and Cultural Order," in *The Social Sciences: Their Nature and Uses*. William Kruskal, ed. Chicago: Chicago University Press, 1982 (reprinted in Marshall Sahlins, *Culture in Practice: Selected Essays*. New York: Zone Books, 2000, 277–91).

———. *Islands of History*. Chicago: Chicago University Press, 1985.

———. "Cosmologies of Capitalism: The Trans-Pacific Sector of 'The World System,'" in *Proceedings of the British Academy* 74 (1988) (reprinted in Marshall Sahlins, *Culture in Practice: Selected Essays*. New York: Zone Books, 2000, 415–69).

———. *How "Natives" Think: About Captain Cook, for Example*. Chicago: Chicago University Press, 1995.

Salas, Elizabeth. *Soldaderas in the Mexican Military: Myth and History*. Austin: University of Texas Press, 1990.

Sale, Kirkpatrick. *The Conquest of Paradise: Christopher Columbus and the Columbian Legacy*. New York: Knopf, 1990.

Salomon, Frank. "Testimonies: The Making and Reading of Native South American Historical Sources," in *The Cambridge History of the Native Peoples of the Americas, Volume 3: South America*. Frank Salomon and Stuart Schwartz, eds., 19–95. New York: Cambridge University Press, 1999.

Salomon, Frank, and Stuart Schwartz. *The Cambridge History of the Native Peoples of the Americas, Volume 3: South America*. New York: Cambridge University Press, 1999.

Sánchez, Joseph P. "African Freedmen and the *Fuero Militar*: A Historical Overview of *Pardo* and *Moreno* Militiamen in the Late Spanish Empire," in *Colonial Latin American Historical Review* 3:2 (1994): 165–84.

Sarmiento de Gamboa, Pedro. *History of the Incas* [1572]. Sir Clements Markham, ed. London: Hakluyt Society, 1907.

Sater, William F. "The Black Experience in Chile," in *Slavery and Race Relations in Latin America*. Robert B. Toplin, ed., 13–50. Westport, Conn.: Greenwood, 1974.

Scholes, France V., and Ralph L. Roys. *The Maya-Chontal Indians of Acalan-Tixchel: A Contribution to the History and Ethnography of the Yucatan Peninsula*. Washington: Carnegie Institution, 1948 (Reprinted by University of Oklahoma Press, 1968).

Schroeder, Susan, ed. *Native Resistance and the Pax Colonial in New Spain*. Lincoln: University of Nebraska Press, 1998.

Schwaller, John F., ed. *The Church in Colonial Latin America*. Wilmington, Del.: Scholarly Resources, 2000.

Schwartz, Stuart B. "Denounced by Lévi-Strauss," in *The Americas* 59:1 (July 2002): 1–8.

Schwartz, Stuart B., ed. *Victors and Vanquished: Spanish and Nahua Views of the Conquest of Mexico*. Boston: Bedford/St.Martin's, 2000.

Seed, Patricia. "'Failing to Marvel': Atahualpa's Encounter with the Word," in *Latin American Research Review* 26:1 (Winter 1991): 7–32.

———. "The Requirement: A Protocol for Conquest," in *Ceremonies of Possession in Europe's Conquest of the New World, 1492–1640*, 69–99. Cambridge: Cambridge University Press, 1995.

Silverblatt, Irene. *Moon, Sun, and Witches: Gender Ideologies and Class in Inca and Colonial Peru*. Princeton: Princeton University Press, 1987.

Simmons, Marc. *The Last Conquistador: Juan de Oñate and the Settling of the Far Southwest*. Norman: University of Oklahoma Press, 1991.

Sousa, Lisa M., and Kevin Terraciano. "The Original Conquest of Oaxaca: Nahua and Mixtec Accounts of the Spanish Conquest," in *Ethnohistory* 50: 2 (2003).

Soustelle, Jacques. *The Daily Life of the Aztecs on the Eve of the Spanish Conquest* [1955]. London: Pelican, 1964.

Sowell, Thomas. *Conquests and Cultures: An International History*. New York: Basic Books, 1998.

Spalding, Karen. *Huarochirí: An Andean Society Under Inca and Spanish Rule*. Stanford: Stanford University Press, 1984.

Steinberg, Stephen. *The Ethnic Myth: Race, Ethnicity, and Class in America* [1981]. Boston: Beacon Press, 2001.

Stern, Steve J. *Peru's Indian Peoples and the Challenge of Spanish Conquest: Huamanga to 1640*. 2nd ed. Madison: University of Wisconsin Press, 1993.

Sullivan, Paul. *Unfinished Conversations: Mayas and Foreigners Between Two Wars*. New York: Knopf, 1989.

Summerhill, Stephen J., and John Alexander Williams. *Sinking Columbus: Contested History, Cultural Politics, and Mythmaking during the Quincentenary*. Gainesville: University Press of Florida, 2000.

Taube, Karl. *Aztec and Maya Myths*. Austin: University of Texas Press, 1993.

Taylor, William B. *Drinking, Homicide, and Rebellion in Colonial Mexican Villages*. Stanford: Stanford University Press, 1979.

Tedlock, Dennis, ed. *Popol Vuh: The Mayan Book of the Dawn of Life*. New York: Simon and Schuster, 1985.

Terraciano, Kevin. *The Mixtecs of Colonial Oaxaca: Ñudzahui History, Sixteenth Through Eighteenth Centuries*. Stanford: Stanford University Press, 2001.

Thomas, Hugh. *Conquest: Montezuma, Cortés, and the Fall of Old Mexico*. New York: Simon and Schuster, 1995.

———. *The Slave Trade: The Story of the Atlantic Slave Trade, 1440–1870*. New York: Touchstone, 1997.

———. *Who's Who of the Conquistadors*. London: Cassell, 2000.

Todorov, Tzvetan. *The Conquest of America: The Question of the Other*. New York: Harper & Row, 1984.

———. *The Conquest of America: The Question of the Other*. Reprint of 1984 edition, with foreword by Anthony Pagden. Norman: University of Oklahoma Press, 1999.

Tozzer, Alfred M. *Landa's Relación de las cosas de Yucatán*. Cambridge: Peabody Museum, Harvard University, Paper 28, 1941.

Trexler, Richard C. *Sex and Conquest: Gendered Violence, Political Order, and the European Conquest of the Americas*. Ithaca: Cornell University Press, 1995.

Trouillot, Michel-Rolph. *Silencing the Past: Power and the Production of History*. Boston: Beacon Press, 1995.

Tuchman, Barbara W. *The March of Folly: From Troy to Vietnam*. New York: Ballantine, 1984.

Vallado Fajardo, Iván. "Cristianos españoles e indios yucatecos en las historias del siglo XVI y XVII." Master's thesis, Universidad Autónoma Metropolitana-Azcapotzalco, 2000.

Vargas Llosa, Mario. *Making Waves: Essays*. New York: Farrar, Straus and Giroux, 1996.

Vargas Machuca, Bernardo de. *Milicia y Descripción de las Indias*. Madrid: Pedro Madrigal, 1599 (copy in JCBL).

Varón Gabai, Rafael. *Francisco Pizarro and His Brothers: The Illusion of Power in Sixteenth-Century Peru*. Norman: University of Oklahoma Press, 1997.

Vásquez de Espinosa, Antonio. *Compendium and Description of the West Indies (c.1620)*. Charles Upson Clark, ed. Washington: Smithsonian, 1942.

Velasco, Sherry. *The Lieutenant Nun: Transgenderism, Lesbian Desire, and Catalina de Erauso*. Austin: University of Texas Press, 2000.

Verdesio, Gustavo. *Forgotten Conquests: Rereading New World History from the Margins*. Philadelphia: Temple University Press, 2001.

Verlinden, Charles. "European Participation in the Portuguese Discovery Era," in *Portugal, The Pathfinder: Journeys from the Medieval toward the Modern World, 1300–ca. 1600*. George D. Winius, ed., 71–80. Madison: Hispanic Seminary of Medieval Studies, 1995.

Veyne, Paul. *Did the Greeks Believe in Their Myths? An Essay on Constitutive Imagination.* Chicago: University of Chicago Press, 1988.

Villagutierre Soto-Mayor, Juan. *Historia de la Conquista de la Provincia de el Itza, Reduccion, y Progressos de la de el Lacandon, y Otras Naciones de Indios Barbaros, de la Mediacion de el Reyno de Guatimala, a las Provincias de Yucatan, en la America Septentrional.* Madrid, 1701 (copy in JCBL).

Vinson, Ben, III. "Race and Badge: Free-Colored Soldiers in the Colonial Mexican Militia," in *The Americas* 56:4 (April 2000): 471–96.

Wachtel, Nathan. *The Vision of the Vanquished: The Spanish Conquest of Peru through Indian Eyes, 1530–1570.* Hassocks, UK: Harvester Press, 1977. (Translation of *La vision des vaincus. Les Indiens du Pérou devant la conquête espagnol 1530–1570.* Paris: Gallimard, 1971.)

———. "The Indian and the Spanish Conquest," in *Cambridge History of Latin America, Vol. 1: Colonial Latin America.* Cambridge: Cambridge University Press, 1984.

Wasserman, Martin. "Montezuma's Passivity: An Alternative View Without Postconquest Distortions of a Myth," in *The Masterkey* 57:3 (July–September 1983): 85–93.

Weinbaum, Batya. *Islands of Women and Amazons: Representations and Realities.* Austin: University of Texas Press, 1999.

Whitehead, Neil L. *Lords of the Tiger Spirit: A History of the Caribs in Colonial Venezuela and Guyana, 1498–1820.* Dordrecht, Holland: Foris, 1988.

———. "The Ancient Amerindian Polities of the Amazon, the Orinoco, and the Atlantic Coast: A Preliminary Analysis of Their Passage from Antiquity to Extinction," in *Amazonian Indians from Prehistory to the Present: Anthropological Perspectives.* Anna Roosevelt, ed., 33–54. Tucson: University of Arizona Press, 1994.

———. "The Historical Anthropology of Text: The Interpretation of Ralegh's *Discoverie of Guiana,*" in *Current Anthropology* 36:1 (February 1995): 53–74.

Wilford, John Noble. *The Mysterious History of Columbus.* New York: Knopf, 1991.

Wilson, Samuel M. *The Emperor's Giraffe and Other Stories of Cultures in Contact.* Boulder: Westview, 1999.

Winius, George D., ed. *Portugal, The Pathfinder: Journeys from the Medieval toward the Modern World, 1300–ca. 1600.* Madison: Hispanic Seminary of Medieval Studies, 1995.

Wolf, Eric R. *Sons of the Shaking Earth.* Chicago: University of Chicago Press, 1959.

———. *Europe and the People Without History.* Berkeley: University of California Press, 1982.

Wood, Michael. *Conquistadors.* Berkeley and London: University of California Press and the BBC, 2000.

Wright, Elizabeth R. *Pilgrimage to Patronage: Lope de Vega and the Court of Philip III, 1598–1621.* Lewisburg: Bucknell University Press, 2001.

Wright, R. R. "Negro Companions of the Spanish Explorers," in *American Anthropologist* 4:2 (1902): 217–28.

Wright, Robert. *Nonzero: The Logic of Human Destiny.* New York: Pantheon, 2000.

Wright, Ronald. *Stolen Continents: The Americas Through Indian Eyes Since 1492.* Boston: Houghton Mifflin, 1992.

Zamora, Margarita. *Reading Columbus.* Berkeley: University of California Press, 1993.

Zárate, Agustín de. *Historia del descubrimiento y conquista del Peru.* Antwerp: Martin Nucio, 1555 (copy in JCBL).

———. *The Discovery and Conquest of Peru* [1555], J. M. Cohen, ed. London: Folio Society, 1981.

Sources in Other Media
(Illustrated Novels, Recordings, Film, Television, World Wide Web)

Bergeron, Eric "Bibo," and Don Paul, dirs. *The Road to El Dorado*. Dreamworks Pictures, 2000.

Berry, Leon "Chu," and Andy Razaf. "Christopher Columbus," 1936. Lyrics quoted with permission and as sung in the 1957 recording by Dinah Washington. On *The Essential Dinah Washington*, Verve 314 512 905-2 (1997), and other compilations.

Brooker, Gary, and Keith Reid. "Conquistador," 1972. Lyrics quoted as recorded by Procol Harum. On *Live*, Chrysalis 1004 (1972), and *Portfolio*, Chrysalis 1638 (1988).

Downs, Lila. "La Llorona," 1998. Public domain. Cited recording by Downs appears on *La Sandunga*, released in the United States on AME/Tolemia 640014-4083-2 (1999).

Hergé. *The Adventures of Tintin: Prisoners of the Sun* [1946–47]. London: Methuen, 1962.

Jones, Kelly. "Mr. Writer," 2001. Lyrics quoted as recorded by the Stereophonics. On *Just Enough Education to Perform*, V2 Records 63881-27092-2 (2001).

lcweb2.loc.gov/cgi-bin/query/r?frd/cstdy:@field(DOCID+mx0013).

Scott, Ridley, dir. *1492: Conquest of Paradise*. Paramount Pictures, 1992.

Shaffer, Peter. *The Royal Hunt of the Sun* [1964]. Film version of 1964 play. Royal Films, 1969.

Rice, Tim, and Elton John. *Elton John's The Road to El Dorado*, Dreamworks Records 0044-50219-2, 2000.

Wallace, David, dir. *Michael Wood's Conquistadors* [four-part television series]. MayaVision and the BBC, 2000.

www.bergen.org/AAST/projects/Cortes/cortes.html.

www.britannica.com/eb/article?eu=7804.

www.nasm.edu/galleries/gal209.

www.whitehouse.gov/history/whtour/blue.

www.yale.edu/ynhti/curriculum/units/1992/2/92.02.01.x.html.

Written for Pennsylvania State University
History Seminar 569 (Spring 2001)

Arndt, Bobbie L. "Destruction, Silence and Oblivion: The Mythic Aftermath of the Fall of Mexico," 2001.

Cesco, Valentina. "The Myth of the Invisible Conquistador: Account of an Eclipse," 2001.

Cowher, Iris. "'A Handful of Adventurers'? The Myth of the King's Army in the Conquest of the New World," 2001.

Frederick, Jason. "Colonizing Columbus: Mythmaking and the Admiral of the Ocean Sea," 2001.

Inclán, María de la Luz. "Plucking the Feathered Serpent: The Debunking of Cortés' Incarnation as the Returning Quetzalcóatl," 2001.

Maldonado, Blanca. "Cultural Diversity, Contact, and Change: Debunking the Myths of Completion of the Conquest and Subsequent Native Anomie in the Americas," 2001.

Nelson, Zachary. "El Cid and the Mexica Reconquista," 2001.

Reese, Christine. "The Myth of Superiority in the Conquest of Mexico," 2001.

Smith, Michael. "'See Those Hideous Men That Rush Upon Us': Dramatic Interpretations of the Conquest of Peru," 2001.

Vincent, Leah. "'We Understood Them So Little': The Use of Signs and Interpreters in the Conquest of Latin America, 1492–1520," 2001.

Index

Numbers in italics refer to illustrations; numbers in bold refer to the main treatment of the entry.